Urban Communication

Production, Text, Context

EDITED BY
TIMOTHY A. GIBSON AND MARK LOWES

ROWMAN & LITTLEFIELD PUBLISHERS, INC.
Lanham • Boulder • New York • Toronto • Plymouth, UK

ROWMAN & LITTLEFIELD PUBLISHERS, INC.

Published in the United States of America
by Rowman & Littlefield Publishers, Inc.
A wholly owned subsidiary of The Rowman & Littlefield Publishing Group, Inc.
4501 Forbes Boulevard, Suite 200, Lanham, Maryland 20706
www.rowmanlittlefield.com

Estover Road, Plymouth PL6 7PY, United Kingdom

British Library Cataloguing in Publication Information Available

Library of Congress Cataloging-in-Publication Data Available

ISBN-13: 978-0-7425-4061-3 (cloth : alk. paper)
ISBN-10: 0-7425-4061-8 (cloth : alk. paper)
ISBN-13: 978-0-7425-4062-0 (pbk. : alk. paper)
ISBN-10: 0-7425-4062-6 (pbk. : alk. paper)

Printed in the United States of America

∞™ The paper used in this publication meets the minimum requirements of American
National Standard for Information Sciences—Permanence of Paper for Printed Library
Materials, ANSI/NISO Z39.48-1992.

For Clara and Leo – *T.A.G.*

For Maya and Marina – *M.L.*

Contents

Acknowledgments

This volume could not have been possible without the efforts of many individuals. The editors would like to thank our contributors for their hard work on behalf of this project. We would also like to thank the editors at Rowman & Littlefield, particularly Brenda Hadenfeldt, Bess Vanrenen, Jenn Nemec, and Anna Schwartz for their counsel and their patience during the process of bringing this book to print. We would like to thank all of our families for their support, and our research participants for their willingness to take time out of their lives to assist us in our research. Finally, we would like to acknowledge that three of the following chapters are revised versions of articles first printed elsewhere. These articles appear with permission from the following copyright holders.

Chapter 2 first appeared in the *Journal of International Communication,* vol. 9 (2003): 35-51. ©Macquarie University, Sydney, Australia.

Chapter 4 first appeared in the *International Journal of Cultural Studies*, vol. 8 (2005): 259-80. ©Sage Publications.

Chapter 9 first appeared in *International Sociology*, vol. 15 (2000): 533-57. ©Asef Bayat.

Introduction

The City as Production, Text, Context

Timothy A. Gibson and Mark Lowes

In December of 2004, in a hotly contested vote, the District of Columbia's city council approved a resolution to spend $440 million on a new major league baseball stadium. Funded largely by a special tax levied on the District's largest businesses, the new stadium would be built on the banks of the Anacostia River—the historical dividing line of class and race in DC—and would serve as the future home for the soon-to-be-moved and renamed Montreal Expos franchise. After a thirty-year absence the national pastime had returned to the nation's capital.

Mayor Anthony Williams, who had long championed the drive to lure baseball back to the District, was predictably ebullient. "Finally and at last . . . the Washington Nationals are rounding third and heading for home," Williams said at a news conference immediately after the vote. "Isn't that great?"[1] Of course many baseball fans in the region shared the mayor's enthusiasm—particularly those in suburban Maryland and Virginia, who would now gain access to major league baseball without having to pay for a stadium. At the same time, according to public opinion polls released before the vote, a clear majority of District residents were deeply troubled by the decision to build an elaborate sports palace entirely with public funds. Although most residents supported in general terms efforts to return major league baseball to the District, the more citizens learned about the specifics of the financing plan, the less they liked the whole idea. In fact, in the days leading up to the council vote, a number of surveys had opponents of the public financing deal leading supporters by a two-to-one margin.[2]

Considering the list of challenges facing the District, the concerns of local residents become clear. During the 1990s, the boom years of the Clinton administration, poverty rates in Washington actually increased, particularly in the city's poorest neighborhoods.[3] In addition, the District's long-suffering public school system has continued to struggle, with clear majorities of eighth-graders scoring at a "below basic" level in both reading and mathematics in recent national tests.[4] Finally, while the District's poor became poorer, a resurgent regional economy and escalating demands on urban space forced rents up across the city, generating an acute affordable housing crisis. In other words, the District government had a long list of priorities competing for the city's scarce tax revenues. But in the end, at that historic council meeting, major league baseball received from the city a promise to spend over $400 million in public funds on the stadium. In fact, by the beginning of 2006, rising land acquisition costs had driven up the estimated public bill to over $600 million.

What's going on here? What could possibly motivate city leaders to pour public funds into a baseball stadium given this context of competing social priorities? Clues to the thinking of city leaders can be gleaned from their public statements. Although all pronouncements from the pro-stadium camp were tailored for local consumption, a cursory review reveals a split between arguments pitched at the "local" and "global" scales. At the local scale, stadium proponents presented the public with visions of a transformed Anacostia waterfront. The stadium was not merely about baseball, wrote *Washington Post* columnist Michael Wilbon, "it's about turning that area, most of it simply blight, into something shining and inviting and productive."[5] The baseball stadium would be a catalyst for urban revitalization and renewal, sending a message to developers and regional businesses that the District was on the comeback trail. It would breathe life into a dead district of the city.

Another set of arguments, however, spoke of the District's relation to an increasingly competitive global economy. For example, stadium proponents took pains to remind District residents that there were other cities vying to become the future home of the Expos—cities that were not quibbling over building a stadium at public expense. Losing this interurban competition would send a powerful signal to the national marketplace that Washington lacked true "world-class" status. On the other hand, a victory in this competition would generate a lot of favorable publicity. Not only would the District receive an immediate burst of positive news coverage upon baseball's return to Washington, but the city would also reap the long-term symbolic benefits of hosting a major league franchise. For eighty-one home games each year, television cameras would broadcast the Nationals across the world, allowing the District to become a backdrop for something other than partisan political wrangling.

More important, the return of major league baseball would contribute to the city's overall stock of cultural capital that could then be strategically deployed to attract investment from a fickle global marketplace. According to officials from the Greater Washington Initiative, the place marketing arm of the Washington Board of Trade, "quality of life" issues play an important role in corporate location decisions, and the presence of major league baseball only enhances the District's image as a world-class residence.[6] Corporate executives are human beings, after all. They, and their spouses, want to like where they live. Many of these same folks are baseball fans. It should thus not be surprising that, as the president of the Greater Washington Sports Alliance put it, "culture, sports, and entertainment are what companies look at when they they're relocating and recruiting."[7]

What we have here, then, is an attempt to communicate. More than just a (highly debatable) source of jobs and revenue, the baseball stadium is, at base, a vehicle for sending strategic messages. Sometimes the audiences targeted by these messages are local: developers, retailers, and pro-baseball citizens. In other cases, the audiences are global: relocation consultants, corporate executives, and the disembodied, hyper-competitive "global marketplace." In all cases, the messages promoted by this effort in spectacular redevelopment include expertly crafted images of the District's revitalization and its resurgence as a leading destination for tourism and investment. In the end, in all likelihood, the stadium will lose money for the city—a point conceded by stadium proponents in their more reflective moments.[8] But, even so, proponents argue that such spectacular redevelopment projects constitute a wise investment in positive urban images. The stadium, in short, will pay off in semiotic, if not economic terms.

It is true that urban revitalization projects have always changed the physical form and the image of the city, the ways in which these are perceived and experienced, and the emotional relationships between the people and the urban environment. It is equally true that urban redevelopment has long been tied to the imperatives of interurban competition and urban boosterism. At the same time, it seems clear that the need to cultivate a positive civic image has assumed a special urgency in major cities over the past three decades. As far as contemporary boosters are concerned, in fact, image is everything.[9] It is not that struggling schools, relatively high tax burdens, and concentrated poverty are fantasies. City leaders acknowledge these challenges are real and consequential. It is rather that the solution to these problems begins, in the view of officials, with a process of changing *perceptions* about the relative costs and benefits of visiting, investing, and residing in cities. The city, in short, has an image problem. This image problem keeps new residents and investment away. It denies city leaders the economic growth they need to build a better future. It locks the city into a perpetual state of underdevelopment. In this context the "image of the vigorous, renascent city is carefully nurtured as the seed of the future material city."[10]

The manipulation of city images, cultures, and experiences has thus become one of the most important arrows in the economic quiver of urban governments and pro-growth commercial interests. More precisely, it is a "world-class" image of the city that civic elites strive to construct. Again, the idea behind this is that the more a city can appear on the same stage with the world's other leading cities, the stronger its civic leaders believe their chances will be of growing and prospering. And so we see city leaders competing madly to win the Olympic franchise so that they can broadcast spectacular urban images to audiences around the world. We see city leaders "branding" their cities and then promoting their brands to potential retailers, investors, and tourists. And we see city officials in Washington and elsewhere pouring public funds into sports arenas and tourist amenities, not so much for their tangible economic value, but rather because their construction may convince potential investors that "our city" is in the "big leagues."

Driving this obsession with urban images, according to many scholars, is a vigorous, globalized interurban competition for economic growth and investment. As David Harvey has argued, cities now understand they are faced with a global field of competitors, and thus they take pains to create a positive and high quality *image of place*, seeking whatever architectural styles and forms of urban design that promise to project the appropriate image. That urban leaders should feel compelled to engage in such image-making and promotion is understandable, notes Harvey, given the grim history of deindustrialization and restructuring that left most major cities in the advanced capitalist world with few options "except to compete with each other, mainly as financial, consumption and entertainment centres."[11]

In short, what we are witnessing is the inauguration of "place wars" on an international scale, as cities fiercely compete to attract the attention of global flows of tourism and investment. The practice of "place marketing" or "urban branding" is the most visible strategy in this competition, as coalitions of public officials and private boosters work tirelessly to circulate representations of their cities that might appeal to tourism brokers and corporate decision-makers. Yet this practice of projecting images involves much more than producing glossy brochures and glad-handing executives at international trade conferences. Advancing one's interests in the place wars also requires a determined effort to reshape the urban fabric to suit the needs of global tourists and multinational corporations. To this end, urban leaders have set themselves the task of building the "spectacular city"—a carefully manicured urban playground with such obligatory components as "festival" marketplaces and shopping malls, elaborately themed restaurants and cafes, world-class entertainment venues (including theaters, sports facilities, museums, live music, casinos), and a downtown-based visitor infrastructure (including hotels, convention centers, and transportation systems). Urban leaders vigorously pursue such big-ticket amenities not merely to generate increased property rents and tax revenue, but more importantly because they help boosters jockey for competitive advantage in the place wars.

If this process of projecting images to local and global audiences for strategic reasons sounds familiar to students of the media, it should. More and more, contemporary urban studies has begun to tackle questions that move the field toward the study of signification and discourse.[12] At the same time, communication scholars from around the world are beginning to pursue research on the nexus between global economic and technological restructuring, local political struggles over economic and social development, and the rise of a rich trade in urban promotional imagery.[13] Yet, as is often the case, until recently an artificial division of academic labor—with communication scholars studying "discourse" and urban studies scholars studying "history and political economy"—has fragmented the exploration of this substantive common ground into the usual disciplinary boxes.

No longer. This volume brings together, for the first time, a growing community of urban studies and communication scholars who are exploring the crucial intersections between critical theory, cultural studies, and contemporary urban political economy. In their essays the contributors to *Urban Communication* each draw upon a synthesis of political-economic and cultural theory to explore how urban revitalization and promotional strategies are forged, circulated, lived, and contested within the contemporary urban landscape. In this introduction, we will therefore attempt to provide a conceptual map of this borderland between urban and communication studies, with a focus on the theoretical and substantive questions one can ask when viewing issues of urban development and politics through the lens of media and cultural theory.

A Framework for Studying Urban Communication: Production, Text, Context

In a seminal essay, the British cultural studies scholar Richard Johnson proposed a model for understanding what he called the "circuit of culture."[14] Drawing on both Marxian political economy and French structuralism, Johnson conceptualized the social flow of cultural forms and meanings as a circuit with four distinct moments: production, text, reception, and lived cultures. Beginning with the moment of their production, cultural forms are encoded into texts, which are then read or interpreted by individuals in concrete social contexts. Taken separately each moment offers insights into the circulation of cultural meanings not available from the vantage of other moments. For instance, while the commercial structures of the television industry may determine the broad range of discourses circulated on the tube (in the moment of production), a careful analysis of television texts can reveal semiotic ambiguities and contradictions which create space for alternative interpretations. And while studying the moment of television reception can reveal the wide range of possible audience interpretations, the fabric of social relations that connect and constitute individuals will determine the social reach and political significance of their readings. Taken together, Johnson's four moments provide a powerful heuristic from which media scholars and cultural theorists can generate a wide range of engaging research questions.

Johnson's model, we believe, can also be productively applied to analyzing the cultural politics of contemporary urbanization. By focusing on the "moment of production," for example, we consider the broad political and economic context that motivates the pursuit of urban promotional and redevelopment strategies. Consider the example of Washington's new baseball stadium. Thinking about the "moment of production" compels us to ask questions about how the plan to build the stadium was forged in the crucible of interurban economic competition and local political struggle. What compelled city leaders to pursue major league baseball with such abandon—so much so that they were willing to build a stadium at taxpayer expense? What were the motives of baseball officials, and how were they in a position to play one city off another for the best possible deal? How was the specific plan to build the stadium, including the site location, negotiated within the local political sphere, and who had access to these deliberations? All of these questions focus our attention of the politics of textual production—in this case the concrete social processes that led to the production of the stadium-text.

The "moment of text," however, requires us to shift focus from the concrete practices of urban redevelopment and promotion toward an engagement with the images and meanings created out of these practices. How, for example, is the stadium signified in local, national, and international media images? How do city officials and boosters transform the stadium into a strategic commodity-sign that can be circulated within the international marketplace, with the ultimate intention of returning economic investment and growth back to the region? What about the discourses and texts produced in the struggle over public financing? What texts were produced in this local political struggle, and what visions of the urban good life were embedded in these texts? What about the architectural design of the stadium itself? What kinds of social experiences and public gatherings are privileged by the stadium's design and its articulation with the surrounding neighborhood? Questions of text, in this way, can range widely from the representation of "the city" in the global media environment to more narrow questions concerning the meanings generated through our encounters with, and within, particular urban spaces and places.

Finally, the "moment of context," as we conceptualize it, actually condenses two distinct moments in Johnson's circuit—the moment of reception, in which individual audience members encounter urban texts (images, narratives, spaces) and produce their own readings, and the moment of "lived cultures," when these individual encounters and experiences with urban texts play back into the social relations that constitute everyday life. The move into context thus compels us to think carefully about how new urban spaces and promotional urban imagery are picked up, used, and interpreted by situated audiences, and how these uses and interpretations of urban texts generate particular social and ethical consequences. How, for example, will the new stadium transform the experience of urban life for those who live within—or were displaced from—the space it will occupy? How, in more general terms, are the risks and rewards of such spectacular redevelopment and promotional strategies distributed within the local public sphere? And how are these strategies, and their risks and rewards, contested through concrete political struggle? And finally, at the global scale, how are such promotional images of an "urban comeback," carefully cultivated by regional elites, picked up and understood within the international marketplace of tourism brokers and footloose global corporations?

In the end, exploring the symbolic dimensions of contemporary urbanization through the moments of production, text, and context helps to clarify the conceptual terrain shared by urban studies and critical communication scholarship. The attempt to secure for one's region a disproportionate share of future global economic growth increasingly takes place through the strategic assembly, construction, and circulation of urban images and texts. In some cases the texts are bold media images of an unparalleled "quality of life," one carefully crafted by pro-growth booster organizations, and circulated through international networks of commerce and promotion. In other cases the texts are concrete urban spaces, conceived, built, and promoted in order to cultivate a sense of urban vitality and rebirth among local, regional, and global audiences of shoppers, investors, and tourists. In either respect, the model of production/text/context forces scholars to simultaneously consider the political-economic contexts that motivate strategies of urban redevelopment and promotion, the specific cultural understandings of the "urban good life" embedded within and expressed by these strategies, and the social and ethical consequences of these strategies at the level of everyday urban life.

A Second Dimension: The Global/Local Nexus

Although conceptualizing contemporary urban development and promotion as, at least in part, an exercise in sending messages can open up an engaging series of questions, the next step lies in specifying the spatial scale upon which these symbolic strategies operate. The audiences targeted by the District's baseball stadium, for example, included a range of actors from local developers to national sporting executives to global corporate relocation specialists. For this reason, we believe it is useful to think of urban promotional strategies as operating along two distinct but intersecting *fields*—a global field and a local/regional field.[15]

The Global Field

For Pierre Bourdieu, a field is a particular social context within which actors struggle over the distribution of the particular forms of "capital" (or social resources) that are central to the field's operation.[16] Some actors within a specific field—say, the academic field—will struggle to maintain the current relational structure of the field and the existing distribution of key resources (such as tenure, research funding, teaching assistants, and salaries). Others, however, will struggle to rearrange existing relations within the field and work to redistribute these resources in some way—as occurs when heterodox academics argue for a more expansive definition of what constitutes "research" and "knowledge" within the academy. The outcomes of these struggles depend, of course, on the already-existing distribution of resources: those with greater access to key forms of capital have a better chance of imposing upon the field a structure that benefits themselves and their allies. In other words, although there are no guarantees of success or failure in these struggles, a pre-existing accumulation of economic capital, cultural knowledge, and social prestige confers enhanced power to shape the field to one's advantage.

With this in mind, it is clear that urban promotional strategies operate, first, within a *global* field marked by an international, interurban competition for investment, jobs, and tourism. To be sure, cities and regions have long jostled with one another for economic advantage, but, as regulation theorists have persuasively argued, the global economic crisis of the 1970s both raised the stakes of this competition and radically expanded the field of competitors. The origins of this global crisis have been described elsewhere in great detail.[17] But, to summarize this literature briefly, by 1973, an unholy mix of inflation, unemployment, and the reemergence of industrial competitors in Europe and Asia had sparked the most severe global recession since the 1930s. During these difficult years, manufacturers in the United States and Canada faced an unpredictable global marketplace saturated with low-priced goods—often produced in nations where low wages and anti-union practices kept production costs low. The confluence of events thus spelled the end of the long postwar economic expansion and what regulation theorists have termed the Fordist regime of capitalist accumulation—a regime based on a virtuous circle of increasing productivity, increasing profits, increasing wages, and an interventionist welfare state.

This global economic crisis set the stage for twenty years of corporate experimentation and economic restructuring that, by the mid-1990s, had coalesced into a new regime of accumulation variously described as "flexible accumulation," "flexible specialization," or "post-Fordism." In this new post-Fordist regime, the firms that survived the global recessions of the 1970s and early 1980s learned to exploit new innovations in transportation and communication technologies in order to impose more "flexible" forms of production and control onto an increasingly globalized workforce.

A key component of this move toward flexible accumulation has been the transformation of the vertically-integrated corporation of the postwar "monopoly capital" years into a more decentralized structure that Robert Reich has called the "web enterprise."[18] In the post-Fordist regime, multinational corporations increasingly use new information technologies to stitch together global networks of subcontracted "inputs"—with each input farmed out to whatever region of the global economy provides the best competitive advantage.[19] For example, when Ford produces its latest SUV, the final assembly may occur in Mexico, but the seats are stitched in China; Malaysian subcontractors produce the electronic components; German engineers assist in the design; a marketing firm in Britain develops the advertising campaign; and, to round it off, Ireland and Barbados share the data processing and customer service work. At the center of this vast global web, of course, a core group of Ford executives and planners coordinate these activities from the home office in Michigan.[20]

Moreover, within each input-category, firms located in different regions most likely competed on a global scale to become the provider of that "input." If the Malaysian firm landed Ford's contract, they most likely had to fend off competitors located in South Korea, Singapore, and elsewhere. The same is true for Ireland's call centers, which face a field of competitors in the Caribbean, India, and the American Midwest.[21] In the end, for multinational capital, reorganizing one's enterprise into a global web can yield profound advantages.

Not only can these complex networks of subcontractors be assembled and then discarded easily when corporate priorities and market conditions shift, but, importantly, global firms can now play subcontractors and even whole regions off one another in search of "the best possible deal."[22]

Urban and regional leaders, of course, know that corporations and tourists have more choices about where to invest their resources. They further realize that, in order to attract jobs, tourism, and investment, they must be entrepreneurial, aggressive even, in their competition with other cities and regions. The stakes of the global field, therefore, are clear. Either develop a strategy to attract a disproportionate share of future economic growth, or risk having your region slide "off the network" and into a profound isolation from global flows of commerce and tourism—as has been the fate of large swaths of the global South.[23]

To this end, within most major urban centers, metropolitan political and corporate leaders have organized themselves an interlocking series of pro-growth, regional trade associations, each charged with the task of contending with the field of competitors for a share of future economic growth. Within this competitive field, these regional pro-growth associations attempt to mobilize different forms of what might be called "urban capital" to attract investment and growth. Some forms of urban capital are economic in the pure sense. Pro-growth boosters, for example, can pull the levers of local government to improve infrastructure, lower taxes, and offer fast-track environment approval for new industrial facilities. They can also focus directly on the labor market, either investing in education to sell the region as rich in human resources, or, alternatively, by advertising their region's history of low wage labor.

Other forms of urban capital, including Washington's baseball stadium, are more cultural or symbolic in nature. Trading on this form of "cultural" urban capital works for cities in much the same way as it works for individuals in the social field. Just as members of the middle and upper classes can trade on their accumulation of cultural knowledge (including knowledge of fine cuisine and fine arts) in order to impress the "right" people and accumulate economic capital, so can cities and regions trade on their image and their "quality of life" to rise in the international urban hierarchy. In this way, the accumulation of cultural amenities like opera houses, symphony halls, elaborate retail environments, and other recreational attractions—and the promotion of these attractions through sophisticated urban branding campaigns—can generate for the city a positive international "image," creating the kind of urban scene which helps boosters sell the city to investors and tourists around the world.

The Local Field

The consequences of urban promotion and image-making do not just play out on the global level, however. As urban historians and sociologists remind us, the effort to transform city space to suit the needs of multinational capital takes place within a local field marked by political contest and struggle. It is therefore at this global/local nexus that the imperatives of interurban competition connect with the dicey politics of urban redevelopment and revitalization.

That such efforts to reshape urban space often meet with the vigorous resistance of local residents and communities should not surprise us. As Logan and Molotch argue, the politics of urban redevelopment often hinge on a fundamental division between *use* and *exchange*—that is, between viewing urban space as a source of accumulation, speculation, and profit, and viewing space as a resource for everyday life. On one side of this cleavage stands an interconnected community of "place entrepreneurs"—that is, a downtown establishment of developers, real estate bankers, landowners, and so on—who work collectively to create conditions conducive to steady increases in "exchange" or property values.[24] This relentless search for increased property values and more lucrative uses of space, however, often throws such place entrepreneurs afoul of average citizens and residents, who are typically the first people affected by the progrowth plans hatched in downtown boardrooms. As a result, when the use values residents derive from their neighborhoods and open spaces are threatened by the plans of developers and investors, average citizens can mobilize around their collective interest in preserving the existing amenities built into their neighborhoods and cities. This view of the local urban field as a struggle between *use* and *exchange* thus draws our attention to the process of coalition formation within the arena of local politics and the tendency for groups to organize around their shared interest in promoting some land uses over others.

Table 1.1 Urban Communication: A Map of the Field

	Global Scale (Urban Promotion)	*Local Scale (Urban Struggle)*
Production	Interurban competition inspires spectacular redevelopment to secure global investment.	Competing alliances struggle to define "urban vitality" and to realize their definitions in the fabric of urban space.
Text	The transformation of redevelopment projects into promotional texts.	The visions of "urban vitality" expressed in political struggles; the semiotics of new urban spaces.
Context	The interpretation of promotions by global actors.	How urban spaces (spectacular, civic, etc.) are lived, appropriated, and contested by residents and visitors at the level of everyday life.

Within the local field, then, the promotional and redevelopment strategies of urban elites can spark heated debates over *whose* vision of the urban good life is to be built into the fabric of the city. If city boosters typically define "urban vitality" metaphorically as growth (i.e., as increasing investment, land rents, and tax revenues), local residents often articulate alternative notions of the urban good life, notions that prioritize the collective meanings invested in already-existing urban spaces and the expansion of public participation in the process of urban planning and design.[25] The outcomes of such struggles over the urban fabric are contingent, determined by the relative balance of symbolic, political, and material resources brought to bear by the players involved in any particular struggle. To be sure, urban boosters and pro-growth coalitions often command a disproportionate share of such resources in the local public sphere, and it is not difficult to find case studies that testify to their ability to shape urban space.[26] Yet community groups are not without resources of their own, and the urban literature is also replete with cases where grassroots opposition successfully forced urban elites to make concessions that worked to the advantage of local communities.[27]

All in all, inspired by the analytic distinctions media scholars draw between production/text/context, and committed to keeping both global and local practices in simultaneous view, we can classify the symbolic issues raised by contemporary urban promotion and redevelopment using the grid displayed in Table 1.1. This grid charts some of the more important symbolic and discursive issues that arise at the intersection of the global and local fields. The left side of the grid describes the process of developing "urban branding" or urban promotional campaigns within the context of an interurban competition to attract global flows of economic investment and tourism. The right side of the grid acknowledges that elite efforts to reorganize urban space to suit the needs of corporate decision-makers and tourists depend upon successful political struggle within the local field. This struggle, however, is contingent and elite city-building efforts often must contend with alternative, grassroots definitions of the urban good life and the appropriate use and distribution of local resources. Each of the essays included in this volume can be located somewhere within this grid, as each chapter explores the symbolic, political, and economic issues raised at this crucial intersection between the local and global fields.

The Structure of the Book

The book that follows is divided into three parts—the city in production, the city as text, and the city in context. Deciding how to classify these chapters was not always easy. Often, the contributors touched simultaneously on all three "moments" in Johnson's circuit. It is, after all, difficult to talk about the process of urban production without referring both to the spaces constructed and how these spaces were picked up and used in everyday life. Likewise, providing an analysis of urban promotional discourse without referring to the organizations that produce this discourse would make little sense as well. Still, when reading the chapters it became clear that each of the authors, while providing rich contextual analyses that transcend easy classification, nonetheless anchored their explorations into urban communication from the standpoint of a particular "moment" within the production-text-context circuit.

Part I: The City in Production

The chapters in this section focus on the motives and strategies of urban elites as they forge promotional and revitalization strategies from within the crucible of interurban competition and local political struggle. In chapter 1, for example, Kevin Fox Gotham and Jeannie Haubert take us to the Louisiana Gulf Coast in the era *before* Hurricane Katrina to explore the revitalization strategies pursued by local elites in Allen Parish and New Orleans. Facing recent histories of disinvestment and decline, local elites in the two localities ultimately pinned their hopes for future economic growth on two seemingly contradictory strategies: casino tourism and prison construction. In their analysis, the authors explore the political-economic context that led local elites to embrace this "casinos and prisons" strategy, the local political struggles and scandals that erupted as a result, and the social and economic costs generated by the headlong pursuit of these projects. In the end, Gotham and Haubert develop the concept of *neoliberal revitalization* in order to help clarify our thinking about the relationship between the global flows of investment, the restructuring federal state, and the articulation of local economic strategies.

Gerald Sussman, in chapter 2, continues the focus on urban economic development in his exploration of the role of the Internet in the development plans of national elites in the city-state of Singapore. In particular, Sussman's chapter explores a fascinating tension between the economic utility of the Internet and its potential as a medium for grassroots activism. On the one hand, as Sussman explains, Singapore's ruling party has seized on Internet broadband as a way to cement the city-state's status as a leading center of global commerce. At the same time, the ruling regime eyes the Internet's unruly political potential with cold suspicion. In exploring this tension, Sussman examines a number of important questions. How can the ruling party make Singapore an "intelligent island" and a leading center of the global multimedia industry, while at the same time preserving the ruling party's tight regulation of political speech? Will Singapore serve as a test case for how other states, including those in the region and even in the West, might foreclose anti-systemic and revolutionary uses of the Internet, while engaging in wholesale political and commercial surveillance of citizens? Or will the Internet prove to be—as it has in other political contexts—a very effective organizing tool for mobilizing civil society, public action, and political change in this small city-state?

Continuing the focus on elite efforts to restructure and reshape the urban environment, in chapter 3, John Hannigan offers an update on *Fantasy City*, his influential account of entertainment-based revitalization strategies in the 1990s. As Hannigan argues, over the past decade, there has been a shift away from urban development policies that rely on the construction of major cultural flagship projects. In its place, a new discourse on revitalization and renewal has emerged—a discourse that counsels urban leaders to nurture lively, neo-bohemian arts districts characterized by a vibrant, diverse, and tolerant street-level culture. Rather than being directed to the usual markets composed of tourists and suburbanites, these neighborhoods are carefully designed to appeal to new generations of innovative knowledge workers who are regarded by urban policymakers as holding the key to future urban prosperity and success. For his part, however, Hannigan notes that this strategy of "cultural incubation" is inherently contradictory: it attempts to reconcile an avant-garde creative spirit with a commercialized homogeneity that plays to the demands of middle-class visitors in search of a safe and secure urban adventure. Terming this ambivalent zone the "controlled edge," Hannigan explores how this cultural incubation model, like the more tourist-focused fantasy city model it replaced, ultimately privileges standardized consumption experiences and "riskless risk" over spaces and activities that nurture a more unpredictable and democratic street culture.

In chapter 4, Timothy Gibson turns the discussion from the production of urban spaces toward the production of promotional urban images. In recent years, in other words, urban leaders across the United States have come to believe that the accumulation of negative images of the American city in the popular imagination—fueled especially by the relentless portrayal of urban crime and social pathology in local news and prime-time television—has become a crucial barrier to revitalization and renewal. To combat these negative images, urban leaders have embraced the tools of marketing and have embarked a series of elaborate "urban branding" campaigns—all in the hope that more positive representations of urban life will translate into increased tourism, a growing population, and a larger slice of the regional and global economic pie. Focusing on one such exercise in urban branding—the "city living, dc style" campaign in Washington, DC—Gibson draws on interviews with the campaign's planners to examine the relationship between the institutional motives of campaign sponsors and the images of the "urban good life" that emerged from their efforts. In the end, Gibson explores the potential of urban marketing campaigns to realize their goals of improving the lives of *all* city residents, regardless of class or station.

Part II: The City as Text

The chapters in the second section of the book turn their attention on the *texts* produced out of these elite urban revitalization strategies. Some of these texts are discursive or rhetorical—including the representations of "the city" encoded into promotional materials and reports produced by city officials and private boosters. Other texts are spatial-material, including the elaborate spectacular entertainment projects of the "fantasy city" or architectural styles that are designed to send just the right message to audiences of tourists, shoppers, and investors. Still other texts are produced not by policy or property elites (or, for that matter, by other city residents with their own ideas regarding the direction of urban development), but rather by third parties, including, importantly, those who work in the media system. Local and national journalists, for example, continually produce representations of "the city" in their reports, and the content of representations can have important consequences for both the political fortunes of urban leaders and the economic futures of boosters and residents alike. A focus on "the city as text" thus narrows our focus on the particular political-cultural meanings both invested in urban space and expressed through representation of those spaces and places in the local, national, and global media systems.

In this regard, chapter 5 opens the investigation of urban texts by discussing the cultural politics of architectural design in Dublin, Ireland. As Andrew Kincaid explains, at the height of the colonial period English powers built Georgian-inspired structures throughout Dublin to communicate the values of hierarchy, order, and English superiority. In the postcolonial period, particularly the 1960s, a modernizing Irish nationalist elite pursued a campaign of Georgian elimination in order to cleanse Dublin of its colonial past. Beginning in the 1990s, however, a curious thing began to happen. With Dublin's emergence as a high-tech destination in Europe, the city's architects—commissioned by developers firmly attuned to the needs and desires of international capital—have begun to design new housing and office developments in mock-Georgian style. In his examination of this post-colonial reversal, Kincaid locates this unlikely Georgian revival in the relationship between Dublin's contested local history and the forces of neo-liberal trade and commerce.

For her part, in chapter 6, Caroline Andrew focuses her own textual analysis not on the interpretation of urban social dramas, but on the symbolic construction of "the city" in urban promotional discourse. As Andrew describes, urban elites in Ottawa, Canada have cycled through a number of branding exercises in the last few decades, with each exercise in self-presentation crafted by different political agents acting on different spatial scales in pursuit of different political objectives. If, throughout most of the century, the presence of the federal government defined Ottawa as a political capital, the City of Ottawa has recently become a more important player in shaping the urban imaginary, culminating in a concerted attempt to reposition Ottawa as a leading technopole (with, as Andrew describes, decidedly mixed results). Most recently, the process of urban self-presentation has become a site of struggle as some actors push for conceiving Ottawa as a space of intercultural comity and high-quality public services, while others hope to reposition Ottawa as a site of a renewed, more muscular Canadian nationalism. As Andrew notes, at stake in this semiotic struggle is the ability to privilege a particular narrative about Ottawa, and, by extension, a particular notion of Canadian national identity.

In chapter 7, Carey Higgins and Gerald Sussman turn their attention to one of the most important producers of urban texts—local television news. However pilloried by media critics, local television news is nonetheless the single most important source of information about urban affairs for most metropolitan residents.[28] Although most local television stations aggressively market themselves as "part of our community," in fact many stations are vertically integrated into or affiliated with media corporations of national and even global scope. These mega-media firms have thus begun to use local newscasts as vehicles of corporate synergy and cross-promotion, a practice known in the industry as "plugola." In their chapter, Higgins and Sussman demonstrate how plugola inserts promotional messages (e.g., a short clip on the making of a newly released film) into local station "news" in ways that displace coverage of urban politics and cultural life. The authors conclude their discussion of plugola with a study of the Portland, Oregon news market. In this analysis, they show how, even in a city known for its vigorous sense of civic engagement, a crucial feature of the local public sphere is being colonized by a commercial logic that leaves citizens less informed about the issues and events that animate their city.

Part III: The City in Context

The final section offers a series of essays that attempt to asses the social and ethical consequences of contemporary efforts at urban revitalization and promotion. In doing so, we turn our attention away from the redevelopment and representation of urban space and instead examine how these spaces and strategies redistribute the risks and rewards of urban life in particular ways, and how this redistribution is picked up, interpreted, and contested in the local public sphere. In chapter 8, for example, Mark Lowes and Paul Tranter examine the public health and environmental risks associated with a particular form of spectacular urban promotion—hosting a major motorsport event. They argue that urban elites pursue such events primarily because their use of downtown street circuits offers many opportunities for the city skyline to act as a backdrop to a glamorous sporting spectacle. However, the location of the race within significant public spaces can generate a host of cultural, political, and environmental costs—most of which are not shouldered by racing executives. Drawing on their analysis of motorsport events in Australia, Lowes and Tranter are particularly concerned about the ideological and cultural consequences of turning key public spaces over to racing executives for large chunks of each year. Such decisions, they argue, explicitly privilege values of profit, excess, and waste, while at the same time subordinating a commitment to democratic policy-making, public health, and a sustainable urban ecology.

For their part, the last two chapters of the book offer an important view of the social and ethical consequences of contemporary urban development from two radically different—but nonetheless intimately connected—vantage points. In chapter 9, Asef Bayat takes readers to the streets of the global South, where expanding legions of marginalized individuals, families, and communities struggle to secure the means of existence under the most difficult of circumstances. For his part, Bayat examines the political-economic forces that have generated this global urban subaltern, including especially the integration of developing nations under a global economic regime that offered access to global flows of capital in exchange for neo-liberal fiscal "discipline." This last, of course, was code for the privatization of state industries and services, and a radical reduction in education, health, and welfare spending. As Bayat describes, for a few, this process of global integration and neo-liberal discipline has resulted in increasing wealth and a heady introduction into the ranks of the global economic elite. For millions more, however, the result of global restructuring has been a steady decline in living standards and an unending struggle for economic survival—a struggle now extended to more and more of the developing world's middle class as they receive pink slips from the contracting state apparatus.

But how do the urban grassroots in the slums of the global South respond to their poverty and exclusion? What kinds of political action, if any at all, do they embrace? Beginning with a critique of existing perspectives on the politics of the marginalized urban grassroots, Bayat offers an alternative outlook on the activism of the urban subaltern in Third World cities. Neither potential revolutionaries nor passively poor, the urban grassroots have embarked, Bayat argues, on a "quiet encroachment of the ordinary," where resistance is expressed not through overt political action but rather through a progressive appropriation of private and public spaces to serve their own survival needs. In his conclusion, Bayat examines both the possibilities and limits of this form of grassroots politics.

Moving the discussion from the streets of Cairo to the heart of the American Empire, Vincent Mosco examines the cultural politics of Ground Zero: the World Trade Center. The story Mosco tells is both enlightening and chilling, as he traces the origins of the World Trade Center in the desire of the Rockefeller family to transform the southern tip of Manhattan into a symbol of America's global economic might. This ideological-architectural project required both a willful disregard of the existing New York property market and the complete obliteration of the working-class and small business neighborhood at its future site. In this regard, from their very origins, the twin towers stood as a stark embodiment of the contradictions and conflicts at the heart of American post-industrialism. Mosco concludes with a discussion of current effort to "re-purify" the site after the terrorist attacks of September 11, 2001, arguing that the current rebuilding plan obscures both the consequences of the attacks and the questions they raised. To read Mosco's account of the rise and fall of the twin towers is to recognize the interpenetration of global geo-politics and local political struggle. In this way his article provides a fitting conclusion to this book.

Common Threads and Future Directions

We offer this volume to draw the attention of communication and urban studies scholars to an emerging point of overlap between their two fields. The diverse disciplinary backgrounds of our contributors—drawn from sociology, urban studies, political science, English, and communication—testify to the ecumenical nature of this area of study. In addition, the geographical scope and substantive range of the volume's chapters—from Cairo, Egypt to Allen Parish, from urban architecture to urban branding—likewise demonstrate the empirical breadth and depth of the urban communication field. At the same time, a close reading of the chapters reveals some recurrent themes and what just might be the vague outlines of a common methodological and theoretical approach.

First, taken both individually and as a collective whole, the contributions demonstrate the utility—even the necessity—of a methodological approach that combines political-economic analysis with the conceptual tools of semiotics and discourse analysis. Cities, of course, are sites of economic exchange and the flexing of political-economic power. The struggle for material resources—and the development of urban space to suit the needs of local and global capital—are fundamental features of life in the contemporary urban landscape. At the same time, however, cities are also centers of cultural life. The urban fabric is not only home to a stunning diversity of cultural practices and traditions, but is itself invested with collectively-produced and deeply-felt images and meanings. At stake in the social struggles that animate urban life are not only economic decisions and policies that distribute access to material resources, but also the question of *whose* particular cultural vision of the urban good life will be realized— literally, made real—in the city's future development. What is required in the analysis of urban life, therefore, is a methodological approach that takes issues of meaning and culture seriously, while embedding this analysis in its material and economic context.[29] In this way, the emerging field of urban communication demonstrates a close affinity with the larger post-disciplinary call for the study of "cultural economy"—a still-emerging field that submerges arbitrary divisions between political economy and cultural studies in favor of a more wide-ranging analysis of both the cultural dimensions of economic life *and* the increasing incorporation of cultural practices within a colonizing logic of accumulation.[30]

Taken together the contributors also take what might be called a *critical* approach to the study of urban life. There is no uniform political position argued across these chapters, and we suspect that the contributors, if gathered in a roundtable, would engage in a spirited debate regarding their views on urban and social policy. At the same time, all of the contributors, in one way or another, draw our attention to the gap between what "is" and that "ought to be" in the contemporary urban landscape. In other words, taken together, the contributors force us to grapple with the widening distance between our actual-existing urban communities—communities that are too often marked by radical economic and social inequality—and the kinds of communities we *could* create, under a more equitable distribution of political, economic, and symbolic resources. Across the varied arguments of our contributors, in short, one can perceive not only a compelling critique of the inequalities of contemporary urban life, but also an implicit political commitment to nurture more participatory urban planning processes, to carve out urban spaces conducive to the performance of civic life, and to defend the principle that urban space should serve social and cultural needs beyond those of accumulation and profit.[31]

Finally, the contributors of *Urban Communication* also point the way toward a reconnection with the *local* practices and struggles. This is not to say that more global economic processes and political relations are somehow less important or less "real" than those we experience closer to home. Indeed, the whole theoretical thrust of the present volume is to explore processes of urban development at the nexus of global economic competition and local political struggle. Yet, at the same time, one can argue that the drift of critical scholarship—within communication studies in particular—has pulled scholars toward a preoccupation on issues of national and global concern (e.g., the "war on terror," the war in Iraq, etc.) and away from a sustained engagement with local communities.

It is not difficult to figure out why a certain "national/global" bias might exist in contemporary critical scholarship, particularly within communication and media studies. University professors are often nomadic: the common practice of moving from job to job likely does little to nurture a close connection to local concerns. In addition, academic publishers undoubtedly encourage a more national or international perspective in scholarship to expand the potential market for their offerings, and one should not discount the more subjective appeal of becoming an oft-cited expert on weighty matters of global import. The result, however, has been a soft spot in the critical media literature when it comes to local media and local politics—a soft spot that mirrors the more general isolation of university life from the surrounding communities in which academics live.

This volume thus offers an example of how critical scholarship—especially communication scholarship—can become more engaged with local communities without losing the ability to situate local concerns within their global political, economic, and cultural context. Throughout this volume, our contributors explore the development of urban policy and the production of urban space at the intersection of global and local fields of struggle. The result is a collection that demonstrates the value of, to paraphrase Clifford Geertz, glimpsing the most global of global processes in the most local of local practices.[32] And if this process brings us closer to an engagement with the concerns of our neighbors and the debates that animate our communities, then so much the better.

Notes

1. David Nakamura and Thomas Heath, "Amended Deal on Stadium Approved: Council Seals Return of Baseball to DC," *Washington Post*, 22 December 2001, 1(A).

2. Ipsos Public Affairs press release, "New Poll for 'No D.C. Taxes for Baseball' Coalition Shows: D.C. Voters Oppose Public Funding, Strongly Oppose Giveaway, Reject Ballpark Tax on Business, Want D.C. Council to Make Major Modification of Contract," www.nodctaxesforbaseball.org.

3. Fannie Mae Foundation, *The Poorest Become Poorer: A Report on Patterns of Concentrated Poverty in Washington, D.C.* (Washington, DC: Fannie Mae Foundation, 2003).

4. Test scores are from the National Assessment of Education Progress, circa 2003. The NAEP is a biannual reading and math test administered to all public school children in the USA. The National Education Association describes these tests as "well-respected," http://nces.ed.gov/nationsreportcard/ states/profile.asp.

5. Michael Wilbon, "D.C. Baseball in Foul Territory," *Washington Post*, 6 November 2004.

6. Personal interview, Greater Washington Initiative, 25 March 2005.

7. *Associated Press*, "Washington's Efforts to Attract Sports Have Been Mixed," 30 September 2004, http://sports.espn.go.com/espn/.

8. Irving Rein and B.R. Shields, "Communication and Sports: Language of the City" (paper presented at the annual meeting of the National Communication Association, Chicago, Illinois, November 2004).

9. This point is more fully developed in Mark Lowes, *Indy Dreams and Urban Nightmares* (Toronto: University of Toronto Press, 2002).

10. H. Braviel Holcomb and Robert Beauregard, *Revitalizing Cities* (Washington, DC: Association of American Geographers, 1981), 52.

11. David Harvey, *The Condition of Postmodernity* (Oxford: Blackwell, 1989), 91-92.

12. See, for example, R. Atkinson, "Discourses of Partnership and Empowerment in Contemporary British Urban Regeneration," *Urban Studies* 36, no. 1 (1999): 59-72; C. Mele "The Materiality of Urban Discourse: Rational Planning in the Restructuring of the Early-Twentieth Century Urban Ghetto," *Urban Affairs Review* 35, no. 5 (2000): 628-48.

13. See, for example, Susan Davis, "Space Jam: Media Conglomerates Build the Entertainment City," *European Journal of Communication* 14, no. 4 (1999): 435-59; Richard Gruneau and David Whitson, "Upmarket Continentalism: Major League Sport, Promotional Culture, and Corporate Integration," in *Continental Order? Integrating North America for Cyber-Capital*, ed. Vincent Mosco and Dan Schiller (Lanham, MD: Rowman & Littlefield, 2001); Steve Macek, *Urban Nightmares: The Panic Over the Post-Industrial City in the Media and Public Discourse* (Minneapolis, MN: University of Minnesota Press, 2005).

14. Richard Johnson, "What Is Cultural Studies, Anyway?" *Social Text* 6, no. 1 (1987): 38-80.

15. See Pierre Bourdieu, *Distinction: A Social Critique of the Judgment of Taste* (Cambridge, MA: Harvard University Press, 1984); *Language and Symbolic Power* (Cambridge, MA: Harvard University Press, 1991); *Practical Reason* (Stanford, CA: Stanford University Press, 1998).

16. J.B. Thompson, "Introduction," in *Language and Symbolic Power*, ed. Pierre Bourdieu (Cambridge, MA: Harvard University Press, 1991).

17. Michael Piore and Charles Sabel, *The Second Industrial Divide* (New York: Basic Books, 1984); Steve Lash and John Urry, *The End of Organized Capitalism* (Madison, WI: University of Wisconsin Press, 1987); Bob Jessop, "Post-Fordism and the State," in *Post-Fordism: A Reader*, ed. Ash Amin (Oxford: Blackwell, 1994); David Harvey, *The Condition of Postmodernity.*

18. Robert Reich, *The Work of Nations* (New York: Basic Books, 1991), and *The Future of Success* (New York: Basic Books, 2000).

19. Allen Scott, *The Cultural Economy of Cities* (London: Sage, 2000).

20. Ford example adapted from Reich, *The Work of Nations*, 90.

21. Mark Wilson, "Information Networks: The Global Offshore Labor Force," in *Global Productions: Labor in the Making of the Information Society*, ed. G. Sussman and J. Lent (Creskill, NJ: Hampton Press, 1998).

22. Reich, *The Future of Success*; see also, Manuel Castells, *The Rise of the Network Society* (Oxford: Blackwell, 2000).

23. To be sure, the discourse of globalization includes its share of hype, and there are real limits to how "global" the global economy actually is. Whole swaths of human geography—including much of sub-Saharan Africa, east-central Europe, and central Asia—are "off the network," as Castells put it, and are not even viewed as likely candidates for routine production. For this reason, it matters less in the long run whether your city or region is in North America, Asia, or Europe. What matters is whether your city (or even your neighborhood) is *on* or *off* the network of global economic flows. In North America, there are geographies that are fundamentally tied into Castells' "space of flows" (Silicon Valley, Wall Street, Omaha's call centers, even the free-trade factories of Northern Mexico), and there are geographies that are fundamentally isolated from the global system (such as the failing resource towns of West Virginia). The same is true elsewhere around the world. In fact, you can argue that neighborhoods within a single metropolis are more or less integrated into global economic networks. For example, policy elites in Washington, D.C. make decisions that can determine the distribution of resources within the global system, while two miles away, the battered communities of Southeast D.C. experience economic and social isolation akin to the "mega-cities" of the Third World. See Castells, *The Rise of the Network Society*; Mike Davis, *The Planet of Slums* (New York: Verso, 2005).

24. John Logan and Harvey Molotch, *Urban Fortunes* (Berkeley: University of California Press, 1986), 29-31.

25. Timothy Gibson, *Securing the Spectacular City: The Politics of Revitalization and Homelessness in Downtown Seattle* (Lanham, MD: Lexington Books, 2004).

26. Kevin Fox Gotham, "Marketing Mardi Gras: Commodification, Spectacle, and the Political Economy of Tourism in New Orleans," *Urban Studies* 39, no. 10 (2002): 1735-56. Again, the ability of downtown business leaders to build sports complexes at public expense testifies to the power they can wield within the local field. In Seattle, for example, a motivated group of pro-growth city officials and urban boosters successfully pushed a stadium funding bill through the Washington State legislature in 1995—even after Seattle voters defeated a similar funding bill at the polls earlier that year.

27. For an account of this literature see Mark Lowes, *Indy Dreams and Urban Nightmares*, chapter 2.

28. Robert Entman and Andrew Rojecki, *The Black Image in the White Mind* (Chicago: University of Chicago Press, 1999).

29. For examples, see Eileen Meehan "Leisure or Labor? Fan Ethnography and Political Economy," in *Consuming Audiences? Production and Reception in Media Research*, ed. I. Hagen and J. Wasko (Cresskill, NJ: Hampton Press, 2000), 71-92; Graham Murdock, "Base Notes: The Conditions of Cultural Practice," in *Cultural Studies in Question*, ed. M. Ferguson and P. Golding, (London: Sage, 1998); Carol Stabile, "Nike, Social Responsibility, and the Hidden Abode of Production," *Critical Studies in Media Communication* 17, no. 2 (2000): 186-204.

30. See especially, Scott Lash and John Urry, *Economies of Sign and Space* (London: Sage, 1994); Paul du Gay and Michael Pryke, eds., *Cultural Economy: Cultural Analysis and Commercial Life* (London: Sage, 2002); Ash Amin and Nigel Thrift, eds.,

The Blackwell Cultural Economy Reader (Oxford: Blackwell, 2004); Allen Scott, *The Cultural Economy of Cities* (London: Sage, 2000).

31. Such views are, of course, indebted to Henri Lefebvre, *The Production of Space* (Oxford: Blackwell, 1991).

32. Clifford Geertz, *Local Knowledge: Further Essays in Interpretive Anthropology* (New York: Basic Books, 1983).

Part I

The City in Production

Chapter 1

Neoliberal Revitalization: Prison Building, Casinos, and Tourism in Louisiana

Kevin Fox Gotham and Jeannie Haubert

Before Hurricane Katrina hit, city leaders in Allen Parish and New Orleans, Louisiana (a county in the state of Louisiana is called a "parish") had long devoted themselves to revitalizing the economies of their struggling localities. Responding to pressures and forces articulated at global, national, and local scales, city leaders in these two Louisiana localities settled upon two ostensibly opposed strategies: prisons and casinos. At first blush, this seems paradoxical. Casinos are spaces of entertainment and consumption. Prisons are spaces of incarceration and deprivation of freedom. But despite their different purposes and functions, both spaces are heavily surveilled, regulated, and policed. They are, in fact, both sites where social control is exercised through design, surveillance technologies, and codes of regulation and enforcement. Our aim in this chapter is therefore to draw upon the pre-Katrina experience of these two Gulf coast localities to provide a better theoretical framework for understanding the relationship between these two forms of local economic revitalization.

As it happens, Allen Parish and New Orleans are by no means alone in their turn to these strategies. City leaders in the United States have long devoted enormous public resources to the construction of prisons and large entertainment projects, including stadiums, convention centers, entertainment districts, festival malls, and casinos. Indeed, the current pattern of local government entertainment and prison investment is unprecedented, amounting to billions of public dollars invested in privately-controlled facilities for consumers and deviants.[1] The justification for building prisons is that such projects will generate economic returns by encouraging the creation of new jobs through construction, service, and maintenance. The justification for building casinos is that these entertainment projects will bolster sales tax revenue and create employment opportunities. Although these different economic expectations are tested in the literature, little attention has been given to the political and social consequences of redeveloping cities to warehouse criminals and accommodate devotees of legal gambling.

We begin by exploring the political-economic conditions that motivated local elites to choose prison building and tourism as strategies of revitalization in Louisiana. We draw upon newspaper sources, data from the U.S. Census Bureau, and government reports and analyses, among other data sources. Specifically, we examine the siting of the Oakdale Federal Detention Center and the building of a Grand casino in Allen Parish, and conflicts over a Harrah's casino in New Orleans. We identify the key actors and organized interests responsible for the planning and revitalization, discussing along the way the lucrative local tax subsidies offered to the federal government (i.e., Bureau of Prisons) and casino interests. We also explain how casinos and prisons operate as strategic components of a larger process of local image building. In the end, to better explain the relationship between these local economic development strategies, national political forces, and global flows of investment, we offer the concept of *neoliberal revitalization*—a concept that refers to the role of state devolution, deregulation, and privatization in pressuring local states to actively pursue new forms of revitalization, including casinos and prisons, to bolster the tax base and generate revenue. Our ultimate aim, in short, is to provide some insight into the motivations for building prisons and casinos, the institutional links between federal, state, and local governments, and the connections between global forces and local actions in the transformation of cities.

The Political Economy of Urban Revitalization

Recent decades have witnessed an explosion of scholarly research on the changing nature of urban revitalization. Several scholars have explored how local leaders have embraced place marketing, theming, and imaging and branding techniques to support inward investment.[2] Other scholars have examined the rise of theme parks, riverfront shopping malls, sports stadiums, casinos, and other sites in enabling people to consume many different commodities. Reflecting Max Weber's thesis on rationalization and disenchantment, for instance, noted sociologist George Ritzer maintains that what unites these "new means of consumption" is that they are rationally designed to have an enchanted character to maximize consumption.[3] For their part, Mark Gottdiener's analysis of the development of a fully themed mass culture suggests that mass advertising, marketing, and other corporate efforts to create consumer demand now fuel the transformation of cities,[4] while John Hannigan's discussion of the rise of the "fantasy city" draws attention to the increasing importance of historic preservation sites, megaplex cinema, themed restaurants, simulation theaters, and virtual reality arcades in constituting a "new urban economy" dominated by tourism and entertainment.[5] This thread is further developed by work that focuses on understanding the social dynamics of entertainment and leisure, and global-local connections in the production of urban space.[6] As David Harvey discussed in the *Condition of Postmodernity,* today, new forms of spectacle, entertainment, and simulation are transforming cities, eroding previous stable conceptions of time and space, and reinforcing a situation of ephemerality, chaos, and fragmentation.[7] Broadly, diverse thinkers imply that the growth of urban entertainment and tourism, new strategies of urban revitalization, and new forms of public-private partnerships are indicators of widespread socio-economic change and cultural transformation, though they disagree over the form, impact, and periodization.

On the whole, however, there has been little critical research up until this point on the ways that political and economic elites have used casinos and prisons to transform urban space. What research has been conducted on casinos and prisons has been dominated by policy-oriented and industry-sponsored work, so the analyses tend to internalize industry-led priorities and perspectives. Few mainstream accounts connect their empirical work on casinos and prisons with a broader analysis of capitalism and state policy. To remedy these limitations, we develop and apply the concept *neoliberal revitalization* as a heuristic device to explain the role of state devolution, deregulation, and privatization in pressuring local states to incorporate new and innovative forms of revitalization, including corporate entertainment venues and carceral institutions to generate inward investment. Neoliberalism is a set of economic principles that promote market-led policy reform, social restructuring, and urban revitalization. In the public sector, this involves privatization, trade and financial liberalization, dismantling of welfare state apparatuses, imposition of entrepreneurial criteria in the state sector, and state withdrawal from macroeconomic regulation. Neoliberalism also implies the devolution or decentralization of state authority and control over policy formulation and implementation to local governments and private sector organizations. In addition, neoliberalism involves a combination of tax cuts and growth in tax expenditures steered by private initiatives based on fiscal subsidies for specific economic activities. Examples of the establishment of market-centered initiatives include enterprise zones, empowerment zones, urban development corporations, and the proliferation of new forms of local tax subsidies such as tax abatements, industrial revenue bonds, and tax increment financing (TIF). As an ideology, neoliberalism is akin to privatism which stresses the supremacy of the private sector in nurturing societal development, with the public sector adopting a "hands-off" (laissez faire) strategy whose principle obligation is to encourage private profit.[8]

The last three decades have witnessed a wholesale reduction in direct federal assistance and funding for urban revitalization projects, thereby putting increased pressure on state governments and local municipalities to adopt more market-centered measures to attract investment.[9] Cities have always used an assortment of legal and financial incentives to attract business. Yet, what is novel in the 1980s and later is the increased role that local governments are playing in promoting economic competitiveness, creating a favorable "business climate," and establishing more organized and long-lasting "partnerships" with the private sector.[10] Furthermore, city governments have become more adept at marketing their cities as sites of commercial investment and tourist attractions. Several scholars have noted the shift in the *selling* cities, where public agencies and private organizations attempt to persuade people to consume what the city has to offer, to *marketing* cities, where local agencies and organizations try to reconstruct the city according to the expectations of the types of consumers they want to attract.[11] Today, competitive marketing practices occur throughout the United States and Europe. These practices include the deployment of advertising, architectural design, environmental engineering, and sophisticated technology in the service of selling an experience along with commodities.[12] In sum, the shift to marketing, reduced federal funding, and the growth of local entrepreneurialism are major factors driving changes in the nature of urban revitalization.

Starting in the 1970s, urban areas in Louisiana that had flourished in the postwar Keynesian boom entered a phase of chronic industrial decline. Cities such as New Orleans, Alexandria, Baton Rouge, Shreveport, and others were forced to deal with the triple problems of deindustrialization, falling tax base, and declining public expenditures in an era of intense interurban competition for capital and consumers. Several trends are notable. First, the 1970s witnessed the beginning of a long-term decline in the domestic oil industry, a development that has resulted in the loss of relatively secure manufacturing jobs and a shift toward lower paying service sector jobs with fewer benefits.[13] Second, state and federal reductions in financial aid combined with other forms of federal policy retrenchment presaged the beginning of an era of fiscal austerity for local governments. In 1974, for example, the Louisiana State legislature passed several laws that imposed constraints on the legal ability of local governments to raise revenue through income taxes. These fiscal constraints had the effect of increasing local reliance on sales tax revenue to undertake governmental activities.[14] On the federal level, urban outlays declined from 12.4 percent of all federal expenditures in 1978 to 7.8 percent in 1984.[15] Third, the passage and implementation of the North American Free Trade Agreement (NAFTA) in the early 1990s exacerbated urban disinvestment as small factories in rural areas of Louisiana closed and moved to other areas of the world.[16] In short, the decline of the oil industry, reduced federal and state monies, and fiscal constraints imposed on municipal governments by the state government have eroded significantly the ability of local governments to raise revenue to fund basic government operations and provide public services. As a result, cities throughout Louisiana have been experiencing a condition of chronic fiscal crisis, forced to slash funding for public services while financially pressured to expend greater funds to leverage capital investment.[17]

In addition to economic and political changes, the state of Louisiana has experienced widespread cultural and aesthetic transformations. These changes include the development of a major tourism industry based on the symbolic commodification of places and their transformation into aestheticized spaces of entertainment and pleasure. The mission of the Louisiana Department of Culture, Recreation and Tourism (CRT), for example, is to provide programs and services for the "preservation, promotion and development of Louisiana's historical, cultural, educational, natural, and recreational resources." The goal of these state activities is to enhance "the quality of life for Louisiana's citizens" and encourage "economic growth while re-imaging Louisiana as a great place to live, work and play."[18] A second organization, the non-profit, private-sector, Louisiana Travel Promotion Association (LTPA), represents the state's travel and hospitality industry by offering education, cooperative programs, and certification training to "enhance the level of professionalism within the industry and raise the industry's overall image." One of their programs, the Tourism Advocacy Leadership Program (TALP), is designed to "enable tourism professionals to develop an understanding and comfort level with the legislative process and the issues that affect the hospitality industry." The program also trains individuals "to actively pursue relationships with elected leaders and become involved in the legislative process." The goal of TALP, in other words, is to train officials in the art of promoting legislation favorable to the state tourism industry.[19] Through the creation of different network forms, the CRT and the LTPA are guided by a logic of standardization, rationalization, and selling of Louisiana and its cities. These organizations and their committees and bureaus design routines to clarify goals, reduce the uncertainty of place promotion, and identify opportunities to enhance consumer demand. Tourism networks extend from the state level to the urban level and operate not only as structures of communication, but also as conduits of resources and information exchange that serve as a basis of collective action.

What is important is that tourism organizations like the CRT and the LTPA are involved in producing and selling tourist "experiences." These experiences are the anticipated outcomes of what sociologist John Urry calls the "tourist gaze," where "places are chosen to be gazed upon because there is anticipation, especially through day-dreaming and fantasy, of intense pleasures, either on a different scale or involving different senses from those customarily encountered."[20] Tourist experiences are transformed into commodities through the processes of standardization and homogenization that emphasize calculability, predictability, and efficiency of control. According to G. Llewellyn Watson and Joseph P. Kopachevsky, keen observers of the tourism industry, "touristic activities are definitely constrained by the prepackaging and staging of activities and experiences, because profitable commodification requires the standardization of inputs, production, clients, and consumption."[21] The various commercial and public institutions designed to commodify and provide tourist experiences make up what tourism researcher S. Britton calls the "tourist production system" that "simultaneously enables tourist experiences to occur, encourages tourists to anticipate their experience and expected social returns, and convinces tourists they have had the requisite experiences."[22] In short, tourism boosters on the state level have defined virtually every region and city as a potential tourist attraction worthy of advertising and showcasing. The important point is that tourism investment and advertising intimates places as commodity-spectacles, images that are produced for global consumption.

Prison Building and Casino Development in Allen Parish

The economic recession of the early 1980s and the subsequent long-term decline of the local economy provided the motivation for government leaders in Allen Parish to establish new relationships and financial connections with corporate capital and the federal government to bolster the tax base. In October 1981, the Vancouver Plywood Company plant in the small town of Oakdale ceased operations due to a depressed construction industry. The wood mill had employed between 200 and 250 Allen Parish residents. One month later, the Calcasieu Paper Company mill located near Oakdale in the town of Elizabeth closed its doors. The paper mill had been a vital part of the parish economy for sixty years, and its closing sent shock waves through the community. Newspaper reports maintained that the mill closed because "replacing its outmoded machinery would be prohibitively expensive and because its products . . . couldn't compete with cheaper plastics."[23] The paper mill closing displaced approximately 350 workers leaving a significant proportion of the population in the small towns of Oakdale and Elizabeth unemployed. Since the mill employees had spent most of their lives in specialized occupations, their skills were not easily transferable to other occupations. The closings also stimulated a significant increase in housing foreclosures and the out-migration of people. Although more than 70 percent of the Oakdale residents owned homes in 1980, the layoffs, and the subsequent years of out-migration, not only made it difficult for unemployed families to pay their mortgages but also made it virtually impossible for families to sell their homes. Broadly, during the 1980s, the population of Allen Parish declined from 21,390 residents to 21,226 residents, while the population of Oakdale plummeted from 7155 to 6832, a 4.5 percent decline. The unemployment rate for Allen Parish was 14 percent in both 1980 and 1990, with 38 percent of the population living in poverty in 1990, an increase of eight percentage points from 1980.[24]

During the 1980s, local leaders launched a major lobbying campaign to attract a Federal Detention Center (FDC) to Oakdale to compensate for the sagging economy and eroding population. Part of the attraction of a FDC was the promise of 600 new jobs. The campaign for the FDC soon developed into a major struggle between Oakdale and El Reno, Oklahoma. Both cities spent much time and effort to win the FDC. To make Oakdale more attractive, Louisiana courted the Bureau of Prisons (BOP) by offering tax exemptions and championing the town as a place of cheap labor and low construction costs. In addition, local and state officials promised to offer bilingual training in special classes at vo-tech schools to help prospective employees work with the mostly Spanish-speaking detainees.[25] In the end, the federal government chose Oakdale and the FDC opened in 1986. According to U.S. Attorney General William Smith, "Oakdale was chosen after an extensive review because of its location and because state, parish, and city officials expressed enthusiastic support for the proposed center." He also noted the "undeniably large and willing work force in the area" as a reason for the siting.[26] Budget constraints resulted in the construction of a facility that employed only 300 people.

Interestingly, there was no strictly "private" side to the local campaign to attract a FDC to Oakdale. Public officials competed with other cities to offer lucrative tax exemptions to the BOP, a federal agency. Nevertheless, this "public-public" partnership still reflected the ideology of privatism, with the BOP operating as a profit-minded organization looking to maximize its financial interests in the most rational and lucrative fashion. Starved for capital investment, the local state placated to competitive pressures and gave in to federal demands offering generous tax breaks to attract the Federal Detention Center.[27]

By the late 1980s, government leaders recognized that the FDC was doing little to alleviate the economic woes of the parish. Continuing manufacturing decline motivated local elites to establish new partnerships with corporate casino interests to promote the growth of a consumption-based tourism infrastructure. The result was the construction of a Grand casino with 400 luxury rooms, six restaurants, 3150 slot machines, 80 poker tables, a golf course, 156 RV hookups, and live entertainment. The resort is owned by seven local families that make up the Cousahtta tribe. As a tribal casino, the Grand casino does not pay state taxes. While the casino has brought new forms of investment to the area along with the creation of 2800 jobs, the wealth is fairly concentrated among a few families, thus reinforcing intense inequalities in the community and region.

The development of the casino reflects larger trends in the region, especially the shift to tourism. As a strategic component of tourism investment, especially in rural towns, casinos reflect elite attempts to project an image of a vibrant and rebounding space of entertainment that will have trickle down effects in the local community. Political officials perceive the Grand casino and resort not only as a site of entertainment but also as a marketing tool with which to change perceptions of Allen Parish from images of disinvestment, dereliction, and emptiness to those of amusement and festivity. Yet this economic revitalization strategy has more to do with concealing depressed areas from visitors than with reversing the massive disinvestment of the parish and region. Casinos embody what Dennis Judd, a noted urban political scientist, calls a "tourist bubble." They provide "entertainment and excitement, with reassuringly clean and attractive surroundings."[28] Where poverty and urban disinvestment make areas of the parish inhospitable to visitors, the specialized areas of the tribal casino and resort operate as tourist destinations. Like other spaces of controlled entertainment and consumption, casinos shield visitors from the unsavory elements of everyday life and enwrap them in a fantasy world of playfulness and festive release.

Rise of Gaming in New Orleans

Like Allen Parish, the rise of gaming in New Orleans in the late 1980s and later is related to the loss of manufacturing jobs, the erosion of the chemical and petroleum industry, and attempts by city leaders to diversify the local economy. In the 1960s and 1970s, dwindling urban population and burgeoning suburban development depressed the local tax base and created the context for city leaders to develop tourism in the city. The result was the construction of a new convention center and the Louisiana Superdome, among other large projects. From 1967 to 1977, manufacturing jobs in New Orleans declined in every year except one. By 1977, only 11 percent of the labor force was employed in manufacturing, a situation that placed the city among the lowest in industrial employment in the nation. The decline in manufacturing in the 1970s paralleled a decline in jobs in the oil and gas industry in the 1980s. In 1982, the oil and gas industry employed approximately 28,000 people in the metropolitan area. By the late 1980s, the city was losing business to other ports, the result of a depressed oil market during the decade. In 2001, only 13,000 people worked in the oil and gas sector in New Orleans.[29] Over the years, local public officials, scholars, and journalists have acknowledged the injurious effects of increasing blight and rising poverty while downtown redevelopment, gentrification, and suburban growth have been taking place.[30] In 1999, six years prior to the arrival of Katrina and the much-hyped "rediscovery" of poverty in America, the poverty rate for the city of New Orleans was 27.9 percent, a rate that was more than ten percentage points above the national average for central cities. In a survey of 216 counties and parishes in the United States with at least 250,000 residents, the U.S. Census Bureau found that Orleans Parish was one of the poorest, ranking fourth, with 25 percent of its working population living in poverty. Only five other counties in the nation had a poverty rate of 25 percent or greater in 2000. In a study of median household incomes in those 216 counties and parishes, Orleans Parish again ranked among the poorest, third from the bottom at 213, with $27,111. In short, crushing poverty was an everyday reality for at least one in four residents of Orleans parish long before the nation's attention was focused on the issue by the arrival of Hurricane Katrina. [31]

Throughout the last few decades, city leaders in New Orleans have implemented policies and established new partnerships with private corporate interests to promote the growth of tourism.[32] The most recent component of this tourism strategy is the legalization of gaming on the state level and the opening of a Harrah's casino in downtown New Orleans, adjacent to the historic Vieux Carre (French Quarter) neighborhood. Initial calls for building a Vegas-style casino in New Orleans came from Governor Edwin Edwards in the mid- to late-1980s. The front stage motivation for building casinos stemmed not only from the depressed local and state economy, but also from the growth of gaming in nearby states such as Mississippi. Edwards, for his part, contended that Mississippi's gaming industry was draining income and jobs from Louisiana and that the state had to legalize gaming to become more competitive with rival states. By the early 1990s, legalized gaming had stimulated the development of the riverboat gaming industry and created additional pressures to expand gaming to land-based casinos.

In 1992, the City of New Orleans began accepting bids from casino operators and eventually awarded a contract to Harrah's to build a casino. During this time, conflicts among local residents and political leaders erupted over whether or not the Harrah's negotiation was a politically-motivated "back room" deal to benefit Edwards's cronies. In addition, anti-gaming groups argued that courting corporate casino interests was the beginning of the "Las Vegasization" of New Orleans—e.g., the conversion of New Orleans into a major gaming destination. Opponents argued that gaming would empower transnational entertainment interests and undermine the cultural charm, ambiance, and historic authenticity of the city. During the early to mid-1990s, the state and local government renegotiated Harrah's lease contract several times in response to Harrah's insistence that the tax burdens were too expensive and constraining its profits. In November 1995, Harrah's filed for chapter 11 bankruptcy. A month later, the City of New Orleans filed a lawsuit against Harrah's to compel the corporation to pay its taxes. After three years of bankruptcy struggles, the state and city governments and Harrah's emerged from litigation and initiated plans to open a permanent casino. In 1999, Harrah's opened at the foot of Canal street, across from the Vieux Carre.[33]

Over the next six years, conflicts between Harrah's and political officials and local hotel and restaurant owners punctuated local debate over the expansion of casino gaming in New Orleans. Two conflicts were especially poignant. First, in January 2001, Harrah's again filed for bankruptcy claiming it could not afford the tax burdens imposed on the corporation by the city and state governments. In response, the state government cut the casino's annual tax payments in half, from $100 million to $50 million. In addition, the City of New Orleans agreed to slash $5 million from annual payments Harrah's made to the city in order to keep 2500 casino jobs. Nevertheless, in July 2001, Harrah's laid off 148 workers, cutting their maintenance staff to the minimum amount required by contract with the city. Second, early negotiations with Harrah's favored local hotel and restaurant interests because the city contract restricted the casino from building any additional hotels or restaurants. In bankruptcy settlements, however, Harrah's emerged with the right to build new hotels and expand food service at the casino. In September 2003, the casino announced plans to demolish five nineteenth century historic buildings to build a twenty-seven story, 450-room hotel, a development that inflamed local preservationist groups. Over the next year, Harrah's appeased some of the preservationists and agreed to salvage two of the five buildings that the corporation originally wanted to demolish. Eventually, Harrah's received city council approval to build the $100 million hotel. When complete in 2006, this hotel will be the twelfth largest casino hotel in the world. Finally, in March 2005, the Louisiana Gaming Control Board approved a massive merger between Harrah's and Caesar's, thereby augmenting the trend of continued expansion of Harrah's, and increasing dominance of the gaming industry in New Orleans and the state of Louisiana as a whole. Although the Harrah's future development initiatives were thrown into some doubt with the destruction wrought by Hurricane Katrina, the gaming giant had planned, by 2006, to operate, in addition to its casino, a steakhouse, a brewery, a buffet, a deli and coffee shop, a Vegas style nightclub, and major hotel.[34]

The development and expansion of Harrah's in New Orleans reflects two major trends. First, it signifies the growth and increased power of corporate tourism and global entertainment firms in the process of tourism-oriented urban revitalization.[35] Since 2003, casino revenue has come to rival oil and gas revenue in importance to the Louisiana state budget. This dependence on the entertainment sector has worried some state legislators who contend that the state budget could be negatively impacted should gambling revenue decrease. According to State Senator Jay Dardenne, chairman of the Senate Finance Committee, a slowing growth rate is "indicative of the inevitable cannibalization of gambling dollars in Louisiana."[36] Second, the growth of Harrah's bespeaks a shift in property ownership away from many small groups and individuals toward a more muted corporate-style control in New Orleans tourism. This corporatization of entertainment has an elective affinity with larger processes of homogenization and rationalization of consumption. Indeed, the growth of corporate gaming expresses the emergence of new global-local connections where the balance of power is shifting from locally-owned entertainment venues and localized consumption patterns toward corporate chains and more standardized patterns of consumption.

In short, the legalization of gaming in Louisiana was never about enhancing consumer choice in gaming but about creating the social and legal conditions for large-scale, corporate-owned casinos to penetrate local economies. Independent and locally-owned gaming venues were criminalized before the early 1990s. Today, the gaming experience is increasingly framed by sameness and sanitation and subject to controlled surveillance of consumer behavior by monopoly firms. Broadly, gaming is a global industry largely driven by mega-sized entertainment corporations who have formed new "synergies" with traditional city boosters (chambers of commerce, city governments, service industries). Corporate casinos like Harrah's are expanding their entertainment operations beyond gaming to encompass music, club and bar venues, and other forms of entertainment. As cities build casinos, locally-owned entertainment spaces may be marginalized and experience what David Harvey referred to as "serial reproduction," losing their local distinctiveness and unique charm.

Prisons, Casinos, and Neoliberal Revitalization

In the end, our analysis of neoliberal revitalization in pre-Katrina Louisiana highlights the importance of situating the study of urban revitalization within larger social and economic processes, including transformations in the nature of state policy. One novel aspect of contemporary urban revitalization is the transformed role of state involvement in local affairs. An important dimension of state involvement is captured by the distinction between direct intervention and regulation. U.S. federal and state governments have never been interventionist states involved in making substantive decisions for many markets. They create agencies to enforce general rules in markets, but they do not decide who can own what and how investment should proceed. The concept of *neoliberal revitalization* draws attention to the new components of state regulation, specifically the impact of privatization, deregulation, and other privatist forms of state policy on the revitalization process. Privatization and deregulation do not represent the withdrawal of the state from regulating the economy but a *reconfiguration* of state involvement in markets.

In Allen Parish and New Orleans, the erosion of both federal and state government revenue over the last few decades means there is a greater reliance on sales tax revenue than ever before, and more intense pressure to invest in speculative ventures. This constrained fiscal environment has reduced the efficacy of redistributive policies, encouraged the adoption of entrepreneurial governance, and created the context for the city government to intensify partnerships with public and private capital to promote prison building and encourage the growth of a consumption-based tourism infrastructure. In short, prison building and casino construction have emerged as strategies of economic development in response to devolution, deregulation, and privatization. For Allen Parish and New Orleans, the rise of neoliberal policies has created a new competitive environment in which local governments are increasingly forced to develop new subsidies and marketing and imaging strategies to attract new investment.

Both public and private prisons and casinos are expanding globally. In the case of prisons, the United States prison population is the world's largest in absolute terms, at more than two million, and is growing larger all the time. Historically, all prisons were private endeavors which gradually came under the control of the government. During the last two decades, however, state and local governments around the world have begun privatizing their prisons, policing activities, and relying more on private security forces.[37] In similar fashion, over the last twenty-five years, commercial gaming has expanded from two states (Nevada and New Jersey) to forty-seven states, an explosive growth that reflects the rise of the entertainment economy and state government efforts to increase revenue and jobs. Today, land-based casinos, large and small riverboat casinos, and Native American reservation casinos are ubiquitous. They exist in all geographic regions in the United States and are spreading throughout the world.[38] In the case of casinos, the local state is increasingly forced into the role of having to supply cheap labor and security forces, including police and fire protection, to sustain corporate entertainment spaces while maintaining the façade of a laissez-faire, privatist, entrepreneurial city. At the same time, city budgets are being set aside for image (re)construction and advertising while institutions like prisons and casinos are increasingly exempted from paying taxes.

Prisons and casinos are a strategic component of local effects to re-imagine and re-package the urban landscape to rejuvenate the economy. Like big-ticket convention centers and sports stadiums, casinos are prestige projects that project an image of progress, optimism, and forward-moving redevelopment. And for cities facing economic annihilation, the lure of hundreds of jobs at a proposed prison can seem like a panacea. Yet the track record of these projects in Louisiana suggests a more sobering reality, including a devastating dynamic of regional economic change, low wages, and strained public infrastructure.

In our view, therefore, the promotion of casinos, prisons, and other forms of urban revitalization as a sort of economic panacea is profoundly shortsighted. The key focus for policymakers should in this way not be on whether casinos or prisons are economically "successful" (although the checkered history of Allen Parish's exercise in "prison-led" revitalization casts some doubt on this score) but that the degree to which these forms of urban revitalization enhance the *quality of life* for local residents. The emphasis on business-led "economic-impact" studies produces much media ballyhoo about the potential of new investment, but they say little about the long-term success. Indeed, more often than not, economic-impact studies function as public relations blitzes and promotional activities.

Instead, as we see it, there is a need to pursue an altogether wider agenda on the "impact" of casinos and prisons. Questions need to be focused on issues of social inclusion, social justice, collective empowerment, and the extent to which urban revitalization offers genuine solutions to the problems of the city. Second, "success" needs to be evaluated not only in economic terms but also in light of social and political implications. We advocate a conception of "success" that evaluates urban revitalization policy on its ability to be democratically inclusive, enhance collective decision-making, and empower marginalized groups. Scholars are constrained in their ability to generalize given the variety of different types of urban revitalization and the unpredictable play of contextual factors. The extent to which different strategies of urban revitalization offer durable and meaningful solutions to the needs of city residents depends on the type of city and nature of investment. Yet what is clear is that development policies which focus narrowly on a one-dimensional definition of "revitalization," or policies that prioritize narrow economic definitions of "success," have little hope of enhancing the broader quality of life for the majority of local residents.

Notes

1. Peter Eisinger, "The Politics of Bread and Circuses: Building the City for the Visitor Class," *Urban Affairs Review* 35, no. 3 (January 2000): 316-33; Kevin J. Delaney and Rick Eckstein, *Public Dollars, Private Stadiums: The Battle Over Building Sports Stadiums* (New Brunswick, NJ: Rutgers University Press, 2004); Tara Herivel and Paul Wright, eds., *Prison Nation: The Warehousing of America's Poor* (New York: Routledge, 2003).

2. For an overview see John Hannigan, "Symposium on Branding, the Entertainment Economy, and Urban Place Building: Introduction," *International Journal of Urban and Regional Research* 27, no. 2 (June 2003): 352-60.

3. George Ritzer, *Enchanting a Disenchanted World: Revolutionizing the Means of Consumption*, 2nd ed. (Thousand Oaks, CA: Pine Forge Press, 2005).

4. Mark Gottdiener, *Theming of America: Dreams, Visions, and Commercial Spaces*, 2nd ed. (Boulder, CO: Westview Press, 2001).

5. John Hannigan, *Fantasy City: Pleasure and Profit in the Postmodern Metropolis* (New York: Routledge, 1998).

6. Richard Lloyd and Terry Nichols Clark, "The City as an Entertainment Machine," in *Critical Perspectives on Urban Redevelopment*, vol. 6, *Research in Urban Sociology*, ed. Kevin Fox Gotham (New York: Elsevier Press, 2001); Paul Chatteron and Robert Hollands, "Theorizing Urban Playscapes: Producing, Regulating, and Consuming Youthful Nighttime Spaces," *Urban Studies* 39, no. 1 (2002): 95-116; Paul Chatterton and Robert Hollands, *Urban Nightscapes: Youth Cultures, Pleasure Spaces, and Corporate Power* (London and New York: Routledge, 2003); Sharon Zukin, *The Cultures of Cities* (Cambridge, MA: Blackwell, 1995); Michael Sorkin, ed., *Variations on a Theme Park: The New American City and the End of Public Space* (New York: Hill and Wang, 1992).

7. David Harvey, *The Condition of Postmodernity: An Enquiry into the Origins of Cultural Change* (New York: Blackwell, 1989).

8. For an overview of neoliberalism, see Neil Brenner and Nik Theodore, eds., *Spaces of Neoliberalism: Urban Restructuring in North American and Western Europe* (New York: Blackwell, 2002)

9. Timothy K. Barnekov, Daniel Rich, and Robert Warren, "The New Privatism, Federalism, and the Future of Urban Governance: National Urban Policy in the 1980s," *Journal of Urban Affairs* 3, no. 4 (Fall 1981); Peter Eisinger, "City Politics in an Era of Federal Devolution," *Urban Affairs Review* 33, no. 3 (1998): 308-25.

10. The literature on public-private partnerships in urban revitalization is vast. For an overview, see Kevin Fox Gotham, ed., *Critical Perspectives on Urban Redevelopment*, vol. 6, *Research in Urban Sociology* (New York: Elsevier Press, 2001).

11. Briavel Holcomb, "Marketing Cities for Tourism," in *The Tourist City*, ed. Dennis R. Judd and Susan S. Fainstein (New Haven: Yale University Press, 1999); Kevin Fox Gotham, "Marketing Mardi Gras: Commodification, Spectacle, and the Political Economy of Tourism in New Orleans." *Urban Studies* 39 no. 10 (September 2002): 1735-56; For overviews, see *Cities and Visitors: Regulating People, Markets, and City Space*, ed. Lily K. Hoffman, Susan S. Fainstein, and Dennis R. Judd (New York: Blackwell Publishing, 2003).

12. Mark Gottdiener, ed., *New Forms of Consumption: Consumers, Culture, and Commodification* (Lanham, MD: Rowman & Littlefield, 2000); Mark Gottdiener, *Theming of America: Dreams, Visions, and Commercial Spaces* (Boulder, CO: Westview Press, 1997); G. Kearns and C. Philo, eds., *Selling Places: The City as Cultural Capital, Past and Present*. (Oxford: Pergamon Press, 1999).

13. Robert K. Whelan, "New Orleans: Mayoral Politics and Economic-Development Policies in the Postwar Years, 1945-1986" in *The Politics of Urban Development*, ed. C.N. Stone and H.T. Sanders (Lawrence, KS: University Press of Kansas, 1987); Robert K. Whelan, "New Orleans: Public-Private Partnerships and Uneven Development" in *Unequal Partnerships*, ed. Gregory D. Squires (New Brunswick, NJ: Rutgers University Press, 1989).

14. The increased reliance on sales taxes is discussed in Michael Peter Smith and Marlene Keller, "'Managed Growth' and the Politics of Uneven Development in New Orleans," in *Restructuring the City: The Political Economy of Urban Redevelopment*, ed. Susan Fainstein et al. (New York: Longman 1986), 126-66.

15. Frank Gaffikin and Barney Warf, "Urban Policy and the Post-Keynesian State in the United Kingdom and the United States." *International Journal of Urban and Regional Research* 17, no. 1 (1993): 67-84.

16. Job losses in Louisiana directly related to the NAFTA totaled almost 7,000 up through year 2001, including over 3,000 in year 2001 in the cities of Abbeville, Port Barre, and St. Martinville by Fruit of the Loom plant closings. See Ed Anderson, "Fruit of Loom Cuts 1,873 Jobs, Abbeville Plant," *Times-Picayune,* 12 November 1997, 1(A).

17. Bureau of Governmental Research (BGR), *BGR Outlook on Orleans: Status Report on the 1998 City Operating Budget* (New Orleans, LA: Bureau of Governmental Research, 1998); Iris J. Lav and Andrew Brecher, "Passing Down the Deficit: Federal Policies Contribute to the Severity of State Fiscal Crisis," *Center on Budget and Policy Priorities,* 2004. http://www.cbpp.org/5-12-04sfp.htm.

18. See Louisiana Department of Culture, Recreation, and Tourism (CRT): http://crt.g2digital.com/secretary.

19. See Louisiana Travel Promotion Association (LTPA): http://www.ltpa.org/index.htm.

20. John Urry, *The Tourist Gaze,* 2nd ed. (London: Sage Publications, 2003), 3.

21. G. Llewellyn Watson and Joseph P. Kopachevsky, "Interpretations of Tourism as Commodity," *Annals of Tourism Research* 21, no. 3 (1994): 643-60.

22. S. Britton, "Tourism, Capital, and Place: Towards a Critical Geography of Tourism," *Environment and Planning: Society and Space* 9: 451-78.

23. John Pope, "As the Mill Stench Left, So did the Town's Jobs," *Times-Picayune,* 14 August 1982.

24. Figures come from the U.S. Census Bureau, Census of Population and Housing, 1980 and 1990; John Pope, "Unemployment in Allen Parish Highest in LA," *Times-Picayune,* 16 May 1982.

25. Associated Press, "Allen Parish Site Chosen for Center to Shelter Aliens." *Times-Picayune,* 11 February 1983; Louisiana State University (LSU) Agricultural Center Research and Extension, "About Allen Parish" 1999. http://www2.lsuagcenter.com/parish/allen/About_the_Parish.htm.

26. Edgar Poe, "Boost For Allen Parish," *Times-Picayune,* 23 February 1983.

27. The ideology of privatism is discussed in Timothy Barnekov and Daniel Rich, "Privativism and the Limits of Local Economic Policy," *Urban Affairs Quarterly* 25, no. 2 (December 1989): 212-38; Timothy Barnekov, Robin Boyle, and Daniel Rich, *Privatism and Urban Policy in Britain and the United States* (New York: Oxford University Press, 1989).

28. Dennis Judd, "Constructing the Tourist Bubble." in *The Tourist City,* ed. Dennis R. Judd and Susan S. Fainstein (New Haven: Yale University Press, 1999).

29. For data and figures on the decline of the petroleum and manufacturing sectors, see City of New Orleans, *Operating Budget for Fiscal Year 1976,* (New Orleans, LA: City of New Orleans, 1976); City of New Orleans, *Operating Budget for Calendar and Fiscal Year 2002* (New Orleans, LA: City of New Orleans, 2002); see also Peter F. Burns, and Matthew O. Thomas, "Governors and the Development Regime in New Orleans," *Urban Affairs Review* 39, no. 6 (July 2004): 791-812.

30. Mickey Lauria, Robert K. Whelan, and Alma Young, "The Revitalization of New Orleans," in *Urban Revitalization: Policies and Programs,* ed. Fritz Wagner, Timothy E. Joder, and Anthony J. Mumphrey (Thousand Oaks, CA: Sage Publications, 1995); Jane Brooks and Alma Young, "Revitalizing the Central Business District in the Face of Decline: The Case of New Orleans, 1970-1990," *Town Planning Review* 64 (1993): 251-71; Robert K. Whelan, Alma Young, and Mickey Lauria, "Urban Regimes and Racial Politics in New Orleans," *Journal of Urban Affairs* 16, no. 1 (1994): 1-21; Robert K. Whelan and Alma Young, "New Orleans: The Ambivalent City," in *Big City Politics in*

Transition, ed. H.V. Savitch and John Clayton Thomas (Newbury Park, CA: Sage Publications, 1991).

31. "Most of the City's Workers Fall into Service Jobs; Orleans Poverty Rate Among the Worst in the U.S.," *Times-Picayune,* 20 November 2001, p. 1. Poverty rate for the city of New Orleans available at U.S. Census Bureau (Census of Population and Housing. Data supplied by the State of the Cities Data System SOCDS). http://socds.huduser.org.

32. Kevin Fox Gotham, "Theorizing Urban Spectacles: Festivals, Tourism, and the Transformation of Urban Space," *City: Analysis of Urban Trends, Culture, Theory, Policy, Action* 9, no. 2 (July 2005); Kevin Fox Gotham, "Tourism Gentrification: The Case of New Orleans's Vieux Carre (French Quarter)," *Urban Studies* 42, no. 7 (June 2005): 1099-1121; Kevin Fox Gotham, "Marketing Mardi Gras: Commodification, Spectacle, and the Political Economy of Tourism in New Orleans." *Urban Studies* 39, no. 10 (September 2002): 1735-56.

33. Peter F. Burns and Matthew O. Thomas, "Governors and the Development Regime in New Orleans," *Urban Affairs Review* 39, no. 6 (July 2004): 791-812; Peter Applebome, "As New Orleans Plans Huge Casino, Some See Promise, Others See Threat," *New York Times,* 7 July 1992; Kevin Sack, "New Orleans Casino Is Halted in Bankruptcy Filing," *Times-Picayune,* 23 November 1995; Ed Anderson and Alfred Charles, "N.O., State Study Options for Dealing with Harrah's," *Times Picayune,* 23 November 1995; Ronette King and Stewart Yerton, "But Long-Term Economic Impact Is Still a Wild Card," *Times-Picayune,* 24 October 1999.

34. Bruce Eggler, "Preservationists Reject Casino Hotel," *Times-Picayune,* 8 October 2003; Rebecca Mowbray, "Harrah's Bill Passed, But Hand Isn't Over Yet," *Times-Picayune,* 15 March 2001; Rebecca Mowbray, "The Art of the Deal," *Times-Picayune,* 18 April 2001; Rebecca Mowbray, "Harrah's In Negotiations to Buy Casino Rival Caesar's," *Times-Picayune,* 14 July 2004; Rebecca Mowbray, "Harrah's Building Nightclub," *Times-Picayune,* 8 March 2005; Rebecca Mowbray, "State Approves Harrah's, Caesar's Merger Plan," *Times-Picayune,* 16 March 2005.

35. We can also see the increasing political power and influence of the gambling industry in overall contributions of the industry to federal elections. During the 1990s, gambling contributions to elections through soft money, political action committees, and individuals increased 447 percent. Sizable portions of soft money have become the dominant form of political giving, rising from 38 percent of the total gambling industry contributions in the 1991-92 election cycle to 64 percent by 1997-1998. From 1999-2001, Harrah's donated over $250,000 in soft money to elections (see Stephen Weissman, Jamie Willmuth, and Frank Clement, "Betting on Trent Lott: The Casino Gambling Industry's Campaign Contributions Pay Off in Congress," *Public Citizen,* June 1999. http://www.citizen.org/congress/campaign/special_interest/articles.cfm?ID=6544).

36. Rebecca Mowbray, "Revenue from Gaming Grows Slowly," *Times-Picayune,* 16 July 2003.

37. Stephen G. Gibbons and Gregory L. Price, "Politics and Prison Development in a Rural Area," *Prison Journal* 75, no. 3 (1995): 380-90; Tim Newburn, "The Commodification of Policing: Security Networks in the Late Modern City." *Urban Studies* 38 nos. 5-6 (2001): 829-48.

38. For an overview of the global spread and socioeconomic impacts of gaming, see James H. Frey, ed., "Gambling: Socioeconomic Impacts and Public Policy," special issue of *Annals of the Academy of Political and Social Science* (March 1998).

Chapter 2

Internet Politics the Singapore Way

Gerald Sussman[1]

> We are right to assume that there is not a point on the globe with which we cannot make a direct link. We now know that the means of real omnipresence are at our disposal. Distance as a cause of uncertainty will disappear from the calculations of the statesman and the merchant.

This effusive assertion of the transformative and dominating power of technology appeared in the American press following the successful telegraphic transmission over the first transatlantic cable in August 1858.[2] Its presumptions about the ascendance of technology over nature and of political and economic hegemony over worldwide communications were, in the mid-nineteenth century, very much a part of the emerging imperial imagination. And the reporter's assessment of the proprietors of this idea of progress, "the statesman and the merchant," was not misguided. What this achievement meant for ordinary people, however, was, and remains, contentious.

A contemporary enthusiast waxing over the marvels of the digital age easily could have uttered a similar declaration of progress. There continues today exhilaration for the commercial, political, and military rewards of geographical conquest. In the colonial era, however, it was telegraphy, especially submarine transmission, that was the strategic informational and communicative tool of empire.[3] British and, later, American regimes of power gained calculated advantage over much of the world's resources, waterways, and peoples—and the infrastructural means to manage and integrate them on a global basis.

Singapore: Spoke of Empire

One of the colonial era's most important outposts was the British naval and commercial station in Singapore, an island territory established in 1819 as an outpost for India- and China-bound cargoes, including valuable opium consignments. In the post-colonial era, it has become an industrial park, oil refinery, free port, and export processing zone run largely for U.S., Japanese, and European capital interests (including the presence of some 5,000 transnational corporations). It is also a modern, wealthy, and materially well-developed (albeit small) city-state run by a rigidly authoritarian bureaucrat-capitalist regime and single political organization, the People's Action Party (PAP). Like the proverbial Big Brother, the PAP carefully watches and regulates almost every aspect of political, economic, and social life on the island.

Singapore represents a challenge to political theorists, inasmuch as it functions, at least nominally, as a democracy and as a successful, relatively open market economy. Yet the PAP imposes a panoptic level of state surveillance, intervention, and repressive supervision over the lives of its citizens. Analyses of authoritarianism found in the literature on Latin America or other parts of Asia commonly rest on assumptions made about either socialist or militarist regimes and do not fit the conditions found in Singapore. Charismatic or liberal democratic types of leadership also do not capture Singapore's governance style. Rather, its political culture is rooted in widely shared conservative and collectivist ideas and values.[4] And unlike its neighboring countries and so many other states attempting to transition to industrial and developed status, Singapore's governing institutions thus far have not been jolted by periodic political and economic instability.

Nonetheless, recent out-migration and a degree of internal agitation for political liberalization suggest that single party rule will not remain without serious challenge, particularly when the state's remarkable economic performance begins to falter. The characterization of the regime as authoritarian is hardly contentious, as it has been widely described as such—indeed, such a depiction is embraced by the ruling party's leadership. Bureaucrat-capitalism refers to a particular regime type in which the top-level administrative class is drawn heavily from leading domestic business and financial interests, who retain their corporate linkages directly or through associates and family members throughout their government service. Former prime minister Lee Kuan Yew, for example, chairs the highly secretive Government Investment Corporation, which manages over S$100 billion of state funds in overseas investments.[5] The state is run on corporatist principles, whereby class, gender, and ethnic identities are suppressed under continuous political socialization and mobilization through nation-building rituals, symbols, and rhetoric. Singapore's national mythos is reinforced, for example, by a grandiose annual "National Day" commemoration, indoctrination about the "Singapore story," and regular official injunctions about personal and family citizenship duties, obligations, and moral values—all laden with references to the country's patriarchic leadership and developmentalist political economic agenda.

There are various explanations for Singapore's brand of authoritarian bureaucrat-capitalist rule, of which six seem most robust. The historical context provides one. Singapore was brought into the international state system and world capitalist market under the colonial dominion of Britain, which established for the island a separate niche status in an imperialist political economy.

British rule imposed on Singapore an administrative regime disciplined by politically repressive acts, some of which are still employed by the successor regime against political challengers.

Second, Lee Kuan Yew, a founder of the state, selectively drew upon Confucianist precepts, particularly those that called for a strict code of political and social conduct and obedience to authority. Third, as a British-trained barrister, Lee infused the political culture with a legalistically-framed hierarchical statist command structure. Hence, political management is maintained not as much through omnipresent police intervention as much as through legislative acts and compliant courts that micromanage the society and impose heavily rule-oriented civic behavior. Fourth, Lee's personal control of the ruling People's Action Party, which has been the main instrument of state policy, was uncontested once he purged the organization of its left wing and established within it a homogeneous political vector that was conservative, business-oriented, and developmentalist.

Fifth, although Singapore has a high per capita income, can boast of a stable political order, and faces no serious internal or external threats, there remains a high degree of dependency on foreign capital and transnational corporate branch plants as the mainstay of its export-oriented industrial economy. This makes the economy and the society highly vulnerable and responsive to economic shifts and downturns in the West, particularly the United States, the country's major investor and trade partner. The PAP thereby sees the need for a strong state, including strict control of mass media and information systems, in order to guide a development strategy that can accommodate changes in the international division of production and labor. And, finally, the regime defends its authoritarianism by citing the need to protect the political order from potential threats arising from the city-state's delicate ethnic balance, a legacy of regional diversity and British colonial practices that it can do little to change.

A central challenge seen by the PAP is how to reproduce the country's standing in the world economy as it shifts to neoliberal restructuring and advanced digital production technologies and services. Since 1995, the PAP publicly has resolved that it must embrace the Internet as an instrument of international commerce, government, and public education and information if it is to continue to succeed as an economically viable state in the midst of much larger state economies and in the context of the increasingly liberalized world trading and investment economy.[6] But how can the ruling party make Singapore a globally competitive "intelligent island" and center of innovation and new, multimedia creative industries, while at the same time preserving the PAP's moral custody and the state's control over print, broadcast, and cyber-media access and content? Is the maintenance of a development agenda consistent with the suppression of political expression? Or has the state's material success activated a popular yearning for intellectual and participatory rights long denied under the regime's rationalizing myths of the "Singapore story" and its anti-liberal, anti-adversarial, so-called "Asian values"?[7]

The "Asian values" pretext for prolonging the PAP's power monopoly and its paternalistic ethos are deeply embedded in its communications policies. Having produced one of the most regulation-thick constitutions in the world, the Singapore state attempts to impose strict supervision over civil society by specifying the approved and legal boundaries of almost every aspect of social interaction—from language use in the home, matrimonial selection, family size, campaigns for cheerful public conduct, and National Day participation, to sanctions on chewing gum. The Party thus assumes the guardianship of correct political and social values, its exclusivity as a political agent, and its authority to monopolize the formation of economic development priorities. There is no room for independent social or political activism, which in its view would disrupt the stability of the society that the PAP has so carefully constructed and contradict its "Asian values," as expounded by Singapore's first prime minister (1959-1990), Lee Kuan Yew.[8]

Digital Dictatorship?

The popular association of the Internet with the idea of unrestricted social, intellectual, and political exchange, even in the most centralized command economies, refutes some of the core governance principles of the PAP. This chapter looks at how the centralized, authoritarian, bureaucrat-capitalist Singapore regime has responded to the Internet challenge in terms of the medium's potential for enabling greater latitude of democratic expression and independent communicative interaction. In what ways does Singapore's Internet policy reflect a *constant* or a *shift* in that country's attitude toward free expression and free association? Will the Internet's open design architecture lead the state to devise and impose more rigid filtering and firewall systems to contain its unruly potential for grassroots democratic politics? Will Singapore, a city-state, thus serve as a test case for how other states, including those in the region and even in the West, might foreclose anti-systemic and revolutionary uses of the Internet, while engaging in wholesale surveillance of citizens to enforce compliance to state rule and commercial exploitation? To help us understand how Internet policy is likely to evolve, it is important to first consider how the Singapore government has treated other modes of information and communication—past and present—and then to consider how these communication policies link up with the broader objectives of the PAP. It also is important to consider the types and effectiveness of resistance to its Internet and broader political policies.

Recent uses of the Internet by politically-minded youth, university students, and adults in Singapore, including those by the Think Centre and Sintercom (Singapore Internet Community), two local electronic forums for political discussion, represent by that country's historical standards remarkable challenges to the government's program of guided public education. Since Singapore's inception as an internally self-governing state (1959), the PAP has actively engaged in the social engineering of school students to channel them into approved subjects and fields and discourage them from engaging in political interests, except where the PAP itself established programs for party leadership training among the "best and the brightest."[9] At the same time, the government has taken certain risks in actively promoting educational and informational uses of the Internet, even if circumscribed by tight legal constraints. By 1999, Singapore boasted a household Internet penetration rate of 46 percent among age 18 and over adults (with nearly 70 percent of households with computers). Its access rate, in fact, was not far behind the United States (59 percent) and Sweden (56 percent), making it one of the most wired cities in the world.[10]

With relatively inexpensive access, Singaporeans have bought heavily into digital networking, not only with the Internet but also with a high use rate of mobile phones, pagers, laptops, short messaging service (SMS), and other communications devices and services. The everyday uses of such instruments diminish the sense of spatial and temporal separation between home and employment and also between citizen and state. A government initiative, Singapore One, was introduced in the late 1990s to wire homes, businesses, and schools with interactive, multimedia applications and services. Beyond extensive surveillance of household telephones and computer use (large corporations with their own leased lines are exempted), the government carries on pervasive electronic monitoring of automobile and ambulatory practices—via required windshield transponders for the island's electronic road pricing system, license plate scanners on expressways and at parking lot entrances, and mounted cameras that observe pedestrian traffic on streets, in public parks and neighborhood centers, and in and outside public buildings. The state also imposes a national identity card system on citizens and permanent residents and has encouraged extensive networks of all varieties of credit and debit card transactions.

The state surveillance potential of such a wired populace is very real. In 1994 the PAP admitted to prying into a government-financed Internet service provider (ISP) in search of pornography and "countersocial activity" among researchers and university staff.[11] In 1999, it was reported (by the British Broadcasting Corporation) that at the behest of Singapore's Ministry of Home Affairs, a local ISP, Singnet, admittedly scanned 200,000 subscribers' personal computers without their consent in what the company said was a search for computer hackers. While the full extent of government surveillance today is not known, Singaporeans generally have been sufficiently forewarned of its existing and potential presence to exercise a high degree of self-censorship.[12] Even without continuous policing of the Internet, a sufficient level of induced fear that leads the citizenry to avoid political discussion on the Web has the intended control outcomes with the added benefit of reduced surveillance costs.

It is no secret, in short, that Internet websites (and other communications media, reportedly including SMS) are regularly scrutinized by the order of government ministries and agencies to track the behavior of citizens and residents. As one Singaporean observer notes, "The government intimidates its critics by collecting information through the surveillance of civil society groups, religious organizations, opposition politicians and whomever else the government perceives to be a threat or considers out of the mainstream. . . . Laws are constantly modified whenever space is found [by citizens] for political expression, mobilisation and action."[13] The Canadian Committee to Protect Journalists found that the Singapore government hired "at least eight censors . . . [to] surf the Internet daily, seeking objectionable material. Sites found with such content are blocked by the local Internet service providers."[14] Surfers receive a "forbidden" message when attempting to reach banned sites on the government's "access control list." Furthermore, the government ruled in 2001 that owners and editors of websites would be held responsible for anonymous postings that violated libel and other laws governing speech. Given the broad sweep of such laws in Singapore, this form of liability poses a major threat to serious website hosts. One website, Sintercom (Singapore Internet Community), which occasionally posts political discussion, effectively was forced to shut down its chat room, and move "offshore," and another, the civil rights group Think Centre, closed its online political forum. Sintercom eventually shut down its site in Singapore altogether when compelled under the Parliamentary Elections Act to register with the Singapore Broadcasting Authority (SBA), but it continued to operate in a limited way outside the country. The threats of lawsuits and prison sentences thus serve as effective instruments in enabling the ruling party to monopolize the political agenda and the distribution of political discussion and information, allowing it "to reap the fruits of electoral legitimacy without running the risks of democratic uncertainty."[15]

In the wake of the September 11 attack in the United States, the Singapore government also has stepped up its surveillance of Islamic activists on the Web, now armed with a "national security" justification for doing so. One controversy in 2002 involved a threat of a criminal defamation lawsuit by the PAP against Zulfikar Mohamad Shariff, the chief executive of a Muslim website (Fateha.com) in Singapore. The website organizers had questioned the government for supporting the U.S. war in Afghanistan, for arresting, at the time, 15 Muslims in an alleged terrorist plot, and for suspending three young Malay Muslim girls for wearing headscarves (*tudung*) to school. Fateha.com also poked fun at the appointment of the wife of then deputy prime minister, Lee Hsien Loong, to a high government post. Zulfikar fled to Australia to avoid prosecution. He reportedly commented, "Looking at the history of the Singapore courts and the court chambers, I do not have that confidence that they are that independent or can act fairly."[16]

In May 2005, the city state's government body in charge of science and technology, A*Star, threatened to bring a lawsuit against a Singaporean blogger Chen Jiahao for making "untrue and serious accusations" about the agency on his weblog. At the time, Chen was a graduate student in physics at the University of Illinois, which raises questions not only about censorship and sweeping libel laws but also about the extraterritorial projection of Singapore's legal and police powers into an American institution that purports to protect the academic freedom of American and international students and university faculty. A*Star insisted it had the right "to protect its reputation and also that of Singapore."

Chen made a hasty apology to avoid prosecution. The New York-based Committee to Protect Journalists expressed concern about "the spectre of costly legal action" by Singapore, as a way to "to chill commentary on the internet."[17]

The reach of government censorship does not extend only to Singaporean citizens. In 1995, a visiting American academic at the National University of Singapore, Christopher Lingle wrote an article for the *International Herald Tribune* in which he critically discussed the human rights conditions in Asia and castigated compliant judiciaries as complicit in the repression carried out by various states in the region. Without ever mentioning Singapore or any Singaporean official, then senior minister Lee Kuan Yew brought libel charges in a Singapore court against Lingle, the *International Herald Tribune*, and its local printing company. All the defendants ultimately were held liable. Lingle hastily fled the country to avoid trial (and $70,000 in damages), taking nothing with him but an overnight bag and his laptop.

As in other countries, many Singaporeans, especially among youth and young adults, share the belief that the Internet represents a vehicle for direct democracy on a global scale. It is seen as an instrument through which people themselves, without the intervention of media institutions, communications corporations, or the government, can act as their own transmitters and interactive agents in information exchange. Singapore's government leaders have shown particular interest in opening space for commercial exploitation of this medium through e-commerce and other Internet services but have no intention of allowing political communication to be part of civil society in the way that some Singaporean net activists imagine. As one study of the Internet found, other authoritarian regimes, especially China, "have taken an active interest in learning form Singapore's example" the ways "that Internet use does not currently pose a significant threat to the stability of authoritarian rule."[18]

The PAP has never been tolerant of the idea of political or public interest groups operating beyond the clutches of the ruling party. In 1987, the Internal Security Act,[19] which allows renewable two-year detentions without trial, was used to arrest 16 "Marxists"—Catholic social workers, young professionals affiliated with the Workers' Party, and theatrical group members—followed by another wave of arrests and rearrests the following year. The *Far Eastern Economic Review* at the time reported this as a move "to quash any possible opposition to its [the PAP] political dominance."[20] In 2001-2002, the ISA was invoked to arrest alleged terrorists without formal charges in conjunction with the September 11 attacks in the United States.

The Political and Legal Context

Since the termination of Singapore's British Crown colony status in 1959, the PAP has retained continuous political control. From the beginning, the PAP and the government have effectively been synonymous terms, and since 1968, there has been almost no organized political opposition. To a great extent, this is a result of the creative efforts of the PAP to eliminate or suppress any political or legal challenges to its rule. The PAP also flexes power through careful control and coordination of the country's economic resources, facilitated by a system of "tight interlocking directorships involving a small coterie of politically-trusted civil servants."[21] In the November 2001 parliamentary elections (in which voting is mandatory and, thereby, precludes no-confidence mass abstention), the four opposition parties together contested only 29 of 84 seats, winning a total of two. The PAP won the rest, securing over 75 percent of the vote in those 29 districts. Lee and his successor, Goh Chok Tong, have used massive electoral victories as "license to engage in whatever action is required to deliver 'good government.'"[22]

The ruling party has instituted various means to obstruct political speech that challenges its monopoly position. Anyone who questions its *dirigiste* prerogatives is regarded as a threat and becomes the focus of intense scrutiny, intimidation, harassment, or arrest. One of the favored means of social control is the liberal use of defamation and libel laws,[23] fines, and tax evasion suits against opposition politicians and political leaders, in effect forcing compliance with the status quo through a legal police state apparatus despite the constitutional (Article 14) guarantee of "the right to freedom of speech and expression" (see Table 4.1). Often, the financial penalties are intended to cause bankruptcy, inasmuch as bankruptcy constitutes a legal barrier against targeted individuals from running for office.

In 1997 alone, one opposition member of parliament, Tang Liang Hong of the Workers' Party, suffered US$5.65 million in libel damages as a result of thirteen suits launched by Lee Kuan Yew and ten other government officials, in addition to thirty-three counts of tax evasion.[24] A leading dissident and former university professor, Chee Soon Juan, was asked to pay more than US$500,000 in court costs and damages, as a result of his public utterances. Chee refused and was reduced to selling his books on the street, risking arrest for not having a permit, and doing so because local bookstores, including the American chain, Borders, fearfully refuse to carry them.

One of Singapore's best-known politicians, Joshua B. Jeyaretnam, first elected under the Workers' Party in 1981, had defamation damages and court costs of US$1.25 million imposed on him in 1998 by a combined action of the country's prime minister, Goh Chok Tong, and ten other government officials, including then senior minister, Lee Kuan Yew. The defamation award stemmed from a factual comment the member of parliament made about "Goh and his people." Bankrupted, Jeyaretnam has been banned from campaigning for political office and practicing as a lawyer. As this was taking place, the National Trade Union Congress was closely collaborating with the government, despite growing economic disparities.[25] The city-state effectively has lost one of its leading opposition politicians.[26] As opposition politicians are eliminated through compliant judiciaries, PAP ministers have been enriching themselves as if they were corporate CEOs. In 2000, the prime minister's salary was raised to S$1.94

million (more than US$1.1 million),[27] by far the highest public official salary in the world.

Table 2.1 Singapore Constitution: Article 14 Freedom of Speech, Assembly, and Association

(1) Subject to clauses 2 and 3
    (a) every citizen of Singapore has the right to freedom of speech and expression;
    (b) all citizens of Singapore have the right to assemble peaceably and without arms;
    (c) all citizens of Singapore have the right to form associations.

(2) Parliament may by law impose
(a) on the rights conferred by clause 1:
    (a) such restrictions as it considers necessary or expedient in the interest of the security of Singapore or any part thereof, friendly relations with other countries, public order or morality and restrictions designed to protect the privileges of Parliament or to provide against contempt of court, defamation or incitement to any offence;
(b) on the right conferred by clause 1:
    (b) such restrictions as it considers necessary or expedient in the interest of the security of Singapore or any part thereof or public order; and
(c) on the right conferred by clause 1:
    (c) such restrictions as it considers necessary or expedient in the interest of the security of Singapore or any part thereof, public order, or morality.

(3) Restrictions on the right to form associations conferred by clause 1c may also be imposed by any law relating to labor or education.

Foreign media have not been spared the PAP's repressive and litigious tendencies. Targeted by the government's unique system of controlling the foreign press, *Time* magazine had its circulation drastically curtailed by government action in 1986, when it edited a lengthy reply of then prime minister Lee Kuan Yew to an article in the magazine about Jeyaretnam. Similar actions were taken against the *Far Eastern Economic Review, Asiaweek*, the *Asian Wall Street Journal*, New York-based Bloomberg news and information service, and the *International Herald Tribune* (all U.S.-owned). The *Tribune* suffered libel suits in 1994 totaling close to a million dollars in damages after publishing articles that offended members of the government—namely, then prime minister Goh Chok Tong, senior minister Lee Kuan Yew, and deputy prime minister, Lee Hsien Loong, Goh's heir apparent.[28] Lee Kuan Yew is now "minister mentor" for the current prime minister, his son Lee Hsien Loong.

In 2002 the same three officials coerced Bloomberg into an apology and paying them US$340,000 in out-of-court libel damages and costs because of a critical commentary that appeared in its online service and in a Malaysian newspaper about the appointment of the deputy prime minister's wife, Ho Ching, as executive director of the state investment agency, Temasek Holdings. At the time, the deputy prime minister himself also held the posts of finance minister and head of the central bank.[29] Since 1990, foreign publications have been required to post a substantial fixed bond for liability and to secure an annual permit.[30] And to this day, the government has continued to use the denial or termination of working visas as another means of disciplining the foreign press.

Despite claims of being independent sources of news, the American media have capitulated to the will of the Singapore government in efforts to either publish or save their circulation and advertising revenue in that island state. Foreign magazines bear the official stamp "approved for distribution" to let readers know that the informational jurisdiction of the state remains firmly in the hands of the ruling patriarchy. The so-called American free press apparently knows the difference between the political line and the bottom line. More recently, the government instructed all foreign television news media in Singapore (BBC, CNN International, Bloomberg, CNBC Asia, and the Chinese Television Network) that any broadcast that it deems unsatisfactory (officially, "interfering in domestic affairs") requires an unfettered right of official reply. Refusal would mean the loss of a broadcasting permit or fines up to $10,000.[31]

Beyond its control over the country's information channels, the ruling party also arranges the machinery and political communication around elections and determines electoral constituency boundaries. Private broadcasting companies are required to provide time to all political parties at election time, but the PAP allocation is much larger than the rest. Just before the 2001 election, the government, leaving nothing to chance, issued detailed and strict rules on election advertising. Parties, candidates, and their agents using email or SMS messages are required to indicate both the sender's name and the person for whom it is being sent; chain letters, polling, and funding appeals are forbidden; non-party political websites can not advertise for candidates during election periods; party chat rooms must be moderated with all messages logged; and all messages must be removed that are "against public interest, public order or national harmony, or which offend good taste or decency."[32]

One Singaporean and devoted "netizen," James Gomez, who has openly challenged state intrusion into public expression and become in the process a person of interest to the police state apparatus, has commented how

> Laws are constantly modified whenever space is found for political expression, mobilisation and action. The ruling party domination of parliament allows for the passage of new laws as well as continual amendment of the constitution so that the legal environment can be constantly revised to serve the ruling party's needs.[33]

An online group and website that Gomez founded, the Think Centre, is listed by the government as a political organization and watched. Upon being labeled "political," organizations are required to register and submit to restrictions, including a Political Donations Act that bans foreign funding and requires the names of domestic contributors giving more than S$5,000 (about US$2,750). The Think Centre is also restricted under the Public Entertainment and Meeting

Act and the Parliamentary Elections Act amendment of 2001, both of which control its political actions and require it to register with the Singapore Broadcasting Authority.[34]

Politics also is banned in film. A Films Act (see Table 2.2), amended in 1998 with fines up to $100,000 and two years in prison for "any person who imports, makes, reproduces, distributes or exhibits 'political films.'"[35] The statute specifies that no film may criticize the government or even a previous government, any member of parliament, any "current policy" or "public controversy," any political party, "or any body whose objects relate wholly or mainly to politics in Singapore, or any branch of such party or body" (see Table 2.1). Covering all bases, the government also has taken steps to ban the distribution of political videos, a move mainly directed at opposition groups. The ruling party's option to call an election as quickly as nine days before the poll date, together with its ban on free political expression via individual or unregistered group websites, renders a polity bereft of meaningful debate or challenge. As several local observers have noted, the intensive level of social engineering practiced by the PAP has brought about a general lack of interest in politics and political participation by the current generation of young adults.

Table 2.2 Singapore Films Act (October 1998)

(2) For the purposes of this Act, a film is directed towards a political end in Singapore if the film:

(a) contains wholly or partly any matter which is intended or likely to affect voting in any election or national referendum in Singapore; or

(b) contains wholly or partly either partisan or biased references to or comments on any political matter, including but not limited to any of the following:

   (i)   an election or a national referendum in Singapore;
   (ii)   a candidate or group of candidates in an election;
   (iii) an issue submitted or otherwise before electors in an election or a national referendum in Singapore;
   (iv)   the Government or a previous Government or the opposition to the Government or previous Government;
   (v)   a Member of Parliament;
   (vi)   a current policy of the Government or an issue of public controversy in Singapore; or
   (vii) a political party in Singapore or any body whose objects relate wholly or mainly to politics in Singapore, or any branch of such party or body.

In May 2005, a Singaporean filmmaker, Martyn See, was brought in for questioning by the police for producing a documentary, *Singapore Rebel*, about political opposition leader Chee Soon Juan. See insisted the film was not made to politically promote Chee but was simply a story about the state of political opposition on the island and therefore not in violation of the country's strict Films Act—a distinction not readily understood by public officials in the essentially single party state. The government forced See to withdraw his film from Singapore's International Film Festival and threatened to impose a jail sentence of two years and US$60,000 in fines if it was shown.[36] See later exhibited his 26-minute documentary at a Malaysian human rights-focused film festival.[37]

Media Concentration and Free Speech Issues

Compliance with the government's propaganda and informational control efforts is further assured through the licensing, management of content, and other news controls in the mass media. The *Straits Times*, the daily newspaper and flagship of the government-controlled monopoly Singapore Press Holdings (SPH), was the result of a media megamerger in 1984. SPH published thirteen newspapers, including all of the dailies, and six magazines as of 1999. Its president, Tjong Yik Min, is a former chief of the Internal Security Department (the country's secret police), and its chairman, Lim Kim San, was a cabinet minister. The dominant telecommunications entity, SingTel, is run by the second son of Lee Kuan Yew, Lee Hsien Yang. Broadcasting is dominated through another government-linked corporation, MediaCorp (via Temasek Holdings), which, with its subsidiaries, runs four television channels and ten of the fifteen radio stations. As a policy encouraging some degree of "competition," SPH was allowed to have up to two TV and two radio licenses by the Ministry of Information to operate web channels, and MediaCorp was given a newspaper permit.[38] Both corporations are widely understood to be instruments of the PAP.

Newspaper operations in Singapore, unlike those of several other countries in the region, are licensed by the state under the 1974 Newspaper and Printing Presses Act (NPPA), and individual ownership of media is forbidden. The NPPA grants the government minister concerned very wide latitude to both grant and "withdraw the license either permanently or for a period as he thinks of." Also, under the Orwellian-sounding Undesirable Publications Act (UPA), the minister concerned can prohibit any publication that is, under this very vague law, "contrary to the public interests." This can refer to either sexual or political content that is deemed to undermine state power.

Government retaliation against the media seems hardly necessary, but this was not always the case. In the 1970s, newspaper owners, including those of the *Singapore Herald*, the *Eastern Sun,* and *Nanyang Siang Pau*, who published criticism of the government were put out of business, and in the case of the last publication, four senior staff were sent to prison as well—for "glamorizing Communism." The *Herald*, on the other hand, was accused of involvement with U.S. intelligence in a "black operation."[39] More recently, the PAP has singled out the opposition Singapore Democratic Party, under the secretary-generalship of Chee Soon Juan, by preventing the latter from distributing political videotapes under the restraints imposed by the UPA.[40]

Embarrassed by international coverage of its suppression of free speech, and in an effort to create a semblance of a discursive public sphere, the Singapore government initiated a Hyde Park-style "speakers' Corner," located in a public park in September 2000.[41] The government also may have entertained the naïve expectation that this opening would help stimulate a more active public voice in civil society ("active citizenship," as it is called in a 1999 government vision statement, Singapore 21) and perhaps induce a somewhat less conformist, more innovative popular culture conducive to fostering the development of new, creative industries. Speakers' Corner varies from the British version substantially, however. To begin with, speakers are required to register with the police, and, according to a human rights report,[42] their speeches are recorded and stored for six years, during which time their words can be used in legal defamation and criminal hearings. Certain topics, such as discussion of ethnic and religious issues, are forbidden. Microphones are not permitted, which means that speakers can reach only audiences within vocal range. Former Minister of Information, Communication and the Arts, George Yeo, stated the limits of Singapore's free speech policy as: "Leave the windows open, but carry fly-swatters."[43]

In such an extremely conservative political environment, Singaporeans understandably tend to exercise profound caution when engaging in political discussions. Although employed infrequently in recent years, the existence of an Internal Security Act, which, among other things, restricts publications that "threaten public order" and gives very wide latitude to the minister concerned to interpret what constitutes such threats, is often evoked as a threat by individuals who would otherwise be more public in their criticisms about the government or the PAP. Free speech is also constrained by a sweeping Official Secrets Act that warns that "any person who divulges any type of information which is prejudicial to the safety or interests of Singapore shall be guilty of an offence." Again, what constitutes the precise criteria of violation is uncertain, forcing upon the politically minded the discreet conduct of self-censorship.

Internet Regulation

The Internet in Singapore, both service and content providers, is regulated as a system of "broadcasting" under the Singapore Broadcasting Authority (SBA), a statutory board under the Ministry of Information, Telecommunication and the Arts (MITA), with the ostensible mandate "to safeguard public morals, political stability and religious harmony."[44] Control is administered in part through the Censorship Section of MITA, which restricts public access by means imposed on both service and content management. The contentious aspect of overall state censorship is that the definition and violation of standards of censorship and the sanctions thereof are left almost entirely in the hands of entrenched government officials and politically acquiescent judicial figures, who make virtually no distinction between the interests of the party and those of the state. The SBA makes clear that no media or Internet content is permissible that "brings the Government into hatred or contempt," a phrase that reveals the true aim of the law and the SBA more generally: protecting not the public interest but instead the ruling party.[45]

The regulation of the Web comes under its "Internet Code of Practice," whereby three general Internet service providers (ISPs), Singnet, Pacific Internet, and Cyberway, all of which are government-owned or government-linked companies with three-year renewable licenses, must set up government-controlled proxy servers and deny access to "material considered by the Authority to be prohibited material if directed to do so by the Authority." All public and private Internet service sites, including Internet cafes, are required to install filters to block access to unsanctioned websites. Because of the scale of Internet use, it becomes necessary for the government to deputize private companies to police the Web, as the SBA does not have the resources to continuously undertake this task by itself. But even for the ISPs, the task of blocking political newsgroups and other prohibited material is far too onerous and impractical an obligation. Under the government's Industry Guidelines, ISPs also are "encouraged to take 'discretionary action against the abusers of chat channels.'"[46]

Among the SBA's catch-all restrictions, Internet users are forbidden to post material that is "objectionable on the grounds of public interest, public morality, public order, public security, national harmony, or is otherwise prohibited by applicable Singapore laws," including material [that] "advocates homosexuality or lesbianism."[47] In July 2001, new regulations were ordered that made rules governing political websites more stringent. The following October, the government added "parliamentary elections regulations" on political advertising, which further restricts the use of the Internet for organizational distribution of political information or analyses. The wide range of laws proscribing speech is intentionally vague so as to have the most chilling effect on political discussion held outside the gates of PAP-controlled channels.

Resistance and Political Change

Although wide-eyed enthusiasts for "digital democracy" often slip into the idealist trap of technological determinism (i.e., technology depicted as an independent, history-making agent), Internet use does represent at least the possibility of facilitating an open and globally-distributed channel for person-to-person communications and a wide range of uncensored interactive discussion. However, even in a materially developed country such as Singapore, one can not assume, as in Maslow's "hierarchy of needs," that satisfaction of basic needs organically gives rise to greater intellectual freedom. Nor can one assume, as does a core tenet of American foreign policy, that open market economies, of which Singapore is certainly one, equate to democratic societies. Rather, the ruling People's Action Party operates on an elitist, social-contractual understanding that as long as it delivers on material standards of living, citizens will forego demands for a more liberal democratic political system. And even if material standards were to decline, there is little reason to believe that the government would relinquish its grip on the media and information channels. The PAP attempts to naturalize this arrangement under its notion of national core values, an argument that considers Western liberalism an alien ideology, even while Western-style corporatism, industrialism, commercialism, and materialism are seen as endogenous. Similarly, the PAP sees no threat from foreign commercialization of the Internet.[48]

When it comes to political information, the government assumes as a matter of "divine right" a position similar to that of the pre-Reformation Church, where all worldly education had to originate within its ecclesiastical chambers. As the self-appointed guardian of civic virtue, the Singapore government publicly defends its right to block websites to protect its citizens from explicit sexual content. It is less candid about censorship of political information that might challenge its monopoly of institutionalized power. The political opposition in Singapore is arguing for political Reformation, allowing citizens to independently register political choices about policies and representation and the freeing up of media and information channels to allow for fuller public discussion and debate.

What explains such political rigidity in a society otherwise without serious external or internal security threats? It is important to keep in mind that although Singapore has officially moved from "developing" to "developed" status, it still bears much of the imprint of a Third World country in the sense that it is extremely dependent on the industrial investment and technology transfers from the West, particularly the United States and Japan. It is just as dependent on crucial resources, including oil and water, coming from its less developed neighbors. Additionally, the ethnic balance in the country presents concerns, real or imagined, that the rise of internal communitarianism or external political-religious influences could foster social instability. The state therefore assumes the need to suppress intellectuals, civic forums, and civil society in general, which has been only reinforced since 9/11. Such practices are inconsistent, however, with the state's stated goal of developing new creative industries, because, even as the neoliberal World Bank would concede, such industries require a political climate that gives wide latitude to free and critical expression and experimental forms of representation.[49]

It is hard to predict where the state's "suppression of radical potential"[50] of the Internet will lead. Those pushing for a politically open Internet system concede that the winds of change are not presently in their favor. According to one study, the adult user population overall in Singapore does not believe that the Internet will help to empower them or effect changes in the political system.[51] This finding should not be surprising, as most people who use the Internet, in Singapore, in the United States, or elsewhere, do not use the medium for political purposes. What has been demonstrated in many places, however, is that once a regime's legitimacy and grip on power begins to falter, and intimidation loses its binding force, the Internet proves to be a very effective organizing tool for mobilizing civil society, public action, and political change.

Notes

1. This chapter is a revised version of an article that first appeared in the *Journal of International Communication* 9, no. 1 (2003): 35-51. With permission of the publisher. The author wishes to thank Portland State University for providing a faculty enhancement grant that funded a visit to Singapore during May and June, 2002 and expresses gratitude to Mark Cenite, Naren Chitty, James Gomez, John Lent, Garry Rodan, and Lyn Tan for their constructive criticisms of this chapter.

2. Jörg Becker, "Internet in Asia: Introduction," in *Internet in Asia*, ed. Sankaran Ramanathan and Jörg Becker, 10 (Singapore: Asian Media and Information Centre, 2001).

3. Daniel R. Headrick, *The Tools of Empire: Technology and European Imperialism in the Nineteenth Century* (New York: Oxford University Press, 1981).

4. Terence Lee, "Emulating Singapore: Towards a Model for Internet Regulation in Asia," in *Asian Cyberactivism: Freedom of Expression and Media Censorship*, ed. Steven Gan, James Gomez, and Uwe Johannen, 162-96 (Bangkok: Friedrich Naumann Foundation, 2004). T. Waipeng Lee, "Singapore," in *Internet in Asia*, ed. Sankaran Ramanathan and Jörg Becker, 148-61 (Singapore: Asian Media and Information Centre, 2001).

5. Garry Rodan, "Asian Crisis, Transparency and the International Media in Singapore," *Pacific Review* 132 (2000): 215-42. To cite just a few other bureaucrat-capitalists, Suppiah Dhanabalan, who served on the government's Economic Development Board (EDB) and as chair of the Development Bank of Singapore, was also chair of a major government holding company, Temasek Holdings, which was invested in more than a thousand government-linked corporations. Lim Kim San had been a banker and industrialist before becoming a cabinet minister (1963-1981). Fock Siew Wah was with the Overseas Chinese Banking Corporation (OCBC), Morgan Guaranty, and the Overseas Union Bank, while he was chair of a mixed public-private body, the Foreign Exchange Market Committee. Yong Pung How went from the OCBC to the government Monetary Authority of Singapore, the Government Investment Corporation, the Currency Board, and the government Broadcasting Corporation. He became Singapore's Chief Justice in the 1990s. Chandra Das was an officer of the EDB and later a member of parliament before he resigned to return to his trading and investment business. See also, Natasha Hamilton-Hart, "The Singapore State Revisited," *Pacific Review* 13 (2000): 195-216.

6. Toward this end, the Goh Chok Tong government initiated a company, Singapore One, in 1996, which started up a year later and went commercial in 1998, by inviting many transnational corporations to participate in developing interactive, multimedia applications and services to homes, businesses, and schools throughout Singapore for "entertainment and news-on-demand, distance learning, on-line shopping and other electronic commerce services, video conferencing capability, government services, as well as fast Internet." See Singapore One, Press Release, accessed online at http://www.s-one.gov.sg/media_rm/press/p_rtcl04.html. In 1998, Singapore One conducted a five-day mass training session for 3,750 people at an indoor stadium to jump-start Internet usage on the island. Such public mobilization campaigns have been common under the PAP's rule, not unlike those in China under the Communist Party. For details, see Lee Waipeng, "Singapore," In *Internet in Asia*, ed. S. Ramanathan and J. Becker (Singapore: Asian Media and Information Centre, 2001), 148-161.

7. The PAP uses the term "Asian values" when it issues a general defensive critique against the West and refers to "core values" when it seeks to promote the idea of national

identity. The definition of "core values" was issued in a 1991 "white paper" which emphasized, among other things, "nation before community and society before self." But nation and society are not the same as state, and many critical Singaporeans challenge the ruling party by asking, "who is watching the watchers?"

8. As the principal spokesperson for "Asian values," Lee Kuan Yew has never systematically discussed its assumptions. The core of it appears to be a selective reading of pre-modern Confucian ideas about the relations and mutual obligations of the state and citizen. Lee has frequently criticized the West for what he sees as its liberal democratic indulgences. Critics have argued that Lee had falsely universalized his most cherished personal political values to Asia as a whole, which is far more complex and diverse than the way that his "Asian values" would suggest, and that he tends to frequently rationalize the most repressive aspects of Singapore governance under this rubric against calls for the protection of human rights (as espoused, for example, in the United Nations 1948 Universal Declaration of Human Rights). See H.E. Wilson, *Social Engineering in Singapore: Education Policies and Social Change, 1819-1972* (Singapore: Singapore University Press, 1978), 238-39.

9. Wilson, *Social Engineering in Singapore*, 238-39.

10. Eddie Kuo, Alfred Choi, Arun Mahizhnan, Lee Wai Peng, and Christina Soh, *Internet in Singapore: Study on Usage and Impact* (Singapore: Times Academic Press, 2002), 100. A study of the Internet in Singapore found no significant divisions of student use of the Internet by gender, but Malays trailed other ethnic groups in usage to a significant degree (10 percent). Income is also a significant barrier, such that those households with above S$7,000 per month income had 92.4 percent usage, while those with S$2,000 and below had 56.3 percent usage levels (72-75). Major gaps also exist according to the level of the mother's or father's education. And for those not fluent in English, both reading and writing, access to the Internet poses major difficulties. Singapore currently claims to have an Internet home access rate of 65 percent (See the *Annual Survey on Infocomm Usage in Households and by Individuals for 2004* at: http://www.ida.gov.sg.)

11. Michelle Levander, "Singapore to Relax Censorship Laws As It Seeks to Expand Internet Access," *Wall Street Journal*, 1 September 1999, 18(A); Philip Shenon, "2-Edged Sword: Asian Regimes on the Internet," *New York Times*, 29 May 1995.

12. James Gomez, *Self-Censorship: Singapore's Shame* (Singapore: Think Centre, 2000).

13. James Gomez, *Internet Politics: Surveillance and Intimidation in Singapore* (Singapore: Think Centre, 2002), 20.

14. Alecks Pabico, "Southeast Asian Regimes Seek to Control Internet: Results Mixed," (March 1998). A special report online at www.freedomforum.org.

15. Andreas Schedler, "The Menu of Manipulation: Elections Without Democracy," *Journal of Democracy* 13 (2002): 37.

16. Cited in James Gomez, "Information Technology as a Tool for Control in Singapore," *Development Dialogue* 1 (2002): 75.

17. John Burton, "Singapore Threatens to Sue Blogger," *Financial Times*, 9 May 2005, 6.

18. Shanthi Kalathil and Taylor Boas, *Open Networks, Closed Regimes: The Impact of the Internet on Authoritarian Rule* (Washington, DC: Carnegie Endowment for International Peace, 2003), 73.

19. The Internal Security Act was originally introduced in Singapore under British colonial rule and covered criminal, religious, and political malfeasance.

20. Gerald Sussman, "The 'Tiger' from Lion City: Singapore's Niche in the New International Division of Communication and Information," in *Transnational Communications: Wiring the Third World*, ed. Gerald Sussman and John A. Lent (Newbury Park, CA: Sage, 1991), 299.

21. Garry Rodan, "The Internet and Political Control in Singapore," *Political Science Quarterly* 113 (1998): 66.

22. Michael Barr, "Lee Kuan Yew and the 'Asian Values' Debate," *Asian Studies Review* 24 (2000): 324.

23. Section 499 of the Penal Code states that "whoever by words spoken or intended to be read publishes any imputation about another person and in so doing knows that it will harm the reputation of that person is said to have defamed that person." Section 501 says, "anyone printing or engraving anything and in so doing knows that such a matter is defamatory of any person shall be punished." Section 505 warns that "Whoever makes, publishes or circulates any statement, rumor or report with intent to cause fear or alarm to the public or which is likely to incite clashes between different communities or class shall be punished." For details, see James Gomez, *Internet Politics*, 33.

24. Garry Rodan, "The Internet and Political Control," p. 68.

25. Garry Rodan, "Singapore: Globalisation and the Politics of Economic Restructuring," in *The Political Economy of South-East Asia: Conflicts, Crises, and Change*, 2nd ed., ed. Gary Rodan, Kevin Hewison, and Richard Robison (Melbourne: Oxford University Press, 2001): 163-64.

26. Associated Press, "Singapore Court Increases Damages for Prime Minister in Defamation Case," 17 July 1998, accessed at: www.freedomforum.org; Singapore Window, "Singapore: Asia's Cuba," accessed at: www.singapore-window.org/sw02/020530hr.htm.

27. Garry Rodan, "Singapore: Globalisation and the Politics of Economic Restructuring," 162.

28. Chee Soon Juan, "Media in Singapore," Paper presented at the Conference on the Media and Democracy, Sydney University, Sydney, Australia, 24 February 2000.

29. Gomez, "Information Technology," 75. Unlike the Muslim activist, Zulfikar Mohamad Shariff, *supra*, Bloomberg chose not to take a stand or leave the country. Apparently, the perception of profit opportunities in Singapore trumped its management's professional and ethical convictions.

30. Rodan, "The Internet and Political Control," 68.

31. Arnold Zeitlin, "Singapore's New Restrictions on International Broadcasters Assailed at Conference," 23 May 2001. http://www.freedomforum.org. Only the Minister of Information, Communication and the Arts is legally empowered to define what constitutes "interference."

32. Tarn How Tan, "Rules on e-Campaigning Spelt Out" *Straits Times*, 18 October 2001, accessed online at http://straitstimes.asia1.com.sg.

33. James Gomez, *Internet Politics*, 20.

34. James Gomez, *Internet Politics*, 11-12, 37.

35. Cherian George, *Singapore: The Air-Conditioned Society* (Singapore: Landmark Books, 2000), 43.

36. John Burton, "Singapore's Arts Ambitions Caught Up in Rights Debate," *Financial Times*, 14 May 2005, 2.

37. *New Straits Times* (Malaysia) "Film Festival to Showcase Human Rights Issues," 26 June 2005, 22.

38. W. Lee, "Singapore," in *Internet in Asia*, ed. S. Ramanathan and J. Becker (Singapore: Asian Media and Information Centre, 2001), 150.

39. Chee Soon Juan, "Media in Singapore."

40. James Gomez, *Internet Politics*, 36.

41. Any public meeting, including political meetings, of more than five persons requires a police permit. When the prominent dissident, Chee Soon Juan, gave a speech in a public park without such a permit in 1999, he was arrested and imprisoned for refusing to pay the fine. A colleague of his also was arrested and jailed for simply adjusting Chee's microphone (an illegal accoutrement). Speakers' Corner was initiated during Chee's legal proceedings.

42. Asia-Pacific Human Rights Network, "Singapore: Asia's Cuba," 30 May 2002. http:// www.singapore-window.org.

43. Cited in Terence Lee, "Emulating Singapore," 184.

44. Indrajit Banerjee and Benjamin Yeo "Reassessing the Internet-Determinism Perspective in Democratization: A Critical Analysis of Singapore," unpublished draft manuscript, 2002, 24.

45. Garry Rodan, "The Internet and Political Control in Singapore," 88, italics added.

46. Samtini Anil, "Re-Visiting the Singapore Internet Code of Practice," *Journal of Information, Law & Technology*, 2001. http://www.elj.warwick.ac.uk/jilt/01-2/anil.html, inner quote from *Guidelines*.

47. Singapore Broadcasting Authority, "Internet Code of Practice, 2002." http:// www.sba.gov.sg/sba/I_codenpractice.jsp.

48 Although no data exist in Singapore for the percentage of Internet domains that are in the commercial sector, worldwide the share as of mid-1999 was 79 percent (.com. or .net extensions), up from 47 percent at the beginning of 1995. The public share (edu., mil., gov., or int.) fell from 48 percent to 17 percent in that period, and non-profit organizations dropped from 5 percent to 2 percent. For details, see Graham Thomas and Sally Wyatt, "Access is Not the Only Problem: Using and Controlling the Internet," in *Technology and In/Equality*, eds. Sally Wyatt, Flis Henwood, Nod Miller and Peter Senker (New York: Routledge, 2000), 25.

48. Shahid Yusuf and Kaoru Nabeshima, "Urban Development Needs Creativity: How Creative Industries Can Affect Urban Areas," *Development Outreach*, November 2003. Accessed online at: http://www1.worldbank.org/devoutreach /nov03.

50. Brian Winston, *Misunderstanding Media* (Cambridge, MA: Harvard University Press, 1986).

51. Eddie Kuo, Alfred Choi, Arun Mahizhnan, Lee Wai Peng, and Christina Soh, *Internet in Singapore*, 51.

Chapter 3

A Neo-Bohemian Rhapsody: Cultural Vibrancy and Controlled Edge as Urban Development Tools in the "New Creative Economy"

John Hannigan

As John Logan and Harvey Molotch demonstrated incisively nearly two decades ago, contemporary urbanization is all about the pursuit of economic expansion by "growth machines": coalitions of politicians, planners, realtors, bankers, industrialists, journalists, and other influential local players that share a common view that the business of cities is development and redevelopment.[1]

While growth coalitions direct the levers of power, nevertheless they find it advisable to periodically legitimate their plans with the wider public. If this task is overlooked there may be a backlash, either at election time or in the form of organized community opposition. As Troutman has observed, the mantra "growth is good" may certainly appeal "to a broad spectrum of the community at least part of the time," but this does not mean that "people respond to cues like automatons." Among competing notions are "fears about the neighborhood changing, accusations that developers are the puppet masters of local government, and environmental concerns."[2]

To legitimate development and secure public approval, urban planners and elites proactively construct "discourses"—interrelated sets of storylines which interpret the world around us and which becomes deeply embedded in societal institutions, agendas, and knowledge claims. These narratives "not only speak of appropriate kinds of growth but also about who should lead it, what public values are compatible with it, who threatens local civility, and who are potential city saviors."[3]

After World War II, a new and dominant discourse appeared for defining and combating urban problems in North America. Gotham notes that this discourse was organized around the interrelated concepts of blight and decentralization. In the United States, decentralization referred to the exodus of middle class whites from the inner city to the rapidly expanding suburbs. Blight described what was left behind, poor black residential areas where the housing was judged to be substandard. Politicians and urban planners denounced blight and decentralization as "cancerous lesions that had to be removed or forced into remission in order to preserve the harmonious function of the city."[4]

This way of conceiving the city and its problems is an integral part of a more extensive narrative of "urban decline" that reached its zenith in the United States in the late 1960s and early 1970s, culminating in what was widely described by media and academic commentators of the day as an "urban crisis." In his acclaimed book *Voices of Decline*, Beauregard argues that this discourse of decline has by no means been self-evident. Nor has it been it uncontested. Rather it is a collective interpretation whose meaning is mediated socially through language. It was designed to serve as a practical guide on how to act, "replete with moral considerations." In the face of central city "decay," a remedial program emerged with the following character:

> On the whole, commentators favor growth; it arrives in the form of office construction and new housing, new business, inflated property values, and rising tax revenues. They want the city to be populated by the middle class. Jobs are important, particularly those that require a college education. Governments are to intervene to spur investment, but not to interfere too much or in any way that constrains the prerogatives of private investors.[5]

According to this narrative the only really effective way to combat the poverty, crime and alienation of America's downtowns is to embrace growth and "lure" the middle class back. This is a "story of progress" where both urban decline and its potential remedies are rendered comprehensible to the public without "undermining widely shared beliefs or the ideological underpinnings that support dominant interests."[6]

This narrative has endured now for half a century. Consider, for example, Tim Gibson's case study of downtown Seattle, Washington, in which he analyzed the successful campaign by a pro-growth coalition, the "Citizens to Restore Our Retail Core" (CROC) designed to convince Seattle voters to approve a major retail project to be situated in the downtown core. The CROC, presented "a coherent and attractive, consumption-driven vision of 'urban vitality' that engaged both voters' desire for an urban renaissance and their fears of continued urban decline."[7] This political discourse hinged on a central trope—downtown is a living but fragile entity. If they rejected the proposed Pine Street pedestrian mall, voters were warned, they would surely sentence the downtown to untrammeled "decay" and eventual "death." As Gibson recognizes, the CROC tapped into the wider discourse of postwar urban decline discussed by Beauregard. For example, in their media campaign, CROC made special note of Detroit, Michigan, a city whose downtown has become infamous for its high crime rate and many boarded-up, vandalized houses. In the Seattle case, discourse was deployed as a symbolic resource in an effort to secure the approval of the media and the public-at-large for a "spectacular" redevelopment project. In his recent analysis of the neoliberal discourse surrounding public housing in the United States, Jason Hackworth identifies a similar strategy.

The dismal state of public housing is often cited as a notable indicator of urban decline. This is typified by the iconic and widely reproduced 1972 photograph of the Pruitt-Igoe apartment building in St. Louis, Missouri being dynamited into rubble, a testament to the folly of modernist, high-rise public housing projects and the failure of public housing in America. This "failed architecture" theme has been paramount in media accounts and critiques of the public housing system. It focuses on "how the physical design of most public housing stigmatizes tenants by forcing them to live in dwellings that stand out from the rest of housing stock; makes crime prevention nearly impossible because of the site design, and makes activities like child care all but impossible."[8]

This being allegedly so, then the HOPE VI program (a federally funded initiative to demolish the country's most "severely distressed" public housing units) becomes inevitable—even progressive—and the federal government emerges as a "savior." Public housing authorities across the nation are encouraged to replace older structures with garden apartments and townhouses, scattered throughout the city. Hackworth argues that the "failed architecture" narrative obscures other important causes of program failure such as inadequate government funding, federally imposed design restrictions, and pressures by the homebuilders' lobby to make public housing stand out. Furthermore, it undercuts efforts by tenant groups to block the destruction of public housing by presenting this as a "design" issue rather than a sociological one.

In each of these cases, the dominant discourse of urban decline and renewal resonated with the media and the public because it framed past events and future possibilities within a consistent, coherent, and comprehensible storyline. In a sense this reconciles "what is" with "what might be."[9] Rather than compelling people to visualize urban progress as a process of overcoming a welter of contradictions, uncertainties, and misgivings, the solution to decentralization and decline is offered up as a program of consumption, growth, and better design that appears as both plausible and non-threatening.

Urban Revitalization Discourses and Cultural Consumption

If, as Beauregard argues, a dominant narrative throughout much of the postwar period has been that of "urban decline," its tag team partner is "urban revitalization." In this account of contemporary urban history, central cities, already "hollowed out" by the flight of the middle class to the suburbs and beyond, have been further battered by tectonic shifts in the global economy that have compelled industry to shift its manufacturing operations "offshore." For cities to survive, it was vital for all segments of the local community to rally around a "new developmental reality" that required cities to be entrepreneurial players in a highly competitive world economy. This theme of "accelerated city competition," Wilson and Wouters have observed, allowed city growth to be reduced to the strategic metaphor of a "clinical challenge" whereby cities were depicted as struggling biological entities in danger of perishing. The antidote or nourishment that would restore good health was entrepreneurial growth of a type that would emphasize "the establishment of posh neighborhoods, high technology growth nodes, elite culture districts, and conspicuous consumption retail zones."[10]

To re-ignite local economies, urban growth machines embraced a strategy of city building that is rooted in sports, tourism, and entertainment. Initially this revolved around what the authors of this volume call *spectacular consumption*. Typically, this relied on taxpayer subsidies and "public private partnerships" to underwrite the construction of urban entertainment centers that included sports stadiums, casinos, megaplex cinemas, virtual reality arcades, aquariums, themed restaurants, and aggressively branded retail outlet.

The inspiration for this "fantasy city" development came primarily from two sources: Las Vegas and the Disney theme parks. To politicians and planners confronted with an eroding tax base, escalating crime and drug abuse, and a crumbling infrastructure, the "Magic Kingdom" appeared to offer a fail safe formula for urban renaissance. Crime was non-existent (or at least hidden); public services such as sanitation and transportation operated seamlessly; and visitors lined up, primed to spend their dollars on products and experiences. Dismissed for decades as an oasis of sin in the desert, Las Vegas now claimed the title of "the fastest growing city in America." Under the direction of a new cohort of entrepreneurial casino czars, notably Steve Wynn, the fabled "strip" was transformed into a postmodern leisure destination featuring faux versions of Paris, Venice, and even ancient Rome.

In the mid-to-late 1990s, planners, builders, and merchants flocked to seminars on urban entertainment development sponsored by the Urban Land Institute and the International Council of Shopping Centers. Energized by the positive hype, they returned home eager to break ground on their own fantasy cities.

Most soon discovered some harsh realities of retailing, finance, and the marketplace. Very few institutional lenders are willing to underwrite projects in which the entertainment component is of significant size as compared to the retail. What dazzles tourists in Orlando, Times Square, or Las Vegas loses its luster when transplanted to Peoria, Dubuque, or Moose Jaw. Megaplexes often only prosper by cannibalizing moviegoers from older, smaller screens in the same theater chain. Attractions such as aquariums need to be significantly renewed every few years, usually at a cost that is affordable only by major leisure operators.

In the face of deep differences with regards to such issues as company scale, time horizons, consumer orientations, branding perspectives, and business models, entertainment giants such as Sony, Disney, and Universal have increasingly stepped back from major downtown projects in North America, leaving shopping center developers and retail chains to spearhead new initiatives.[11] As a result themed entertainment has increasingly taken the role of a supporting player in jumbo, off-price, retail malls such as those operated by Mills Corp., the top outlet mall developer in the United States. The star attraction in these mega-malls is Bass Pro Shops, a retailer of outdoor recreational products whose stores include indoor waterfalls, climbing walls, and fishing ponds. Although it may never actually materialize, plans have recently been announced for the C$500 million Lac Mirabel mega-mall, to be located at the side of Autoroute 15, a highway that winds north from Montreal to the resort communities in the Laurentian mountains. Among its proposed sports and entertainment components are a 150,000 square foot indoor aquarium with 20,000 marine species, a 100,000 square foot European spa modeled after one in the principality of Andorra, an indoor Formula One racetrack amusement ride, a butterfly and hummingbird sanctuary, and Kidtropolis, a giant educational and games-based theme park.[12]

This framing of urban growth as spectacular consumption has consistently concealed the negative fallout of fantasy city development for surrounding populations. In particular, the discourse "muffled potentially controversial issues of hopelessness and anger in inner-city neighborhoods."[13] Contrary to the prevailing metaphor ("a rising tide lifts all ships"), mega-entertainment complexes were of little help to the small local businesses and services. Afraid of being mugged and murdered, most tourists and suburban visitors avoided neighborhood bars and restaurants, remaining within entertainment center, festival marketplace, or sports venue for the duration of their stay.

Culture-led Urban Regeneration

In recent years, the notion that an urban renaissance can be generated through the arts and creative industries has gained considerable currency in planning circles. This has come to be seen as "one of the few remaining strategies for urban revitalization which can resist (or embrace) the effects of globalization and capture the twin goals of competitive advantage and quality of life."[14]

In the North America, the strategy of linking the arts to economic regeneration dates back to the 1960s when arts-led coalitions began bringing together corporations, banks, property developers, arts organizations, and local government officials.[15] In a survey report commissioned by Vancouver's Social Planning Department in the early 1980s entitled "Arts Mean Business," the authors concluded that the arts and the activities that are related to them "constitute one of the few growth industries in the city," and, thus, "the city's economy can be said to depend on the vitality of its cultural life."[16] Particular attention was paid to the "multiplier effect" whereby attendance at cultural events creates additional spin-offs and ancillary expenditures on such things as transportation, parking, dining, etc.

This strategy was explicitly imported into Britain in the 1980s, as that country moved toward a neoliberal agenda during the Thatcher years. Among its chief attractions, it was argued, the arts could:

provide a focus for community renewal and cohesion; provide jobs for artists and ancillary workers; attract people back to downtown areas, making other consumer developments more profitable; attract national and international tourists; and enhance a city's image in the competitive struggle with other cities for investment. [17]

Within a space of just over two decades, "the initiation of culture-driven urban (re)generation has come to occupy a pivotal position in the new entrepreneurialism" and "the idea that culture can be employed as a driver for urban economic growth has become part of the new orthodoxy by which cities enhance their competitive positions."[18] In particular, it has become intertwined with place marketing strategies whereby older industrial cities seek to "re-present" themselves to the world as centers of artistic excellence, cutting-edge style, and globalized consumption.

Until recently, most culture-led regeneration assumed a shape comparable to the fantasy city development discussed above, often featuring *grands projets culturels*—major flagship projects (new museums, arts complexes, theaters, opera houses) said to be a powerful stimulus for tourism and civic renewal.[19] In the official discourse on culture-led urban regeneration, three examples are routinely cited as evidence that a "cultural turn" can deliver the renewal of post-industrial cities: the Guggenheim Museum in Bilbao (Spain), the Tate Modern Gallery in London, and the designation of Glasgow as a "European City of Culture" (ECOC). The first two refer to the impact of a new flagship cultural institution, while the third focuses on the catalytic effects of a cultural program/competition.

It is probably fair to say that the Guggenheim Bilbao has been the most influential of the three. Previously, Bilbao was an aging Spanish port city in the Basque region, mired in the economic doldrums. Then, in 1997, a branch of the Guggenheim Museum in New York opened its doors. Designed by "superstar architect" Frank Gehry, the titanium-clad building was heralded in architectural and design magazines. Soon, this positive assessment spilled over into more mainstream publications, most notably in the travel pages of the weekend newspapers. Tourists began insisting on a side-trip to Bilbao as part of their itinerary. The success of Bilbao Guggenheim illustrates the appeal of "flagship museums" that attract visitors because of the "radical, dramatic and spectacular nature" of their architecture rather than for the art they contain.[20] Indeed, the phrase "Bilbao effect" has now entered the lexicon of urban and cultural planning, referring to the imagined economic boost that will ensue for cities that build their own version of the Guggenheim Bilbao.

Another "flagship" museum that has been cited as a successful example of the efficacy of culture-driven urban regeneration is the Tate Modern. In its inaugural year, the gallery attracted five million visitors. According to one estimate, it has created an economic tsunami worth £100 million ($150 million) and 3,000 jobs.[21] In contrast to the Guggenheim Bilbao, its cachet resides less around its architectural reputation as in its instant reputation as a "cool place to be." As Malcolm Miles explains, the Tate succeeded in moving the cultural center of

London across the Thames River to the South Bank to Southwark, not by converting London's diverse publics to modern art, but, rather, by "becoming a new social space, a place to meet, eat, buy books and be seen."

When Glasgow was unexpectedly nominated in 1986 as the 1990 ECOC, the first to win this competition after an open national competition, it had the reputation for being a gritty, industrial backwater with a host of social problems: deteriorated housing, high unemployment, youth gangs, and rising heroin use. It was often contrasted to Edinburgh, which was depicted as a city of universities, galleries, and music festivals. City officials saw the ESOC designation as an unparalleled opportunity to reverse this unflattering image, spending over £50 million and hosting over 3,800 cultural activities in 1990. The Year of Culture was an important platform for the city. It both provided a hook onto which the achievements of prior regeneration projects could be hung and opened the door for the use of the arts as a component of economic planning.[22] A re-branding campaign with the slogan "Glasgow Miles Better" struck a chord, with some commentators even putting it in the same league as the iconic "I ♥ New York" campaign. Glasgow's former reputation of a city suffering from deprivation was replaced by "one honed by renewed civic confidence and a critical mass of cultural attractions to attract international tourism."[23]

Many cities worldwide continue to pursue a growth strategy that revolves around building flagship cultural institutions and hosting hallmark events, from the Olympics to international film festivals. In some regions, however a "cultural incubator" approach has flourished. Mommaas describes this as involving a shift from a policy emphasizing big statements and flagship projects aimed at organizing occasions for spectacular consumption to a more finely tuned policy of "cultural clustering" designed to create "spaces, quarters and milieus for cultural production and creativity."[24] This takes the form of cultural districts that are meant to breathe new life into declining neighborhoods and communities by "using arts and cultural services to attract people, to contrast economic industrial decline, and to design a new image of the city."[25] Cultural incubation or clustering thus constitutes another, albeit more grassroots, form of place marketing with the object of attracting tourists and other visitors.[26]

"Creative City" Thesis and the Culture of Neo-Bohemia

In America, the popularity of urban development policies that favor fantasy city development and the construction of major cultural flagship projects have recently begun to wane. In their place a new discourse has arisen which plays up the advantages of nurturing lively, "neo-bohemian" neighborhoods characterized by an active arts scene and a vibrant, diverse, and tolerant street-level culture. The authors of this "creative city" thesis, most notably economist Richard Florida, have created their own "buzz circuit" among municipal officials, planners, and arts consultants, bringing their message "to just about every corner of the

United States,"[27] as well as in Europe and Asia.[28] These discourses of creativity and the creative city, Chatterton notes, "have made their way into the centre of urban policy debates."[29]

Table 3.1 "Spectacular Consumption" and "Creative City" Models of Urban Economic Development

Element	Spectacular Consumption	Creative City
Guiding Trope	flagship development projects "brand" a city internationally and secure investment	technology, talent, and tolerance = building blocks of a "creative" and strong local economy
Prototypes	Bilbao, Baltimore	Austin, San Francisco
Target Market	tourists, suburban day-trippers, corporate investors	super-creative labor force
New Urban Spaces	fantasy cities' *grands projets culturels*	neo-bohemian neighborhoods
Favored Metaphors	decay and regeneration, rising tide lifts all ships	cultural ecosystem, cutting edge
Consumption	administered consumption	collaborative consumption
Permeability	tightly sealed and regulated "tourist bubble"	permeable; neo-bohemians active in cultural production
Security/ Adventure	riskless risk	controlled edge

The creative city approach differs from other forms of culture-led regeneration in several fundamental ways (see Table 3.1). First of all, unlike other strategies for urban revitalization, the target population consists of neither tourists nor investors. Rather, arts and culture are deployed in order to attract a specific fragment of the middle class that are said to hold the key to prosperity in the "new economy." This "creative class" or "creatives," as Florida calls them, combine technical skills in computers with the ability to think in an original fashion. For example, computer animators, website designers, video producers, and software developers are highly valued in the growing knowledge economy and represent the type of migrants that cities need to attract.

Florida frames the emergence of this creative class within the framework of changing corporate norms and values in America in the late twentieth century. Whereas the 1950s and 1960s were characterized by the dominance of giant

"Fordist" organizations such as IBM and Xerox in which white collar work was regimented, dress codes were rigidly enforced, and conformity was the order of the day, the new "creative economy" is much more flexible and decentralized. The model for this can be found at the high-tech start-up firms in Silicon Valley. In Florida's account, the microchip revolution was created here by a cohort of "eccentric technology types from Berkeley and Stanford" that were fiercely entrepreneurial, idealistic, and bohemian in their personal tastes and dress styles. Flexibility for these creative workers, Florida notes, "means more than the freedom to show up at the office at 10 A.M. wearing a nose ring."[30] Rather, it involves having input in designing your workspace and your role in the organization and the right to pursue side projects and outside interests with the support of the company.

This new generation of white-collar workers are said to have very definite views about the type of urban environment and lifestyle they prefer. According to Florida, they don't like major league sports, opera, mega-malls, flagship museums and galleries, and large dance clubs—in other words, everything that defines both fantasy city development and culture-led regeneration of the sort that features *grands projets culturels*. Instead, they favor neighborhood art galleries, performance spaces and theaters, small jazz and music clubs, bike trails, cool cafes, and coffee shops.

Creatives are said to be especially attracted to cities and neighborhoods that are diverse and tolerant. Signs of this include "people of different ethnic groups and races, different ages, different sexual orientations and alternative appearances such as significant body piercings or tattoos."[31] One surefire way of identifying a diverse community, Florida claims is to look at the size of the gay community. Cities that have large homosexual populations also rank high on tolerance and creativity. To test this, Florida plotted rankings on his own index, which ranks the presence of high-tech industry by urban region, with rankings on a "Gay Index" devised by a colleague, Gary Gates, to measure concentrations of gay people.[32] The results indicate that Gay Index regions rank among the nation's top high-tech regions and that the Gay Index "did better than any other individual measure of diversity as a predictor of high-tech industry."[33]

Neo-Bohemians

Another strong predictor of a region's high technology base is another census-based scale devised by Florida and his colleagues called the "Bohemian Index." This is a measure of "artistically creative people" that includes authors, designers, musicians, composers, actors, directors, painters, sculptors, artist printmakers, photographers, dancers, artists, and performers.[34]

It is not entirely clear from Florida's book what exactly the relationship is between creatives and bohemians. Statistically the two overlap, although the former are more concentrated in professional jobs. When he uses census and other quantitative data Florida reports that the creative class encompasses around 30 percent of the American population. However, when he cites anecdotal comments solicited in focus groups and in individual conversations, most seem to come from young males in their late twenties that are employed as computer analysts, video game designers, and the like. Little attention is given to either gender or lifecycle.[35] To muddy the waters even further, Florida identifies "the super creative core of this new class," which includes "scientists and engineers, university professors, poets and novelists, artists, entertainers, actors, designers, and architects."[36]

Nowhere does Florida acknowledge the widely recognized distinction between the new middle class (social workers, lawyers, professors) whose members tend to challenge materialist values and the more traditional professional class (engineers, accountants, managers) whose members generally strive to uphold the status quo. Engineers, for example, are grouped with professors as part of the "super creative core." This omission is especially puzzling because Florida does at one point cite political scientist Ronald Inglehart, whose research on "post-materialist values" is central to any discussion of this "new middle class thesis."[37] Indeed, he goes so far as to attribute the swing to a new set of postmaterialist values which "revolve around the quality of life, self-expression, and personal freedom" to "the rise of the creative economy," a hypothesis that most certainly doesn't arise from Inglehart's work.

Creatives are said to have no difficulty slipping into artistic roles in their leisure hours; that is, the software designer by day that becomes a techno musician at night. Florida reports that the people he interviewed reported being able to seamlessly integrate multiple interests and personae, thereby "establishing a unique creative identity." Elsewhere, however, he treats creatives and bohemians as separate species in a "creative ecosystem" that radiates a culture of tolerance and open-mindedness, thereby stimulating creativity among highly coveted knowledge workers:

> So how do gays and bohemians fit into my analysis? I'm not saying that these people literally "cause" regions to grow. Rather, their presence in large numbers is an indicator of an underlying culture that's conducive to creativity. . . . The places where they feel at home and thrive tend to have a culture of tolerance and open-mindedness. Gays and bohemians are leading indicators of a place that has a "creative ecosystem"—a regional habitat which is open to new people and ideas, where people easily network, connect; where bright ideas are not shot down or stifled, but are turned into new projects, new companies and new growth. Regions and nations that have such an ecosystem—that can do the best job of tapping the diverse creative talents of the most people—gain a tremendous competitive advantage.[38]

Florida's ideas on neo-bohemia emanate from two sources. First, he is reacting to a critical mass of writing by some well-known American cultural commentators who argue that the bohemian has now effectively merged with bourgeois culture, robbing the former of any meaningful sense of countercultural edginess. These authors share pretty much the same thesis: that the bohemian value system has gone from being the bane of the bourgeoisie to becoming nothing less than the engine that drives contemporary capitalism.

This idea was introduced by cultural critic Tom Frank, editor of the satirical magazine *The Baffler.* In his book-length essay, *The Conquest of Cool,* Frank argues that 1960s underground culture was barely out of the gate before it was absorbed into the rapidly developing "creative revolution" that was transforming the advertising industry. Out of this merger came a "hip consumerism" that still lingers. Today, counterculture and business culture have essentially become the same thing.[39]

Next up was David Brooks, now a columnist for the *New York Times*, who describes himself as a "comic sociologist." In *Bobos in Paradise*, Brooks identifies the emergence of a new elite in American society that he brands the "Bobos" (short for Bourgeois Bohemians).[40] As the name suggests, this social grouping seamlessly combines both bourgeois and bohemian values, creating a life style that allows them to become "rebels with stock options." Even as they avoid the old clichés of conspicuous consumption such as gas-guzzling cars and marble Jacuzzis, they are willing to pay more for politically correct products and experiences ranging from organic coffee to luxury holidays in the Costa Rican rainforest. As with the hip consumerism described by Tom Frank, what's socially enlightened is cool and vice versa.

Most recently, two Canadian academics, Joseph Heath and Andrew Potter, have reprised Frank's thesis. In the ongoing conflict between old-fashioned bourgeois values (hard work, self-discipline, materialism) and a competing set of bohemian values (hedonistic experience, self exploration, and expression), the latter has emerged triumphant. In the process bourgeois culture may have been shattered, but consumer capitalism has been re-invigorated. What makes this apparent paradox possible, Heath and Potter conclude, is that symbols of rebellion from rap to tattoos are really not anywhere nearly as subversive as they appear. Since all that corporations really care about are profits, they're just as happy to merchandise biker jackets as gray flannel suits. Any "rebel style," then, is soon ripe for commodification, and no subculture remains immune from being co-opted.[41]

All of these writers—Brooks, Frank, Leland, Heath, and Potter—are convinced that the cool, the hip, and the bohemian have more or less merged and, in turn, have been totally subsumed by mainstream consumer culture. This new convergence, they say, now represents the center of gravity of consumer culture in the early twenty-first century.

Florida both challenges and reinforces this thesis. On the one hand, he argues that cultural critics at the conservative end of the spectrum, most notably, David Brooks, have erred by focusing exclusively on the consumer lifestyle dimensions of the "bohemian-bourgeois synthesis" while ignoring more substantive aspects. In particular, he chastises Brooks for overlooking "the deep economic shifts that shaped his Bobos and made them possible" and "the ways in which work has become fundamentally different, in content and meaning, to the people at the heart of this synthesis." At the liberal end of the spectrum, he denies the claim made by Frank and others that bohemianism has been totally co-opted. What was mass marketed, Florida tells us, was just window dressing, not the core ideologies of "true political movements." Nonetheless, mass marketing has its uses, insofar as it brings alternative culture to a much wider audience than would otherwise be the case.

In Florida's version, the real legacy of the sixties revolution was passed on to the current generation through the software developers and circuit designers of Silicon Valley. Steeped in the bohemian counterculture of the San Francisco Bay Area, they melded bohemian values with the Protestant work ethic to produce a new "creative ethos." This synthesis, he emphasizes, implies more than "sticking a bohemian lifestyle onto an organizational man value set." Rather, what we have here are "'creative people' with creative values, working in increasingly creative workplaces, living essentially creative lifestyles." As we have seen, this means that cities that have been fast off the mark to recognize this and nourish neighborhoods that are edgy, diverse, and tolerant will win the competitive sweepstakes for high-technology workers.

A more empirically grounded inspiration for Florida's treatment of creatives and cities is sociologist Richard Lloyd's research on the culture of "neo-bohemia" in Chicago's Wicker Park neighborhood. In the early 1990s, Wicker Park was transformed from an area "mired in postindustrial decay" to "a site of hip urban culture with a thriving music and art scene." This was highlighted by its selection in 2001 as the location for MTV's popular reality television series *The Real World*, thereby "reaffirming its ongoing importance to a generation of hip media images."[42]

Lloyd identifies "gritty" urban spaces such as old warehouse and industrial districts that are flowing with "creative energy."[43] These operate as magnets for artists and musicians, thereby also attracting the much desired high-technology knowledge workers. Lloyd stresses that this is essentially an interactive relationship. Local artists, he says, "are not just color for tech designers who favor a countercultural ambiance," but rather, both groups collaborate in a creative project that centers around "harnessing the aesthetic potential of digital technology."[44] This is confirmed by the dense concentration of media companies in the Wicker Park neighborhood. At the same time, media firms locate here to tap into an available labor pool of digital artists who are willing to work as subcontractors at scaled-down salaries.

Rather than becoming regulated and hermetically sealed "tourist bubbles" which are "cut off from the everyday routes of lived experience," as is characteristic of fantasy city development, neo-bohemian spaces are said to thrive in older city neighborhoods at the intersection of cultural innovation and economic development.[45] Lloyd describes this as the product of "more evolutionary processes of cultural development" in which the production of new urban space is more likely to be found in the hands of its users than in that of developers and political elites.[46]

Another writer whose ideas partially overlap those of Florida and Lloyd is journalist Joel Kotkin. He too buys into the thesis that high-tech companies are locating in neighborhoods and communities with a creative edge and a concentration of creative talent. Citing "fading" industrial areas such as New York's Hudson Square and Flatiron districts and Chicago's Wicker Park and Bucktown, Kotkin identifies the recent emergence of "knowledge-value neighborhoods" that "thrive on specialized, art-based production" and "recall the urban economy before the advent of mass industrialism."[47]

Recently, however, Florida and Kotkin seem to have fallen out. Florida now accuses Kotkin of engaging in "a superficial misreading of my research group's findings and theories."[48] He especially objects to Kotkin singing "new tune" whereby America's "new growth spots" (exurban, traditional families, basic industries like construction, distribution, and retail) are privileged, as against the creative downtown neighborhoods of the high-tech economy that incorporate Florida's "3Ts" of economic growth—technology, talent, and tolerance.

Neo-Bohemia as "Controlled Edge"

What Florida reveals here is an inherent tension between neo-bohemian cultural production and middle-class consumer demand. Insofar as most middle-class consumers (and this includes both the Bobo class identified by Brooks and Florida's creative class) prefer to take their bohemian culture light rather than straight up, there is a constant pressure toward what I have called "controlled edge."[49] By controlled edge, I mean the process whereby bohemian culture is captured and made safe for gentrifiers, tourists, art collectors, suburban day trippers, and other middle-class consumers by a cadre of real-estate entrepreneurs, leisure merchants, fashion designers, restauranteurs, record producers, television and movie directors, casino czars, tourist operators, and advertising agencies. Controlled edge and its analogue "riskless risk" constitute a central organizing framework for a wide array of leisure and entertainment domains in contemporary society.

On the one hand, cultural tourists are eternally in pursuit of "safe adventure," on the other, bohemians strain toward challenging the forces of commercialized homogeneity. The two are not always compatible and this leads to a certain level of discontent. For example, in Wicker Park, local artists "often articulate their ideological antagonism toward an imago of the privileged urban resident—the yuppie," even though they themselves often come from middle or upper class homes and seek out both "fringe" culture and access to "galleries, good bars, and school at the Art Institute (of Chicago)."[50]

The production of controlled edge has its genesis in a long-standing tension in the metropolis between the desire of middle-class residents for novelty and diverse experience and their parallel desire for security. This duality has been the subject of some of the most thoughtful and challenging writing on the contemporary city.

Richard Sennett argues that urban residents are acutely conflicted. Whereas the diversity of people, places and activities offered up by inner-city neighborhoods promises a wealth of spontaneous and unscripted interpersonal encounters, it also entails a measure of risk, even menace. Ultimately, Sennett writes, middle-class Americans, especially suburbanites, are intimidated by the latter prospect, retreating into private spaces that promise to provide a refuge from the perceived dangers posed by difference and diversity.[51]

Zygmunt Bauman concurs, observing that a common response to fears of risky urban encounters is to construct "voluntary ghettoes." Echoing Tajbakhsh, he describes the conflicted quest of the urban dweller for "the magic blend of security and adventure—of supervision and freedom, of routine and surprise, of sameness and variety."[52] Bauman calls city living "a notoriously ambivalent experience" in which the urban scenery alarms, charms, and seduces. He identifies two contrasting processes: *mixophobia* and *mixophilia*. The former manifests itself in the pull toward a "community of sameness," for example a gated residential community. The latter exerts the counter-lure of novelty, surprise, danger, and diversity. Mixophobia and mixophilia, Bauman, observes, "co-exist in every city, but they co-exist as well inside every one of city residents."[53]

The duality described by both Sennett and Bauman is front and center in the controlled edge zones of neo-bohemian neighborhoods in the contemporary city. Furthermore, this sense of safe adventure is socially constructed by entrepreneurs seeking to exploit the desire of Florida's "creatives" to experience a vibrant, diverse, and cool "street edge" minus the potential risk associated with crime and other threats to personal safety.

A good example of this commercial manufacture of "controlled edge" can be seen in the overwhelming success of the Drake Hotel in Toronto. Owner Jeff Stoller, who turned his recruitment agency for high-technology workers into a multimillion-dollar business, has transformed a seedy flophouse into a sleek boutique hotel done up in a retro-modern fusion décor, the only place in the city "where you'll find office workers and quasi-bohemians sipping Stella [premium Belgian beer] and messaging on cell phones." Among the amenities at the "new" Drake are nineteen crash pads (smallish hotel rooms), a raw sushi bar, and "The Underground," a subterranean entertainment space equipped with two video projectors, and a full concert-level audio system. Enter the front lobby and you will find a "Video Peep Hole" that allows artists to create "short-form, time-based concept works." Opened in early 2004, the Drake instantly generated an avalanche of buzz. During the 2004 Toronto International Film Festival, an impressive array of celebrities dropped by, including Neve Campbell, Tom Green, Darryl Hannah, and Jeremy Irons. A month later, Denmark's Prince Joachim was guest of honor at a reception during the autumn "superDanish: Newfangled Danish Culture" Festival. So far, Stoller has successfully maintained this balance between a more upscale clientele that favors the Sky Lounge and the main floor restaurant, and the more bohemian types who stage conceptual and performance art down below. A year after it opened, the alternative Toronto weekly newspaper *Eye* concluded that the Drake was less "a theme-park monument to the wannabe hipster" than "a performance space and hangout where punk bands and fashionistas feel equally at home."[54] On a smaller scale, this mirrors the "ecological balance" that Richard Lloyd attributes to the Wicker Park neighborhood in Chicago.

Whether or not this constitutes "gentrification" as such is unclear. On the one hand, Florida suggests that where "creatives" reside in the metropolitan area is not of crucial importance. As evidence of this, he cites the Bay Area in California, where some creative people (gays and urban singles) commute from San Francisco to work in Silicon Valley while others (family-oriented professionals) live in Silicon Valley suburbs and work in downtown San Francisco.[55]

Elsewhere, however, Florida both recognizes and rues the creeping gentrification (and "Disneyfication") of neo-bohemia. This threatens the diversity and creativity that are said to drive the new urban economy. It is "a well-known fact," he says, that increasing wealth for a city or region brings increasing gentrification and this, in turn, triggers an out-migration of bohemians, especially those in the low-wage sector.[56] Florida worries that "real" buildings, people and history and "unique and original" experiences are giving way to generic landscapes populated by generic and inauthentic chain stores, restaurants, and nightclubs.[57] This, of course, is the very same criticism that is often directed at "spectacular consumption," a form of urban development that proponents of the creative city thesis tell us is passé.

In a similar key, Richard Lloyd reports that some of those he interviewed insisted that "Wicker Park's bohemian moment is over, squelched by gentrification." This represents an upsetting of the "ecological balance" between working artists, the deviant fringe, and bourgeois settlers. Not surprisingly, perhaps, those most upset with these events are not longtime residents but relative newcomers that had lived there for only a few years.[58] This recalls, he says, Rosaldo's concept of "imperialist nostalgia" where "people mourn the passing of what they themselves have transformed."[59] Still, Lloyd remains confident that Wicker Park can support *both* residential gentrification and a host of thriving new media enterprises.

Florida, Lloyd, and other purveyors of the creative city discourse on urban revitalization are fond of employing an "ecosystem" metaphor that celebrates the dynamic interaction between cultural producers and consumers in neo-bohemians (as against fantasy city development where experience is prepackaged by corporate leisure merchants). However, when this enters the realm of strategic urban planning, it begins to look much like more conventional methods of culture-led urban regeneration.

For example, in Syracuse, New York, where a giant 7.5-million-square foot mega-mall is scheduled to open in 2007, local business leaders drafted a blueprint for economic development that was written in consultation with Florida's company, Catalytix Inc. At a cocktail reception at a downtown Syracuse art gallery, Florida told those assembled that the creative use of historic buildings such as those in nearby Armory Square was the best way to stop the export of talented young people from Syracuse and keep the local economy "healthy."[60]

All too often, however, these attempts at cultural incubation drift into rough waters because, deep down, their primary authors, local urban growth machines, don't really either trust or value edge culture. Loretta Lees describes this as a clash between the goal of fostering a genuine public culture on the street and ongoing efforts by planners and politicians to secure urban space by stifling its diversity and vitality. In Portland, Maine, this led to clashes between authorities and downtown youth and to sharp debate over what differences should be tolerated in a planned arts district. Teenaged skateboarders, in particular, came to be regarded as major disruptions at cultural and commercial sites in regenerated districts. In particular, "reckless" skateboarding became the focus of conflict in the small public square outside Green Mountain Coffee in downtown Portland. Shopkeepers complained especially about several dozen teens who had adopted the name commonly wielded against them, "The Untouchables." This is one indication of a growing contradiction in Portland's official marketing strategy: in order to further urban regeneration, diversity and edge are promoted, but planners and politicians soon come to the conclusion that they can only secure that same urban space by stifling its diversity and vitality.[61]

In Barcelona, Spain, the marginal, inner city neighborhood of el Raval was once a bohemian hot spot but had descended into becoming the city's red light district, as well as a notorious drug haven. In an attempt to "turn-it-around," civic officials formally designated el Raval a "Cultural Quarter." The Museum of Contemporary Art, designed by superstar architect Richard Meier was built on land formerly dedicated to working-class housing, within steps of the Centre for Contemporary Culture. Despite the inflow of new designer bars, art galleries, and trendy clothing shops (which have led to skyrocketing real estate values), the new "social mix" hasn't instantly gelled. Tourists, cultural workers, and students have been hesitant to regard el Raval as a desirable or safe place to live. As in Portland, teenagers from varied ethnic backgrounds have subverted the "designer heritage aesthetic" by skateboarding on the slopes of the Museum, weaving through the tourists and office workers. Consequently, the latter tend to visit the area for specific sites or events, then leave. Furthermore, they deliberately restrict their movements to the "corridors of regeneration" that cross the neighborhood and avoid the non-regenerated back streets.[62]

In the London (England) neighborhood of Brixton, efforts by the local council in the 1990s to commercialize and market the "funky, hedonistic and alternative night-time economy" as part of an economic strategy alienated a variety of local constituencies (black youth, club owners, recent gentrifiers) because it was interpreted as an attempt to institutionalize and sanitize what was essentially a "culture of resistance," stripping it (and the area) of its edginess, and killing off the spirit that attracted clubbers and other pleasure seekers in the first place. As in el Raval, the middle class display little enthusiasm for engaging in anything but the most fleeting interactions with local people who were demographically different. While gentrifiers in Brixton highly value the funky character of the neighborhood, they express minimal interest in actively interacting with its diverse population. As it happens, most are geographically separated from the entertainment zone, which clusters around the underground (metro) station, and rarely, if ever, patronize the clubs.[63] Their opposition to the commercialization of Brixton's nightlife by the council parallels the "panic" felt in Wicker Park by first-generation gentrifiers over recent neighborhood redevelopment.

In each of these cases (Brixton, el Raval, Portland, Wicker Park), planners, politicians, and developers have embraced a model of urban revitalization and growth that pivots on creating of a sense of "controlled edge." Public planners in these regenerated areas do not hesitate to trumpet their diversity as a major selling point, even a distinctive brand, but mandate that this diversity be tightly controlled. This is especially the case where youth subcultures are involved. On the one hand, these are promoted as "sexy signs of urban vitality and cosmopolitanism associated with the cultural industries that have come to increasingly dominate urban regeneration strategies. At the same time, as can be seen in both Portland and Barcelona, teenagers are often seen as troublemakers whose actions violate the comfort zone of tourists and other visitors.[64]

At first glance, the "creative city" approach appears to sidestep much of the criticism leveled at the discourse of spectacular cultural consumption. Rather than requiring the construction of flagship buildings or the organization of mega-events, it celebrates the advantages of creating lively, neo-bohemian arts districts characterized by a vibrant, diverse, and tolerant street culture. Instead of being directed to leisure markets composed of tourists and weekend visitors from the suburbs, it targets a new "talent class" that is said to be the key to prosperity and success in the knowledge economy.

At closer range, however, the creative city solution can be recognized as a continuation of the interrelated discourses of urban decline, crisis, and revitalization that were profiled at the beginning of this chapter. As Hoe Lim pointed out over a decade ago,[65] culture-led revitalization strategies essentially "reward" segments of the upper and middle classes for their commitment to the city. As such, they are congruent with the cultural and consumption patterns of these influential groups. Lim was referring to a rising service sector in Britain composed of young, well-paid, professional and managerial workers employed in the commercial and financial sector, but the same holds true for the "creative class" discussed by Florida and his colleagues.

In a piece provocatively entitled "Will the real Creative City please stand up?" the British geographer Paul Chatterton critically explores a number of issues within the concept of "creative urban renewal." The creative city, Chatterton observed is "all about presenting a sanitized picture of urban life" that will satisfy the consumption needs of middle-class consumers and "placate the hearts and minds of local councilors and politicians that they are actually doing something." Much of the agenda here, he observes "is still elite-led and we have to question whether we are serious about opening up the creative process to the most marginalized groups in society."[66] This is not to say that the kind of cultural incubation devices that are encouraged here, for example, "creative lofts" (combined living and working units for young entrepreneurs), are necessarily a bad thing. Nor is the way forward likely to be found in championing the occasional outburst of "undemocratic and illegal creativity," an option Chatterton considers with some degree of sympathy.

Rather, we need to take care not to blindly embrace a "sanguine story of urbanism" that is "written through the lens of the creative city"[67] while overlooking other narratives, for example those that unmask the structural problems of poverty and inequality. This divergence has been especially spotlighted in the aftermath of Hurricane Katrina, when media discourses about New Orleans as a creative cradle of American culture have bumped up against another competing discourse of the city as being seriously in decline. Some commentators, for example, have even drawn parallels between New Orleans after the flood and cities such as Detroit and Newark that were scarred by urban riots in the 1960s and never recovered. Ideally, creativity can be preserved in the rebuilding of that city so that generic consumption experiences do not reign supreme and exclude those local spaces that involve an edgier, more indigenous, and democratic spirit.

Notes

1. John Logan and Harvey Molotch, *Urban Fortunes: Toward a Political Economy of Place* (Berkeley: University of California Press, 1987).

2. Parke Troutman, "A Growth Machine's Plan B: Legitimating Development When the Value-Free Growth Ideology Is Under Fire," *Journal of Urban Affairs* 26, no. 5 (2004): 620.

3. David Wilson and Jared Wouters, "Spatiality and Growth Discourse: The Restructuring of America's Rust Belt Cities," *Journal of Urban Affairs* 25, no. 2 (2003): 128.

4. Kevin Fox Gotham, "Representations of Space and Urban Planning in a Post-World War II U.S. City," in *Constructions of Urban Space*, ed. Ray Hutchison (Stamford, CT: JAI Press Inc., 2000), 156-57.

5. Robert A. Beauregard, *Voices of Decline: The Postwar Fate of U.S. Cities*, 2nd ed. (New York & London: Routledge, 2003 [1993]), 244.

6. Beauregard, *Voices of Decline*, 244.

7. Timothy A. Gibson, *Securing the Spectacular City: The Politics of Revitalization and Homelessness* (Lanham, MD: Lexington Books, 2004), 131.

8. Jason Hackworth, "Progressive Activism in a Neoliberal Context: The Case of Efforts to Retain Public Housing in the United States," *Studies in Political Economy* 75 (Spring 2005): 44.

9. Beauregard, *Voices of Decline*, 244.

10. Wilson and Wouters, "Spatiality and Growth Discourse," 127-31. This metaphor of the "city as a diseased body" is discussed at greater length in David Wilson, "Metaphors, Growth Coalition Discourses and Black Poverty Neighborhoods in a US City," *Antipode* 28, (1996): 72-96. See also Troutman, "A Growth Machine's Plan B," 612; and Gibson, *Securing the Spectacular City*.

11. M.S. Rubin and C. Bragitikos, "Destination Development Arrives," *Urban Land* 60, no. 2 (2001): 40-49, 111.

12. Hollie Shaw, "Mega-mall for Mirabel?" *Financial Post*, 27 August 2005: 5(FP1).

13. Wilson and Wouters, "Spatiality and Growth Discourse," 128.

14. Graeme Evans, "Measure For Measure: Evaluating the Evidence of Culture's Contribution to Regeneration," *Urban Studies* 43, no. 5/6 (2005): 960.

15. See J. Whitt, "Mozart in the Metropolis: The Arts Coalition and the Urban Growth Machine," *Urban Affairs Quarterly* 23, no. 1 (1987): 15-36.

16. S. Backerman, *Arts Mean Business: An Economic Survey of Vancouver's Non-Profit Cultural Industry*, ed. A. Niwinske. Social Planning Department, City of Vancouver, March 1983, 2.

17. K. Bassett, "Urban Cultural Strategies And Urban Regeneration: A Case Study and Critique," *Environment and Planning A*, 25(12), 1993, 1779.

18. Steven Miles and Ronan Paddison, "Introduction: The Rise and Rise of Culture-Led Urban Regeneration," *Urban Studies* 42, no. 4/5 (2005): 833.

19. Graeme Evans, "Hard-Branding the Cultural City—From Prado to Prada," *International Journal of Urban and Regional Research* 27, no. 2 (2003): 417-40.

20. Chris Hamnett and Noam Shoval, "Museums as Flagships of Urban Development" in *Cities and Visitors: Regulating People, Markets and City Space*, ed. Lily M. Hoffman, Susan S. Fainstein, and Dennis R. Judd (Malden, MA: Blackwell Publishing, 2003), 222.

21. S. Wilks-Heeg and P. North, "Cultural Policy and Urban Regeneration: A Special Edition of Local Economy," *Local Economy* 19, no. 3 (2004): 305-11, cited in Miles and Paddison, "Introduction," 836.

22. Hoc Lim, "Cultural Strategies for Revitalizing the City: A Review and Evaluation," *Regional Studies* 27, no. 6 (1993): 592.

23. Steven Miles and Malcolm Miles, *Consuming Cities* (Houndsmills, Basingstoke, Hampshire: Palgrave Macmillan, 2004), 55.

24. Hans Mommaas, "Cultural Clusters and the Post-Industrial City: Towards the Remapping of Urban Cultural Policy," *Urban Studies* 41, no. 3 (2004): 208.

25. W. Santagata, "Cultural Districts, Property Rights and Sustainable Urban Growth," *International Journal of Urban and Regional Research* 26, no. 1 (2002): 19.

26. John Hannigan, "Boom Towns and Cool Cities: The Perils and Prospects of Developing a Distinctive Urban Brand in a Global Economy" (paper presented at the Leverhulme International Symposium 2004: The Resurgent City, London School of Economics and Political Science, 19-21 April 2004).

27. Michael Indergaard, *Silicon Alley: The Rise and Fall of a New Media District* (New York & London: Routledge, 2004), 170.

28. In a recent posting on the *Metropolis* magazine website, Kerrie Jacobs cites a conversation with John Thackara, a conference organizer in Amsterdam and New Delhi who founded the Netherlands Design Institute. "It's quite remarkable," Thackara notes, "how many city planners and developers I've met over the last couple of years who walk around either carrying or quoting this book [*The Rise of the Creative Class*] as if it were a bible of how to make their city hip and modern and successful." See Jacobs, "Why I don't love Richard Florida," *Metropolismag.com*, 22 February 2005.

29. Paul Chatterton, "Will the Real Creative City Please Stand Up?" *City* 4, no. 3 (2000): 390.

30. Richard Florida, *The Rise of the Creative Class* (New York: Basic Books, 2004), 93.

31. Florida, *Creative Class*, 226.

32. See Daniel Black, Gary Gates, Seth Sanders and Lowell Taylor, "Demographics of the Gay and Lesbian Population in the United States: Evidence From Available Systematic Data Sources," *Demography* 37, no. 2 (2000): 139-54.

33. Florida, *Creative Class*, 256-57.

34. Florida, *Creative Class*, 333.

35. B. Donald and D. Morrow, *Competing for Talent: Implications for Social and Cultural Policy in Canadian City Regions* (Hull, Quebec: Department of Canadian Heritage, 2003).

36. Florida, *Creative Class*, 34.

37. Florida, *Creative Class*, 173.

38. Richard Florida, "Kotkin's Fallacies—Why Diversity Matters to Economic Growth," http://www.creative class.org/baffler_response.shtml.

39. Thomas Frank, *The Conquest of Cool: Business Culture, Counterculture and the Rise of Hip Consumerism* (Chicago: University of Chicago Press, 1997).

40. David Brooks, *Bobos in Paradise: The New Upper Class and How They Got There* (New York: Simon and Schuster, 2000).

41. Joseph Heath and Andrew Potter, *The Rebel Sell: Why Culture Can't Be Jammed* (Toronto: HarperCollins, 2004).

42. Richard Lloyd, "'Neo-Bohemia': Art and Neighborhood Redevelopment in Chicago," *Journal of Urban Affairs* 24, no. 5 (2004): 521.

43. Richard Lloyd, "Grit as Glamour: Neo-Bohemia and Urban Change," unpublished manuscript, University of Chicago, 2000.

44. Lloyd, "Neo-Bohemia," 527.

45. Lloyd, "Neo-Bohemia," 519.

46. Lloyd, "Neo-Bohemia" 527.

47. Joel Kotkin, *The New Geography: How the Digital Revolution Is Reshaping the American Landscape* (New York, Random House, 2000), 114-15.

48. Florida, "Kotkin's Fallacies."

49. Hannigan, "Boom Towns and Cool Cities."

50. Lloyd, "Neo-bohemia," 528-29.

51. Richard Sennett, *The Conscience of the Eye* (New York: Knopf, 1991); *The Uses of Disorder: Personal Identity and City Life* (London: Faber & Faber, 1996).

52. Zygmunt Bauman, *City of Fears, City of Hopes* (London: Goldsmiths College, University of London, 2003), 25.

53. Zygmunt Bauman, *City of Fears*, 34.

54. "The Drake Works," *Eye*, 30 December 2004, 11.

55. Florida, "Kotkin's Fallacies"; "Cities and the Creative Class," 22.

56. Florida, *Creative Class*, 25.

57. Florida, *Creative Class*, 228.

58. Lloyd, "Neo-Bohemia," 525, 529.

59. R. Rosaldo, *Culture and Truth* (Boston: Beacon Books, 1989), 69, cited in Lloyd, "Neo-Bohemia," 529.

60. Tim Knauss, "MDA Seeks to Marry Creativity and Renewal," *(Syracuse) Post-Standard,* 26 February 2004.

61. Loretta Lees, "The Ambivalence of Diversity and the Politics of Urban Renaissance: The Case of Growth in Downtown Portland, Maine," *International Journal of Urban and Regional Research* 27, no. 3 (2001): 613-34.

62. Monica Degen, "Fighting for the Global Catwalk: Formalizing Public Life in Castelfield (Manchester) and Diluting Public Life in el Raval (Barcelona)," *International Journal of Urban and Regional Research* 27, no. 4 (2003): 867-80.

63. Tim Butler (with Gary Robson), *London Calling: The Middle Classes and the Re-making of Inner London* (Oxford and New York: Berg, 2003).

64. John Hannigan, "Diversity Without Tears: Marketing the Multicultural in the Gentrified City," (Paper presented at the Seminar on "Takeaway Cultures," Centre de Cultura Contemporània, Barcelona, December 2004).

65. Lim, "Cultural strategies," 590.

66. Chatterton, "Will the Real Creative City," 393.

67. Chatterton, "Will the Real Creative City," 392.

Chapter 4

City Living, D.C. Style:
The Political-Economic Limits of
Urban Branding Campaigns

Timothy A. Gibson

This chapter examines a curious trend in the political economy of contemporary
cities. As many contributors to this book have argued, cities all over the world
now confront a global competition for future growth and investment.[1] Unfortunately, the sober reality is that there is only so much growth and prosperity to go
around. Some cities and regions—what Castells might call the "technopoles"
and "command centers" of the global economy—will find a way to secure a
disproportionate share of this growth.[2] Others, particularly the sprawling mega-
cities of the developing world, have been increasingly consigned to labor at the
bottom of the international urban hierarchy.[3] For urban policy and property elites embroiled in this global competition the stakes are enormous. Accordingly,
civic boosters across the world have cast about for strategies that might secure
for their cities a favorable position in the international marketplace.

What is remarkable, as argued in the introduction to this book, is that so
many of these urban development and growth strategies are largely symbolic
and ideological in nature. The logic goes something like this: if city leaders can
find a way to project "world-class" images of "urban vitality" into the international marketplace, then maybe they can improve their chances of convincing
tourists, suburban shoppers, and multinational corporations to invest in *their*
city, and *not* the city down the interstate or across the ocean. For this reason
place marketing is now a fundamental feature of contemporary urban governance, and most cities have created (usually with a complex brew of private and
public funds) an integrated network of trade, economic development, and tourism organizations devoted solely to the task of cultivating, projecting, and man-
aging urban images.[4]

The practice of urban marketing is a complicated one, however. Cities are
not like sweaters. They are not empty vessels into which an infinite number of
meanings can be poured. Cities have histories. In the American context this his-

tory includes fifty years of disinvestment, population loss, and anti-urban policy-making. This history also includes fifty years of a discourse—circulated in the national media system—that positions the city as an amoral space of social decay and disorder.[5] Represented most concretely in both the relentless news coverage of local crime and the equally omnipresent cop shows on television (invariably set in major cities), this discourse of decay invests urban space with stigma. Time and again, the city is presented as a space of violence, drugs, and prostitution, a space of failed government initiatives and intractable poverty. That this anti-urban discourse, in an American context, is tightly articulated with the politics of race should surprise no one. The demonization of the city has long been code for the demonization of the poor, the black, and the immigrant.

None of this makes the job of selling the city easier. But if one major problem facing urban leaders is the circulation of such negative images about the American city, then, as many leaders have concluded, the solution is symbolic as well. The city's brand has been stigmatized, and now it must be repositioned.[6] To this end, officials in most major cities pour substantial amounts of public money into marketing and advertising campaigns designed to spread the good news about their metropolis and attract tourists, suburban shoppers, and corporate investment.[7] These institutionalized efforts to draw in the consumption dollars of tourists and suburbanites are by now familiar and have been the subject of extensive research.[8]

Of particular interest in this chapter, however, are those marketing campaigns designed explicitly to attract new *residents* into the city. Often targeted to suburban audiences, such campaigns are best viewed as form of semiotic warfare pitched against an amorphous enemy: the image of urban decay that has dominated American discourse about "the city" since at least the mid-nineteenth century.

It is clear that such campaigns to attract new residents are nothing if not ambitious. Convincing a tourist to invest a weekend in your city is one thing. Convincing a suburbanite to buy an urban condo is something else again. More than likely the suburbanite has been raised on a steady diet of urban crime news.[9] More than likely they have concerns about the schools, the taxes, and the quality of city services. They may also have been cautioned against moving into the city by real estate agents when they first relocated to the region. Still, if the challenges facing such promotional campaigns are significant, city leaders believe the potential payoff might be equally impressive. If city leaders can convince some of our suburban neighbors—maybe just 5 percent of them—to embrace the possibilities of city living, the logic goes, then they can broaden the tax base, improve the funding of public schools, inspire new retail and housing development, and, if it all comes together, spark a virtuous circle of economic growth that will benefit all city residents, rich and poor alike.

But can urban branding campaigns—particularly campaigns targeted to affluent suburbanites—achieve these lofty civic aims? On the whole, critical scholars are rightly suspicious of claims to represent the universal civic good, and, in fact, much effort within critical media studies is devoted to plumbing the gap between symbolic assertions of the universal interest and a lived reality marked by an unequal struggle to access symbolic and material resources.[10] In this spirit, this chapter examines the potential for urban marketing campaigns to live up to their promise to advance the universal civic interest. In doing so, I offer a case study analysis of the District of Columbia's "city living, dc style" campaign—a campaign designed to sell a particular vision of city living to the Washington metropolitan region.

Drawing on eleven in-depth interviews with campaign planners and housing advocates, a close reading of key campaign texts, and two days of field research conducted at the campaign's annual housing exposition, this chapter details the emergence of a profound gap between planners' promises to conduct an inclusive campaign that would yield tangible benefits for all District residents and the actual performance of the campaign itself. As we will see, by offering an account of the campaign as it moved through three key moments in Richard Johnson's "circuit of culture"—the moments of production, text, and context—this analysis finds that the workings of class power and privilege both structured the execution of the campaign and ultimately exerted powerful limits on the campaign's ability to achieve its civic aspirations.[11]

In the end, I will draw upon this analysis of urban branding in Washington, D.C. to discuss the prospects of building a more productive dialogue between political-economic and cultural-discursive approaches to media studies. The stereotypes on either side of this intramural and often sterile debate are by now well-known. Cultural studies scholars are often accused of losing themselves in jargon-filled analyses of text and discourse, thereby cutting themselves off from the material forces that structure both media production and the contexts of reception. Political economists, for their part, are said to focus with single-minded ferocity on the consequences of for-profit ownership and commodification, thus neglecting studies of text and audience that might reveal spaces of complexity and contradiction within the circulation and consumption of cultural commodities. That these stereotypes fail to capture the nuances of the best work in either tradition has unfortunately not lessened their purchase in the pages of our leading journals.[12]

The time has come to work through this divide. Fortunately movement toward a more productive dialogue between cultural studies and political economy is already underway along several fronts.[13] To this end, the study of the symbolic politics of urban development offers a good opportunity for exploring the benefits of a *synthesis* of cultural and political-economic analysis. It is my view, in other words, that a careful study of urban marketing campaigns—one that follows a specific campaign through the Johnson's "circuit of culture"—will demonstrate the utility of an approach that offers a detailed analysis of textual structures and cultural discourses, while at the same time situating the text within the material context of both its production and reception.[14] In the end, the chapter will draw our attention to an important, but underdeveloped, point of overlap between these important critical traditions.

City Living: The Moment of Production

By all accounts, in the winter of 2003, Mayor Anthony Williams looked across the District of Columbia and liked much of what he saw. After decades of population decline and economic stagnation, signs of renewed investment in the District abounded—particularly in the commercial districts adjacent to the federal center. The MCI center had opened next door to Chinatown, marking the return of the NBA's Wizards to downtown D.C. Construction of a new publicly-subsidized Convention Center in Mt. Vernon Square was well underway for a 2003 opening. In such times, mayors tend to think about legacy, and Williams was no exception. Addressing dignitaries assembled to hear his second inaugural address, Williams thus issued perhaps his most ambitious policy goal to date: finding a way to attract 100,000 new residents to the District in the next ten years. "We must lure back residents who fled the city in the past," he said. "But not at the expense of those who today call the District home. We can do this. We will do this."[15]

This would be no small task. After the end of World War II, the District could boast 750,000 residents. By the year 2000, that number would shrink to 570,000—all during a time when the regional population expanded exponentially. Although the population of the District had stabilized since the late 1990s, attracting 100,000 new residents over the next decade would require a dramatic turnaround from a thirty-year slump.[16] At the same time, however, demographers were projecting that over one million residents would descend upon the Washington metro area during that ten-year span. So, as one planner put it, all the District was asking for was ten percent of this future growth. "We think it's really reasonable," he said.[17]

In addition, from this city's perspective, attracting new residents from the suburbs was about more than merely boosting numbers and repairing urban pride. New residents, particularly new homeowners, would expand the District's notoriously narrow tax base and provide much-needed revenue for improving city services and schools. Of course, most mayors would like a wider tax base, but in the nation's capital the thirst for funds is especially acute. With acre after acre occupied by federal offices and foreign embassies, close to 40 percent of the District's geography is exempt from property taxes.[18] Even worse, although non-residents (read: suburban commuters) earn approximately two-thirds of all income in Washington, D.C., the U.S. Congress has prevented the District from applying a modest "commuter tax" that would recapture some of this income.[19] The result of these unique restrictions is a District tax base that relies disproportionately on a narrow range of personal income and local business taxes, with the predictable result: schools and services are chronically underfunded, while at the same time the District runs a structural deficit that prevents long-term planning and investment.[20] Attracting more residents would therefore widen the tax-base and spread the load of funding basic services among more citizens.

In short, the mayor's goal was an understandable response to the District's fiscal woes. It would fall, however, to his Deputy Mayor for Planning and Economic Development, Eric Price, to find a way to bring the 100,000 new residents back into the city. Faced with this task, Price immediately called on his contacts in the urban development community, including, importantly, the DC Marketing Center and the Downtown Business Improvement District (BID). Both organizations offered the city staffing support and supplemental funding, and, together with a private event-planning firm, Price's task force began to plan a marketing campaign that would reach out to suburbanites and convince them to "come home" to the District.

It is at this point—with the inclusion of business booster organizations—that the motives for conducting the campaign began to multiply. The DC Marketing Center, for example, is a public-private partnership funded jointly by the District government and the DC Chamber of Commerce. As staffers explained, the DC Marketing Center attempts to generate jobs and economic investment in the District by promoting the District's business climate to retailers, financial institutions, professional service firms, and other potential investors. For its part, the Marketing Center became involved in the mayor's campaign to attract new residents as part of their larger commitment to attracting new retailers to the District. Like many large urban centers, the District suffers from a relative lack of national-chain retailers which long ago followed the flight of middle-class residents to the suburban fringe. Drawing these retailers back to the city requires convincing them not only that the District is attracting new residents, but that these new residents have money to spend. "Retailers follow rooftops, and average household income," as one Marketing Center official said.[21] In short, if the deputy mayor's campaign succeeded in drawing in new residents—particularly middle-class or upper-income residents—then the Marketing Center might make more headway convincing the Targets, Home Depots, and Barnes & Nobles of the world that "city living" in the District was indeed for them.

The Downtown BID—an organization of downtown property owners and retailers—had its own motives for getting involved. In 2003, after decades of stagnation, things in the downtown residential market were heating up fast. Encouraged by resurgent regional economy and a targeted tax abatement program, residential developers had descended en masse upon once-vacant downtown lots. As a result, in just a few short years, the downtown residential market exploded from essentially zero in 1996 to over five thousand units of upscale housing built or under construction by 2003. In fact, it was almost too much, too fast: approximately two thousand of the units were scheduled to hit the housing market in a single two-month span in the fall of 2003. "We wanted to make sure we filled these units quickly," one BID staffer said.[22]

Why the rush? For development experts, the risk was clear: if these units remained unsold or vacant for long, future residential developers might draw that conclusion that downtown was overbuilt and then steer clear—a point also emphasized by officials at the DC Marketing Center. So it occurred to the Downtown BID that they might want to do some marketing "to tell people about the new residential development downtown." There was only one problem, as one BID staffer recalled. "We couldn't get our guys [BID members] to pay for it."[23] The developers and residential property owners within the downtown district basically told the BID's staff that they were happy with their individual marketing efforts and did not feel the need to help fund a collective "come and live downtown" campaign—a campaign that might help their competitors as much as themselves.

For these reasons, when Deputy Mayor Price called the Downtown BID and the Marketing Center for help, it all seemed to click into place. The city needed 100,000 new residents to expand the tax base. The Marketing Center needed middle-to-upper-income "rooftops" to attract new retailers. The BID wanted to conduct a marketing campaign to absorb downtown's 2,000 new housing units. Maybe they could meet all their goals by working together to market city living to suburban audiences. How, as one planner put it, could we get people excited about living in the District? And how could we channel this excitement toward a decision to relocate?[24]

One idea grabbed the group right away as it met in February 2003. "Our first thought," as one city official recalled, "was that . . . we would just do a big housing Expo."[25] At the Expo, visitors could wander from booth to booth and learn about the new apartment and condo developments coming on-line in the District. At other booths, mortgage brokers would be available to offer advice on financing. At still other booths, city planners would tell visitors about the city's distinctive neighborhoods, and housing officials would promote the incentives available for first-time homebuyers in D.C. The event could even feature a series of presentations on the cultural and recreational advantages of living in the District. The Expo, in other words, would "give you everything you need to move to the District except the keys to your new house."[26]

Soon, however, planners concluded that putting on an Expo was well and good, "but if you hadn't educated people beforehand, they would come with the same misconceptions they had already."[27] And so here we arrive at the crucial ideological challenge facing campaign planners. If suburbanites raised on a diet of local crime news and anti-urban gossip believed that violence raged on the streets, or if they believed there was no nightlife beyond the floodlit memorials, then why on earth would they come to an Expo? In order to make the Expo a success, the planners therefore needed to address, even if obliquely, the long-term accumulation of negative imagery about the District.

Thus began additional plans for a year-long advertising campaign on television, print, and radio. This campaign would only promote the Expo but would also mobilize image, sound, and text to promote something less tangible—the unique advantages of the urban good life. In doing so, it would begin to offer alternative images of the District to those broadcast on the nightly news. By June 2003, the official kickoff of the campaign, the basic framework was in place. Throughout the summer months, the planners would promote "city living, dc style" through targeted print, radio, and television advertising. These activities would culminate in the year's signature event: the City Living Expo held in late October 2003—just when those units in downtown were coming "on-line."

At this point, one last decision remained. What audiences would be targeted by the campaign? With limited funds, the task force focused immediately on what one planner called the "low-hanging fruit"—in other words, those groups, identified through marketing surveys, which were most open to the idea of moving and buying a home in the District.[28] Right away, as numerous planners conceded, this excluded families with kids. "Schools definitely are a concern for a lot of people," one planner said.[29] "We're not advertising, 'bring your children in here to go to school,'" agreed another, "because we wouldn't be honest with ourselves if we did that."[30] For this reason, the campaign crafted specific appeals for three major suburban audiences: young professionals, suburban commuters, and "empty-nesters" (parents whose kids have moved out).[31] For young professionals, the message was, of course, "the District: it's hip, it's hot, it's happening."[32] Empty nesters, for their part, would hear about the world-class museums, and commuters, stuck in the region's notorious traffic jams, would be encouraged to dream of a life with a ten-minute commute.

At the same time, it is in the selection of suburban target audiences that the class politics of the campaign is most clearly revealed. For instance, when asked what these three target groups had in common, one city official replied:

[I]t was two main . . . things. The first was that those groups had the ability, both physically—in terms of mobility of life—and financially to move. So it just, it made the most sense to focus on them. *You know, we have all this housing on-line. We want to make sure that it gets picked up* [emphasis added].[33]

In another interview, when asked if income played any consideration in the selection of target markets, a DC Marketing staffer said:

Not in the sense that we were targeting any particular class of people, or anything like that. We were aware that the cost of real estate here is expensive, and so we, we were sort of looking for, I mean we weren't targeting any particular income, but we knew that certain, that people that had jobs, that had money, would be more likely to, and so, you know, we were looking for like the dual income, no kids families that have more disposable income. . . . *What we were trying to do is to be practical about the market rate units that are here, who's going to buy them? Who's going to lease them?* [emphasis added][34]

These comments are worth quoting at length not merely because they demonstrate the clear discomfort informants felt when confronted with the issue of class, but also because they illustrate how the motives of the campaign's private players—in particular the need to fill the "market rate units" (especially those located downtown)—profoundly shaped the actual performance of the campaign. By the summer of 2003, the primary goal of the campaign was no longer the mayor's sweeping call to attract 100,000 residents. Fully in the realm of the "practical," the campaign's texts would instead focus on attracting only a particular kind of new resident—those willing and able to "pick up" the market-rate housing coming "on-line."

City Living: The Moment of Text

The "city living, dc style" campaign is not a single text. It is instead a loosely bounded collection of texts that includes everything from television, newspaper, and radio advertisements, to key chains and knick-knacks, to the "city living" website and the weekend-long Expo itself. What unifies this complex intertextuality is, of course, the brand.[35] Campaign planners were quite determined to develop for the District a strong brand within the regional marketplace, a brand that would distinguish the city from its competitors in the Virginia and Maryland suburbs. Indeed, the language of branding and consumer product marketing was often quite explicit in planners' discourse. "It's just like marketing a pair of jeans," said one planner.

> I'm sorry but it's true! It's no different. You market a pair of jeans by saturating people with your brand until they can't think of anything else to wear. This is just the same. We're going to saturate them with our brand until they can't think to live anywhere else. . . . It's my job to market this brand.[36]

Planners began the branding process by first imposing a consistent design upon each and every text in the campaign. Every textual element used the same font. Every printed text—flyers, ads, posters, even the final frame of the television spot—included a white background framed by two horizontal blue stripes. Every text included the brand's signature—the "city living, dc style" tagline, always in red letters, always in lowercase. These consistent, repetitive design elements create a semiotic environment in which a single text within the campaign—say a key chain—can immediately set off a chain of associations with every other element of the campaign, all of which share the same basic design template.

The content of these semiotic associations formed a second important element of the branding of city living. Nike, for example, has an almost universally recognized logo: the omnipresent swoosh. But the swoosh acts as more than a corporate identifier. Over the years, through the relentless assault of television advertising, the logo has been associated with a limited range of images dramatizing and romanticizing individual achievement (i.e., "just do it"). From Nike's perspective, this relentless strategy of symbolic association pays of in semiotic economy: consumers merely have to see the logo to evoke a chain of dramatic connotations and images related to high-performance sports. In a similar way, the challenge facing the District's campaign planners lay in selecting a limited set of recurring and positive images that would not only illustrate and dramatize the benefits of city living (especially for the designated targets) but would also make the urban brand stand out as distinct from, and superior to, other brands (Arlington, Bethesda, Fairfax County) in the regional field.[37] The ultimate goal would thus be to create conditions in which a single encounter with the brand— even just the tagline in its familiar lowercase red letter—would evoke a consistent set of images about the urban good life.

It is in these consistent images of the urban good life that we encounter the implicit boundaries of class and income encoded within the various texts of the campaign. As Budd, Craig, and Steinman note, media texts—particularly advertisements—mobilize images, sounds, and script to create a preferred viewing position from where the text should be read. This viewing position is best viewed as an invitation.[38] In other words, the advertisement, by addressing us in a particular way and positioning us in a specific relationship to the text, *invites* us to adopt the social traits and desires inscribed within the viewing position. If we answer this invitation, we are encouraged to adopt these social traits and desires as our own, and are thus more likely to produce a reading of the text in line with the producer's intentions.[39] Our reading of the ad, therefore, will depend upon how willingly or profoundly we consent to occupy this position and the desires and perspectives inscribed within it.

Given the overlapping motives of the campaign—motives that, as we have seen, led planners to focus narrowly on upscale suburban audiences—it is important to focus on the intersections between ideologies of class and the discursive viewing positions inscribed into campaign texts. In other words, how did the twin goals of expanding the tax base and filling upscale downtown housing play into the discourses of class mobilized within the campaign texts themselves? In creating preferred viewing positions within the text, who—in terms of social class—do these ads think "we" are? What social traits do these texts assume we have? And finally, what desires and perspectives are inscribed within these preferred viewing positions? When analyzing the texts produced by the "city living" campaign, then, it behooves us to begin by investigating how the texts attempt to position readers in terms of the location they occupy within a social field structured profoundly by class divisions.[40]

Print Advertisements: "Morning Commute" and "Board Meeting."

Let us begin with the print ad entitled "Morning Commute" (see Figure 4.1). This black-and-white ad features a single image with a two spare lines of text. The black and white image shows a bicyclist (we see only the bicycle and the biker's legs) wearing spandex shorts speeding along a bike-only pathway. The roadway, the foliage along the path, and the cyclist him or herself (the gender of the cyclist is unclear) are a blur across the page, evoking connotations of speed and motion. Across the bottom of the ad, in lowercase, the text reads "morning commute." The focus on motion was quite intentional, planners said.[41] They were guessing that suburban commuters stuck in the nation's third worst traffic might identify with a desire for motion, speed, and convenience.

So far so good. But by choosing cycling to represent the ideal commute, planners position readers as "the kind of person" who might bike to work. This obviously excludes working families with children, which in itself is strategic given the campaign's focus on the professional and the childless. More subtly, however, the practice of cycling itself carries class connotations that, in the context of this ad, serve to address some potential audiences while excluding others.

Figure 4.1 Morning Commute

morning commute

city living, **dc style! EXPO**
get moving. www.citylivingdc.com

washington convention center · october 24-26, 2003

As Bourdieu observes, while working-class residents tend to participate in competitive team sports, the middle and upper classes tend instead to embrace individual sports like cycling, running, or cross-country skiing. This is not merely because the costs of participation in such sports can often exclude subordinate classes (especially in the case of skiing and cycling), but also because the performance of these activities has become invested with a moralistic discourse of health and exercise common among such class fractions. Within middle-class discourse, the body becomes something to be worked upon and sculpted as an external display of one's self-discipline and intrinsic worth. The goal of these individual sports is therefore not merely winning but something "higher," the achievement of health and the display of this achievement to others.[42]

Perhaps not surprisingly, then, a look at the marketing demographics of cycling magazines reveals an audience skewed toward the middle-to-upper reaches of the class structure. *Bicycling* magazine, for example, reaches a subscription base with an average age of forty and an annual average household income of $83,000. For their part, subscribers to *Bicycling's* sister magazine, *Mountain Bike*, are even younger (an average of thirty-six years old) and command more wealth ($94,000 average annual household income). In their relations with others, marketing surveys conducted by the magazine reveal a class segment accustomed to exerting influence and giving rather than receiving orders and advice. For instance, between two-thirds and three-fourths of subscribers say they are "independent thinkers who rarely follow the crowd," that "people rely on me for advice," and that they "influence the buying decisions of others."[43] In other words, by positioning the viewers as "the kind of person" who might cycle to work, the text addresses an upscale audience while at the same time subtly excluding those potential residents for whom a cycle to work holds little practical or sensual appeal.

A second print ad, "Board Meeting," (see Figure 4.2) offers a more complex set of class discourses. The central black-and-white image of this ad shows an outdoor chess match in progress. An African-American man sits at a small concrete table, dressed in a dark t-shirt and white baseball cap. He is reaching across the board, arm blurred, seemingly in the midst of taking one of his opponent's pieces. Along the edge of the board stand two more black pieces: evidently the seated figure is winning. Of the unfortunate opponent, we only see his arms, clad in a dark business suit jacket and white dress shirt, his (white) hands, and his wedding ring. Though the rest of his body is cut off, the opponent appears to be leaning on the table, hands clasped to its rim. In the background, an ornate fountain anchors the location: this is the small park at the center of DuPont Circle. Across the center of the image, a line of text, again in lowercase, simply reads: "board meeting"

It would be easy to point to the chessboard and loudly pronounce the class-bias of the ad. After all, isn't chess a game for the intellectual elite? It would also be wrong to do so. The scene depicted here—an outdoor chess match—is a common one in DuPont circle, and the protagonists in these matches seem to be, from anecdotal observation at least, distributed more or less evenly across ethnic and class lines.

Of more interest is the relationship between the two figures. This is, first of all, an interracial match. As one planner argued, in a city historically divided along lines of race as much as class, such images of racial comity send an important message to suburban audiences who may view the District as a divisive racial war zone.[44] In addition to representing racial comity, another reading of the relationship between the figures suggests a playful take on class relations.

Here the historical class and racial hierarchy is not neutralized but inverted. The (working-class) African-American man is the dynamic player, hand in motion, about to capture his opponent's piece—for the third time, no less. The business-clad white guy can only grip the edge of the table in frustration.

However, the addition of the tag "board meeting" quickly overlays these playful, inverted, "race-and-class comity" readings with a class-specific mode of

Figure 4.2 Print Advertisement: Board Meeting

address. Indeed, perhaps for this reason, the insertion of the "board meeting" tag was a matter of some debate among campaign planners. One city official in particular pushed to replace the "board meeting" tag with "community meeting"— precisely *because* he felt the reference to corporate boardrooms carried connotations of exclusive wealth and power. Only professionals and executives may be invited to board meetings, he argued.[45] But community meetings are open to everyone. The other planners, drawn from the city's private partners, disagreed, and ultimately the "board meeting" tag was re-inserted. "It just played [better] off the [chess] board," as one planner explained.[46]

Maybe so. But the tag also has the effect of specifying who, in class and racial terms, is addressed by the ad—a matter left ambiguous by the image itself. With the more inclusive "community meeting" tag, in other words, viewers could conceivably identify with either figure. If anything, one would most likely identify with the seated African-American man. He is the player in motion. He is the player who is winning. But adding the "board meeting" text works against the reader's ability to identify with the seated player. Instead, the "board meeting" tag privileges a reading in which the viewer identifies with the faceless figure leaning on the table and good-naturedly losing the chess match. After all, it is the man in the business suit who most likely attends "real" board meetings. Read this way, the ideal viewer is presumed to be "the kind of person" that attends board meetings (and would therefore "get" the joke). This ideal viewer is then positioned alongside the standing (white, male, professional) player, and is encouraged to imagine that they have stopped for a quick game with a friendly neighbor on their way home from work—where presumably the real board meetings are held.

In the end, by inserting the "board meeting" tag, a reading of class/race comity is not obliterated, but transformed. The ideal vantage point from which to view the scene now shifts from an ambiguous position, in which the scene of class and racial solidarity can be viewed from either position (black/white or working-class/professional) in favor of a reading that firmly addresses the reader as a suit-clad executive. In doing so, the preferred meaning of the scene shifts from a playful inversion of class/race relations that can be read from a variety of social positions toward a class-specific reading that subordinates this inversion and labors to reassure the potential concerns of white suburbanites. Look at this scene, dear professional white suburbanite. You needn't be concerned about class and racial antagonisms in the District. We all get along just fine. In the end, the overall effect is that the "urban good life" promoted by the text is one narrowly constructed to engage the desires and assuage the fears of the professional class.

The City Living Expo as Text

Within the campaign, these two print ads played a dual role. On the one hand, they were designed to present an image of city living that might appeal to the campaign's affluent targets. On the other hand, the lifestyle ads also had a more utilitarian purpose: drumming up attendance at the campaign's flagship event, the City Living Exposition, held on the floor of the Washington Convention Center. At this event, then, the public would be invited to participate in the performance of the campaign's über-text within which the District would attempt to close the deal with its preferred target markets.

What I present here, therefore, is my own reading of this über-text as I wandered the convention floor and engaged with some of the participants in the scene. Upon arrival, my first task was to pursue the booths themselves, representing all of the public and private organizations who paid a fee to rent space at the conventional hall. After browsing a bit, I began to conduct ad hoc interviews with exhibitors and patrons, focusing on those booths marketing condos and apartments. After all, these were the folks with whom the planners were most concerned. Would these new units—in downtown and elsewhere in the District—be "absorbed" quickly enough to sustain a good climate for real estate investment? In chatting with these firms, then, I was mostly interested in determining *who* these property developers were attempting to reach. What was their "market"?

The PN Hoffman booth was my first stop. PN Hoffman is, as one representative told me, a residential developer that focuses mostly on "urban infill"—that is, the practice of buying a "property that is either vacant or under-utilized," razing it, and then constructing a new building in its place. When asked about her target market, she said, "it's the D.C. market. Professionals. Empty nesters. People moving to D.C. and who only plan to be here two to five years and who don't want to spend a lot of time maintaining a residence." These folks, she said, "want something new. New is a big deal. . . . They don't want the hassle of an older house." What PN Hoffman offers this market is therefore "premium" housing. "We do premium," she said. "I don't like to say luxury. But it's certainly high-end finishes like granite countertops, stainless steel appliances, and urban contemporary design. It's definitely high-end."

As I moved to other booths, this pattern of a focus on "premium" units for "high-end" markets continued, with a couple of interesting exceptions (see below). For instance, across from the PN Hoffman booth, two young salespeople presided over the MassCourt booth. Located downtown, at Massachusetts and Seventh NW, MassCourt was at that time nearing completion. "[It's] really three separate buildings," the staffer described. "One loft. One traditional. One historic. The loft apartments are like nothing else in the District. They're going to have concrete floors, exposed pipes, loft ceilings. Very New York style. Very unique. I think people will love the amenities, the yoga room, the rooftop pool with spectacular views of the Capitol Building, [and] the rooftop track and fitness area." But how much would it cost to rent a two-bedroom apartment? "$2,033 [a month] for a two-bedroom," she replied.

After she had listed off the amenities and handed me promotional materials with images of young single people, in impeccable clothes, enjoying the yoga room and fitness area, I asked about the kind of "audience" she was trying to attract to her building. In reply I received a long, uncomfortable pause and then simply, "anyone, really." Later I would learn from another booth that real estate firms are forbidden by housing anti-discrimination laws to talk about the "kind of person" they want as tenants. For this reason, the question of "preferred target markets" asked sales staff to move into dangerous socio-political territory, and accordingly few took the bait. At the same time, however, it was equally clear in the developers' promotional materials that they were in fact aggressively marketing to a particular slice of the housing market, to a particular "kind" of person—in class terms at least, if not in terms of race or ethnicity. Let us be frank. Yoga rooms emphatically do not appeal to just "anyone." They appeal, as Mass-Court's own marketing images attest, to college-educated, upward-climbing, young professionals whose particular stock of cultural capital includes both an appreciation of Eastern philosophical pursuits and a taste for haute couture.

While most other booths pitched buildings of equal distinction, there was one notable exception to this focus on the "premium" market: the William C. Smith booth. Although William C. Smith develops and manages housing units all across the District, close to one-third of their properties are located in Southeast D.C., an area home to the highest concentrations of poverty and joblessness in the city. But, interestingly, these were the units that generated the most enthusiasm from the sales staff. As Smith's PR director put it, "southeast is where all the exciting stuff is going on." She then described her firm's redevelopment of "the Parklands" neighborhood in Southeast:

> When we bought that . . . it was 60 percent boarded up, crime, drugs, you name it. We restored the apartments. We partnered with the community. We partnered with the police to let the drug dealers know they were no longer welcome. We built the first for-sale townhouse community in Ward 8 [the poorest ward in the city], [and] we targeted first-time homebuyers.[47]

She described, in other words, a transformed physical and social landscape, with the development firm playing a leading role in turning the neighborhood around. When asked about William Smith's target market for this development, the PR director said, "affordable housing. Our market is affordable housing." So how much would a townhouse in Parklands cost? After selling initially for $105,000, she said, owners are now re-selling them for $160,000. They are, in her words, "truly affordable."

That she would describe these properties as affordable reveals much about the District's more general housing crisis. Put simply, $160,000 (US) is still a lot of money. According to the National Low-Income Housing Coalition, the median annual income for renting households in the District is just under $33,000.[48] At this income, the Fannie Mae Foundation estimates that the median renting household looking to buy in the District would only be able to afford a $128,000 mortgage and a monthly payment of $990 a month—and this figure assumes that the buyers had saved $8,000 for a down payment and could secure a lender at a 5 percent interest rate. [49] In other words, if Smith's townhouse developments were what passed for affordable housing within the Expo "text," then this effectively excluded more than half of all renters in D.C.

And so we arrive at the key contradiction within the Expo über-text. Despite planners' stated commitment to conduct an inclusive campaign, one that addressed not just upscale suburbanites but also encouraged current District renters to buy their first home, the vendors pitching granite countertops and "prime"

locations vastly outnumbered the William C. Smith's of the Expo. And despite
the claim that the campaign would show the public that "there are ways you can
make living here an affordable reality,"[50] the text of the Expo contained little
evidence that this "affordable reality" was either real or affordable.

Perhaps this explains one last notable feature of the Expo: the unexpected
popularity of the District of Columbia government. By mid-afternoon, huge
crowds pressed into the D.C. government's booths to ask officials questions
about the city's affordable housing programs. I met two members of this crowd
over lunch. They were two friends, both African-American women in their for-
ties, and both were commuters currently living in Maryland. They had traveled
to the Expo to explore the idea of buying a home in the District, and they were
frustrated. Everything was too expensive, they said, and sometimes, "they don't
even list the price"—a bad sign by all accounts. It was for this reason that they
spent a lot of time at the government booths looking into housing subsidies and
incentives. Ultimately, they left disappointed. "They want people like us to
move here to repopulate," one friend said. "But what do they consider affordable
housing? They're not meeting us halfway." Said her companion, "show us the
programs!"

City Living: The Moment of Context

What I term here as "the moment of context" actually condenses two distinct
moments in Johnson's circuit of culture—the moment of reception, in which
individual audience members receive the text and produce their own readings,
and the moment of "lived cultures," when these individual readings play back
into the social relations that constitute everyday life. [51] With this in mind, my
comments with regard to the reception and social consequences of the "city living" campaign are necessarily speculative. I have yet to conduct any reception
analysis, and because the campaign is still underway, any attempt to explore its
material effects would be premature. What this section offers, then, is an analysis of the broad economic and political context into which *any* interpretation of
this campaign, and any analysis of its consequences, would have to be inserted.

And what is this political and economic context? In other words, what are
the likely results of this campaign, if it indeed succeeds and attracts new residents to the District? Posing the question of context in this way requires us to
explore the possibility that even a campaign specifically designed to attract single affluent professionals might nonetheless benefit *all* residents by expanding
the tax base and thereby improving schools and services—just as the planners
had claimed. To a person, however, the housing advocates I interviewed were
quite skeptical of this claim, and their skepticism hinged on the likely effects of
attracting large numbers of affluent residents to an already superheated housing
market.

The rental market in particular is a hostile place for middle- and low-income households. According to the Urban Institute, between 2001 and 2003, low vacancy rates and high housing demand pushed up the average advertised rent for a two-bedroom apartment by 84 percent.[52] Given these figures, it should not surprise anyone that market-rate apartments in the District are now renting at levels beyond the means of most working families. To put the crisis into perspective, in the current housing market a worker earning the District's minimum wage would have to work for 152 hours every week to afford a typical, market-rate, two-bedroom apartment (currently renting at slightly over $1,200 a month).[53]

Now, argue housing advocates, the mayor proposes adding an additional 10,000 residents into the District housing market each year for the next ten years. Not only would this increase the total number of households bidding for housing, but, if the "city living" campaign hits its target, these households would command significantly more resources on average than existing residents. In the free housing market, the newcomers would be able to outbid many existing residents for the District's existing housing stock. To be sure, this rapid increase in demand for housing would likely stimulate additional construction, but these new units would come in slowly and at the prevailing market rate—in short, at rents beyond the means of most existing District renters. The long-term result would be the rapid turnover of lower-income households with upper-income households—particularly in working-class neighborhoods adjacent to downtown and other city amenities.[54] District residents without the means to keep up in the bidding war would be forced to either crowd into the few remaining affordable neighborhoods east of the Anacostia River (further exacerbating the problem of concentrated poverty in these areas) or to flee the District entirely, most likely to the low-income areas of Maryland's Prince Georges County.[55]

Furthermore, the particular geography of class power in the District will ensure that this process of displacement and gentrification is concentrated in some neighborhoods and not others. As one housing advocate argued, the target markets potentially attracted by the campaign may be affluent in comparison to current D.C. renters, but even they cannot afford to break into the District's most desirable neighborhoods, including Cleveland Park, DuPont Circle, and Georgetown. The search will then be on for housing in neighborhoods either immediately adjacent to these hotspots or in shouting distance of downtown's retailing and cultural amenities. The ensuing displacement of existing residents will therefore accelerate in the "borderland" neighborhoods of Columbia Heights, Shaw, and Southwest D.C.—in other words, those areas of the city more affordable than Georgetown, adjacent to the amenities of downtown, but without the stigma of "decay" long associated with neighborhoods east of the Anacostia River.[56]

The likely effect would be that the frontier of gentrification would progressively extend from the über-affluent environs of Northwest (Georgetown, DuPont Circle, Cleveland Park) and colonize more and more working-class or low-income areas in Northwest, Northeast, and Southwest D.C., particularly in the neighborhoods closest to downtown like Shaw, Columbia Heights, and Logan Circle. As one advocate put it:

> Look, they're not trying to attract the people they are displacing. They are try-
> ing to attract the people they think will add to the tax base. And where are these
> people going to go? They can't afford to live in Woodley Park. It's going to be
> Mt. Pleasant, Columbia Heights, Shaw in the future. That's where they're go-
> ing to go.[57]

This was certainly the strategy of one couple I spoke with at the Expo. This childless, twenty-something couple lived in suburban Alexandria (which was "pretty cool" but was a bit heavy on "kids and dogs" for their taste), but they were looking for "something with a little more nightlife, more edge." They wanted to relocate to the District, and had two criteria: cost and safety. This meant that, for them, Southeast was out of the question, while the more glamorous districts in Northwest would be well beyond their means. Within these constraints, their strategy was to speculate. "We're looking for the next great 'hood . . . the next place to be gentrified, frankly. I know that's a bit controversial, but there you have it. . . . We're looking for the places that will be the next frontier."

Even in the years prior to the District's "city living" campaign, the effects of such "urban pioneers"[58] as this young Expo couple were already being felt in the "middle-ground" neighborhoods of Shaw/Cardozo and Columbia Heights. In Shaw, not far from a new luxury condo development promoted at the Expo, single family homes that sold in 1996 for $80,000 sold for 87 percent more just three years later. In the same neighborhood, small townhouses on 13th and O Street sold for $249,000 in 2000. By 2001, such townhouses in the same development were selling for $373,000.[59] Nearby in the Columbia Heights/Mt. Pleasant neighborhood, the median housing sale price for a single-family home or condominium increased by 45 percent from 1998 to 2002, while at the same time, the neighborhood lost 24 percent of its public and subsidized housing units due to reconversion and redevelopment.[60]

By the time of the city living Expo, in short, the super-heated housing market in the District had focused advocates' attention on a fundamental question: how should the city define "revitalization"? Should revitalization "pertain only to increasing the tax base by attracting upper-income new residents, or should it mean ensuring that low and moderate-income working class families can afford to live in this city and contribute to its development?"[61] In the end, then, the performance of the "city living" campaign is the District government's own answer to this question, for it is into this volatile affordable housing crisis that the city living campaign would pour, if everything went well, another 10,000 affluent residents every year for the next ten years. In the absence of a sustained commitment to subsidized and affordable housing—a commitment that my advocacy informants suggested was long on words and short on funding—the result would be a predictable acceleration of housing costs and a spiral of displacement and neighborhood gentrification.[62]

So what should we conclude from this effort to persuade affluent suburbanites on the benefits of city living? We can, I believe, draw both substantive and theoretical conclusions. Substantively, it seems clear that, as the campaign moves forward, planners' inability to confront the realities of class power in the regional housing market will likely undermine any claim that their efforts serve the universal civic good. If planners initially intended to produce an inclusive, broad-based campaign, the more immediate desire to absorb new upscale housing units and to attract national-chain retailers ultimately exerted a more profound influence. Produced out of this "mission creep," the campaign's texts thus focused attention on a narrow slice of the suburban regional market and collectively presented the District as the stage upon which the dreams and desires of affluent professionals could be performed.

In the end, it is this pursuit of a class-specific target that promises to undercut the civic aspirations of campaign planners. Even if the campaign succeeds admirably in attracting its prized single professionals and empty nesters, the likely result of this process, as advocates suggest, would be an accelerated cycle of real estate speculation, ending in the displacement of long-time residents and the progressive gentrification of District neighborhoods.[63] The District that would emerge from this process would be a revitalized city with a broader tax base, enhanced city services, better schools, and a stunning variety of retail and cultural amenities. But, in the process, many working families who sustained their neighborhoods through the difficult years would be unable to compete for housing and would ultimately be excluded from participating in their city's revitalized future.

For this reason, the true realization of the planners' civic aspirations ultimately depends upon more than mobilizing images and re-positioning brands. It will require instead a sincere commitment to grapple with the realities of class privilege in the contemporary urban landscape. In short, if indeed all residents are to enjoy the benefits of the District's rebirth, then the Mayor's ambitious goal of attracting new residents must be coupled with an equally ambitious goal of expanding access to low-income and affordable housing. This is by no means a small undertaking. Such a commitment would require the city to devote more resources to public housing programs. It would require measures that force developers to include affordable units within each and every housing development. It would undoubtedly require antagonizing powerful interests in the local business community—including some of the same actors who contributed to the "city living" campaign. None of this would be easy, and, according to housing advocates, the Williams administration has sent decidedly mixed signals regarding its commitment to affordable housing.[64] But without such a commitment, the planners' promise that *all* citizens will share in the city's revitalization will be of little comfort to families priced out of their homes and displaced from their neighborhoods.

There are theoretical conclusions to be drawn as well. In particular, the "city living" campaign offers an opportunity to discuss how critical media scholars might build a more productive dialogue between political economy and cultural studies. Specifically, this case study highlights an important but underdeveloped point of overlap between the two traditions: the study of the production-text relation. That cultural studies has drifted away from an engagement with the material practice of textual production is by now a familiar critique.[65] As Livingstone argues, the turn toward poststructuralist approaches to textual analysis in the late 1970s shifted the focus of cultural interpretation from the text itself (within which analysts armed with the tools of structuralism could locate its "true" meaning) to the text-audience relation.[66] Texts, as Barthes famously noted, were inert until interpreted or realized by actual, rather than ideal, readers. Authorship thus migrated from the *producer* to the *audience*, and the interpreter—not the multinational media conglomerate—thus became the true "producer" of textual meanings.[67]

This poststructuralist turn slowly pulled cultural studies away from the social practices of media production (the moment of "encoding") and toward a singular focus on the moment of "decoding."[68] The crucial analytical question was not, therefore, "how do producers encode a 'preferred' reading into the text?" but rather, "how do situated audiences exploit the necessary polysemy of the text to produce divergent readings?" The furthest extension of this logic can be found in the often-criticized "semiotic democracy" promoted by John Fiske, whose work often celebrates the ability of media consumers to appropriate and transform the meaning of popular culture to advance their own interests and perspectives.[69] If the best cultural studies work on the dynamics of audience reception did not join Fiske in such celebrations,[70] the post-structuralist turn toward the question of polysemy nonetheless had the effect of repressing an engagement with the production-text relation and how the concrete practices of cultural production place important limits of the range of discourses circulated in the media system in the *first* (rather than last) instance.[71]

As it happens, cultural studies is not alone in the neglect of the production-text relation. It may, at first, seem odd to accuse political economists of neglecting a careful analysis of the "moment of production." After all, the tradition's fundamental purpose, as Meehan explains, is to trace the "processes by which corporations routinize, commercialize, and commoditize both cultural expression and cultural consumption."[72] At the same time, political-economic analysis often moves quickly from a macro-study of corporate structures—often expressed in lists of "who owns what"—to detailing the thoroughly commodified output of corporate media and the proliferating sins of hypercommericalism, including brand integration, product placement, and cross-marketing synergies.[73] What's often missing from political-economic work, as Vincent Mosco (a leading figure in the field) notes, are close analyses of the mediating processes of textual production that provide the missing link between economic structures, commercial motives, and the end-products, the media-texts themselves.[74] While political economists have begun to make strides toward the careful, even ethnographic study of concrete production practices,[75] too often the tradition has relied on sociologists to do this sort of legwork.[76]

In the end, as the "city living" case demonstrates, focusing analytical attention on the relationship between production and text can yield insights not available at other moments in the circulation of cultural commodities. The inclusion of the DC Marketing Center and the Downtown BID into the planning process had, in other words, an explicit and demonstrable effect on the images and experiences produced by the campaign. And ultimately, it was this class-specific vision of the urban good life—one strategically designed to attract the sorts of residents that could advance the economic goals of the downtown development community—that promised to spark a cycle of gentrification and undermine the civic aspirations of campaign planners.

This case therefore suggests that both cultural studies and political economy scholars would do well to focus more attention on the concrete practices of cultural producers. For cultural studies scholars, this will require a re-connection with the early history of the discipline, in which works like *Policing the Crisis* contributed importantly to the understanding of how particular ideological premises are woven into media texts through the professional codes that structure the practice of journalism and other forms of cultural production.[77] For political economists, this will require overcoming the tendency to equate institutional analysis with charting the transformation in ownership structures over time.[78] Instead of farming out the concrete analysis of media production to media sociologists,[79] political economists need to get their hands dirty and study how cultural commodities are actually produced in historical contexts and how this process enables and delimits the circulation of particular images, discourses, and ideologies. In either case, a re-engagement with the production-text relation would not signal the return of a crude economism. Instead, it would build upon Raymond Williams' conception of economic determination as the "setting of limits and exertion of pressures" on cultural and political expression, mostly by ensuring that some discourses and not others have preferred access to the powerful storytelling machinery of the contemporary media.[80]

Notes

1. Saskia Sassen, *The Global City: New York, London, Tokyo* (Princeton, NJ: Princeton University Press, 1991); Dennis Judd and Todd Swanstrom, *City Politics: Private Power and Public Policy* (New York: HarperCollins, 1994); Manuel Castells, *The Rise of the Network Society*, 2nd ed. (Oxford: Blackwell, 2000).

2. Castells, *Network Society*.

3. Mike Davis, "Planet of Slums: Urban Involution and the Informal Proletariat," *New Left Review,* 26 (March-April 2004): 5-34.

4. See Timothy Gibson, *Securing the Spectacular City: The Politics of Revitalization and Homelessness in Downtown Seattle* (Lanham, MD: Lexington Books, 2004), especially chapter 4, for a description of some of these image-management activities.

5. Robert A. Beauregard, *Voices of Decline: The Postwar Fate of U.S. Cities,* 2nd ed. (New York & London: Routledge, 2003 [1993]); Timothy Gibson, *Securing the Spectacular City.*

104   *Timothy A. Gibson*

6. John Hannigan, "Symposium on Branding, the Entertainment Economy, and Urban Place Building: Introduction," *International Journal of Urban and Regional Research*, 27 (2003): 352-60; G. Kearns and C. Philo, *Selling Places: The City as Cultural Capital, Past and Present* (Oxford: Pergamon Press, 1993).

7. M.C. Boyer, "Cities for Sale: Merchandising History at South Street Seaport," in *Variations on a Theme Park*, ed. M. Sorkin, (New York: Hill and Wang, 1992); Kearns and Philo, *Selling Places* (Oxford: Pergamon Press, 1993).

8. John Hannigan, *Fantasy City: Pleasure and Profit in the Postmodern Metropolis* (New York: Routledge, 1998); Kevin Fox Gotham, "Marketing Mardi Gras: Commodification, Spectacle, and the Political Economy of Tourism in New Orleans," *Urban Studies* 39 (2002): 1735-56.

9. D. Lowry, T. Nio, and D. Leitner, "Setting the Public Fear Agenda: A Longitudinal Analysis of Crime Reporting, Public Perceptions of Crime, and FBI Crime Statistics," *Journal of Communication* 53, no. 1 (2003): 61-73; D. Romer, K.H. Jamieson, and S. Aday, "Television News and the Fear of Crime," *Journal of Communication* 53, no. 1 (2003): 88-104.

10. Pierre Bourdieu, *Language and Symbolic Power* (Cambridge, MA: Harvard University Press, 1991); J.B. Thompson, *Studies in the Theory of Ideology* (Berkeley: University of California Press, 1984).

11. Richard Johnson, "What Is Cultural Studies, Anyway?" *Social Text* 6, no. 1 (1987): 38-80.

12. See especially Nicholas Garnham, "Political Economy and Cultural Studies: Reconciliation or Divorce?" *Critical Studies in Mass Communication* 12 (1995): 62-71.

13. Douglas Kellner, "Overcoming the Divide: Cultural Studies and Political Economy," in *Cultural Studies in Question*, ed. M. Ferguson and P. Golding, (London: Sage, 1998); Eileen Meehan, "Leisure or Labor?: Fan Ethnography and Political Economy," in *Consuming Audiences? Production and Reception in Media Research*, ed. I. Hagen and J. Wasko, (Cresskill, NJ: Hampton Press); Allen Scott, *The Cultural Economy of Cities: Essays on the Geography of Image-Producing Industries* (London: Sage, 2000).

14. For a good example of this approach, see Carol Stabile, "Nike, Social Responsibility, and the Hidden Abode of Production," *Critical Studies in Media Communication*, 17 (2000): 186-204.

15. Anthony Williams, "Mayor Williams' Second Inaugural Address: One City, One Future," http://www.dc.gov/ mayor/speeches/speech.asp?cp=1&id=76.

16. U.S. Census Bureau, "State and County Quick Facts: District of Columbia," http://quickfacts.census.gov/qfd/states.

17. Interview, Deputy Mayor's Office, 1 October 2003.

18. Office of the Chief Financial Officer, *Tax Rates and Tax Burdens in the District of Columbia—A Nationwide Comparison* (Washington, DC: Office of the Chief Financial Officer, District of Columbia, 2004).

19. C. O'Cleireacain, and Alice Rivlin, *Envisioning a Future Washington: A Brookings Institution Research Brief*, http://www.brook.edu.

20. U.S. General Accounting Office, *Report to Congressional Requesters: District of Columbia Structural Imbalance and Management Issues.* (Washington, DC: U.S. General Accounting Office, 2004).

21. Interview, DC Marketing Center, 8 October 2003.

22. Interview, Downtown Business Improvement District, 9 April 2004.

23. Interview, Downtown Business Improvement District, 9 April 2004.

24. Interview, Deputy Mayor's Office, 1 October 2003.

25. Previous three quotes, Interview, Deputy Mayor's Office, 1 October 2003.

26. Interview, DC Marketing Center, 8 October 2003.

27. Interview, Deputy Mayor's Office, 1 October 2003.

28. D. Nakamura, "Selling a Hipper Image: Marketing Campaign Seeks to Attract Upscale Residents," *The Washington Post,* 19 June 2003, 10(T).

29. Interview, Deputy Mayor's Office, 1 October 2003.

30. Interview, TCI Companies, 6 November 2003.

31. A fourth target audience included current residents within the District. This audience was not featured in the advertising campaign; however, some booths at the Expo were designed with the needs of current residents in mind.

32. Interview, DC Marketing Center, 8 October 2003.

33. Interview, Deputy Mayor's Office, 1 October 2003.

34. Interview, DC Marketing Center, 28 October 2003.

35. K. Ono, and D. Buescher, "Deciphering Pocahontas," *Critical Studies in Media Communication* 18, no. 1 (2001): 23-41.

36. Interview, Deputy Mayor's Office, 1 October 2003.

37. Pierre Bourdieu, *Practical Reason* (Stanford, CA: Stanford University Press, 1998).

38. Mike Budd, Steve Craig, and Clay Steinman, *Consuming Environments: Television and Commercial Culture* (New Brunswick, NJ: Rutgers University Press, 1999).

39. Louis Althusser, *Lenin and Philosophy and Other Essays* (New Left Review, London, 1971).

40. Pierre Bourdieu, *Practical Reason.*

41. Interview, TCI Companies. 6 November 2003.

42. Pierre Bourdieu, *Distinction: A Social Critique of the Judgment of Taste* (Cambridge, MA: Harvard University Press, 1984).

43. Rodale Publishers, "About *Bicycling*/About *Mountain Bike*," accessed online at http://www.bicycling.com/aboutus/0,3291,s1,00.html.

44. Interview, TCI Companies, 6 November 2003.

45. Interview, Deputy Mayor's Office, 1 October 2003.

46. Interview, TCI Companies, 6 November 2003.

47. Fieldnotes, City Living Exposition, 24 October 2003.

48. National Low Income Housing Coalition, *Out of Reach 2003: America's Housing Wage Climbs*, http://www.nlihc.org/oor2003.

49. Fannie Mae Foundation, "Calculators: How Much House Can You Afford?" www.fanniemae.com.

50. Interview, Deputy Mayor's Office, 1 October 2003. Previous two quotations.

51. Richard Johnson, "What Is Cultural Studies, Anyway?"

52. M.A. Turner, G.T. Kingsley, K. Pettit, and N. Sawyer, *Housing in the Nation's Capital, 2004.* (Washington, DC: Fannie Mae Foundation and the Urban Institute, 2004).

53. National Low Income Housing Coalition, *Out of Reach 2003: America's Housing Wage Climbs.*

54. Interview, DC Tenants Advocacy Coalition, 10 December 2003.

55. Interview, Washington Regional Network for Livable Communities, 16 March 2005.

56. Interview, Committee for Indigenous Solidarity DC, 9 December 2003.

57. Interview, Committee for Indigenous Solidarity DC, 9 December 2003.

58. For an insightful analysis of the "frontier" metaphor in the context of urban gentrification, see Neil Smith, *The New Urban Frontier: Gentrification and the Revanchist City* (London: Routledge, 1996).

59. Lois Athey, *The State of Latinos in the District of Columbia: Trends, Consequences, and Recommendations,* (Washington, DC: Council of Latino Agencies, 2002).

60. DC Agenda, *Issue Scan Full report: An Annual Report Examining Changes in Neighborhood Conditions in the District of Columbia,* http://www.dcagenda.org/

61. Lois Athey, *The State of Latinos in the District of Columbia,* 80.

62. T. Knott, "Mayor's 'City Living, DC Style' Vision Shortsighted," *Washington Times,* 6 November 2003, http://washingtontimes.com.

63. M. Kennedy and P. Leonard, *Dealing with Neighborhood Change: A Primer on Gentrification and Policy Choices: A Discussion Paper Prepared for the Brookings Institution Center of Urban and Metropolitan Policy,* http://www.brookings.edu./urban; C. O'Cleireacain and Alice Rivlin, *Envisioning a Future Washington: A Brookings Institution Research Brief.*

64. Interview, Washington Regional Network for Livable Communities, 16 March 2005

65. Nicolas Garnham, *Capitalism and Communication: Global Culture and the Economics of Information* (London: Sage, 1990); Vincent Mosco, *The Political Economy of Communication: Rethinking and Renewal* (Thousand Oaks, CA: Sage, 1996).

66. Sonia Livingstone, "The Rise and Fall of Audience Research: An Old Story with a New Ending" *Journal of Communication* 43, no. 4 (1993): 5-12.

67. Roland Barthes, *S/Z,* trans. Richard Miller (New York: Hill and Wang, 1974); see also, John Fiske, *Television Culture* (London: Routledge, 1987).

68. Hall, S., "Encoding/Decoding."

69. Fiske, *Television culture*; John Fiske, "Ethnosemiotics," *Cultural Studies* 4 (1990): 85-100.

70. Sut Jhally and Justin Lewis, *Enlightened Racism: The Cosby Show, Audiences, and the Myth of the American Dream* (Boulder, CO: Westview Press, 1992); Janice Radway, *Reading the Romance: Women, Patriarchy, and Popular Literature* (Chapel Hill: University of North Carolina Press, 1984); Andrea Press and Elizabeth Cole, *Speaking of Abortion: Television and Authority in the Lives of Women* (Chicago: University of Chicago Press, 1999).

71. Stuart Hall, "The Problem of Ideology—Marxism without Guarantees," in *Marx: 100 years On,* ed. B. Matthews (London: Lawrence and Wishart, 1983); David Morley, "Active Audience Theory: Pendulums and Pitfalls," *Journal of Communication* 43, no. 4 (1993): 13-21; Graham Murdock, "Base Notes: The Conditions of Cultural Practice."

72. Eileen Meehan, "Leisure or Labor?: Fan Ethnography and Political Economy," in *Consuming Audiences? Production and Reception in Media Research,* ed. I. Hagen and Janet Wasko, 72 (Cresskill, NJ: Hampton Press, 2002).

73. Robert W. McChesney *The Problem of the Media: U.S. Communication Politics in the 21st Century* (New York: Monthly Review Press, 2004); Janet Wasko, *Understanding Disney* (Cambridge, MA: Polity Press, 2000).

74. Vincent Mosco, *The Political Economy of Communication,* 158.

75. Timothy Havens, "'It's Still a White World Out There': The Interplay of Culture and Economics in the International Television Trade," *Critical Studies in Media Communication* 19 (2002): 377-91; E. Levine, "Toward a Paradigm for Media Production Research: Behind the Scenes at *General Hospital,*" *Critical Studies in Media Communication* 18 (2001): 66-82.

76. I am indebted to Vincent Mosco for this point; see *The Political Economy of Communication.*

77. Stuart Hall, Chas Critcher, T. Jefferson, John Clarke, and B. Robert, *Policing the Crisis: Mugging, the State, and Law and Order* (New York: Holmes & Meier, 1978).

78. Mosco, *The Political Economy of Communication.*

79. Gaye Tuchman, *Making the News: A Study in the Construction of Reality* (New York: Free Press, 1978); Todd Gitlin, *Inside Prime Time* (New York: Pantheon, 1983).

80. Raymond Williams, *Marxism and Literature* (Oxford: Oxford University Press, 1977); see also, Kevin Carragee, "Interpretive Media Study and Interpretive Social Science," *Critical Studies in Mass Communication* 7 (1990): 81-97.

Part II

The City as Text

Chapter 5

"They Stand for All the Things I Hate": Georgian Architecture and Cultural Memory in Contemporary Dublin

Andrew Kincaid

Architecture is a form of narrating history. Buildings exist in their historical contexts, as well as in the milieu of the structures that surround them. A winged, dynamic Calatrava museum, for example, tells its neighbors that they are stodgy, and that the future has arrived (at least until something more innovative and *du jour* is built down the block). The debates over architectural style have often been about the thorny historical problem of national identity: modernism, with its stripped, planar uniformity, consciously rejected references to the parochial, divisive past in an attempt to strike off and form a brave new world of internationalism and universal appeal; more recently, new urbanism reflects a specific selection of new and restored buildings culled from an eclectic range of premodern architectural styles and motifs (palladian, renaissance, and the medieval marketplace, to name a few) in order to imprint nostalgia onto a contemporary city that might otherwise be perceived as harsh and profit-driven. History is written on the city.

Architectural battles over issues ranging from preservation to gentrification and renewal underscore this truth. Changing political and economic situations, along with their attendant reinterpretations of the past, are mirrored in the production of space. The rise of the "bourgeois villa," a single house on a parcel of private land, in early eighteenth-century England, for example, represented the emerging values of individualism, selfhood, and economic success. The denizens of these homes were then all-the-better positioned to view themselves, and their class, as the natural, entitled heirs to the legacy of decades of internecine warfare. Likewise, the modern American skyscraper imprinted both street and history with a corporate mark: if the present looked powerful, and business-like, then the less prosperous past was necessarily inferior and, at the same time, evocative of simplicity. Architecture illustrates not only the power of institutions—state, church, crown—but also the way it can be used to show how each era regards those that went before it.

The relationship between memory and the city has long been debated. All the major thinkers of modernity have used the city as a metaphor for their theories. Moreover, their lives and work were rooted in the actual, changing environment of the city: Joyce and Dublin, Freud and Vienna, Benjamin and Berlin, Marx and the English industrial city. For Freud, the structure of the unconscious was topographical, mirrored in the archaeologically layered cityscape. In *Civilization and Its Discontents*, Freud imagines Rome with all its layers of history exposed, existing simultaneously, where nothing has disappeared or been destroyed. For Joyce, Dublin is fragmented but connected, at the same time modern and traditional, colonial and proudly independent, particular and universal. In its contrasts and serendipities, Joyce finds the raw material for expressing the everyday, yet elevated, practice of everyday life. For Marx and Engels, Manchester represented the disconnection between a displaced rural working poor, along with an immigrant Irish underclass, and their memories and traditions. Each of these writers, who used the city as working metaphor, was also rooted in a rapidly transforming city; their theories could not have come about outside of their immediate urban lives. As these writers worked, their cities changed around them, undergoing waves of modernization, renewal, and demographic expansion. In turn, these urban upheavals enabled modern forms of personal experience (sexual freedom, personal consumption, artistic expression, loneliness), along with new social possibilities, from the construction of collective identities (worker, feminist, ethnic) to the articulation of a new universalism. Many of these theories—from Freud's belief that the pressures of contemporary life create ever greater repression, through Marx's notion that modern capitalism leads to increased alienation, to Joyce's argument that urban engenders increased complexity and the lack of perceptual tools to understand it—focus on the city, because it is there that the rift between progress and tradition, possibility and confusion, is most stark.

In modern Ireland, contrary to popular conception, the city has always been a contested site, one whose physical structure and more ephemeral character have represented ideological victory to all sides of the lengthy contest over political and national identity. Colonialism, fundamentally, rests on a distinction not simply between people—these differences can blur with time—but between concepts. When English settlers in the seventeenth century constructed a series of market towns across the north of Ireland as part of the Ulster Plantation, they were also demarcating a set of divisions between the new arrivals and the native population, between inside and outside, urban and rural, civilization and barbarism. The planning, architecture and founding of Londonderry made these distinctions concrete. A walled town, Londonderry was laid out on a grid pattern with a formal public space and market building at its center. Land was reserved for a school and a church, representatives of the institutions that would subsequently play an important role in maintaining difference.

At another pivotal point in Irish history, several centuries later, when the Irish Free State gained autonomy from Britain in 1922, the city was again a flashpoint, and control over its spaces represented a crucial means for the new state to consolidate its authority. The construction of new suburbs served to win support from the city's middle and working classes, the latter of whom had played a leading part in the anticolonial movement and who would, therefore, potentially be most volatile in expecting concrete results from their victory. Each of these examples—Londonderry and postcolonial Dublin—works to re-fashion the environment in the interests of ideology, an act that is, in itself, a form of history-writing, inasmuch as the past is seen as needing correction, and the future becomes a receptacle for these improvements.

Georgian architecture, in particular, and particularly in Dublin, has been freighted with controversial ideological significance. Stylistically, Georgian architecture displays classical columns, pedimented porches, planar walls of granite, and large windows. The form arose during the eighteenth century in England, and its symmetry, classical references, and suggestion of wealth spoke to the confidence of the age, colonial expansion, the objectivity of science and reason, and the splendor of Empire. When it was introduced into Ireland in the mid-eighteenth century, Georgian architecture had both an urban and a rural manifestation. In the countryside, English landlords stamped their pedigree on the landscape by building large houses, ranging in size from extensive farm-houses to Palladian and neo-classical mansions. These Big Houses, as they would come to be known, with their surrounding demesnes, were a powerful symbol of the new Anglo-Irish Ascendancy class (which had consolidated its political and military hold on Ireland in the wake of the Williamite Wars of the 1690s) and of the shift in culture, language, and power that had occurred. As well, then, it was no coincidence that Georgian architecture was an import to Dublin in the early 1700s. In Dublin, a group of landlords, parliamentarians, and Protestant businessmen joined together to create an early and powerful urban renewal authority called the "Commissioners for Making Wide and Convenient Ways, Streets and Passages." These commissioners carved out a series of broad boulevards from the medieval city, connecting notable structures of the colonial state to each other. Along the new routes, new administrative institutions, repre-senting trade, communications, and democracy, were constructed in Georgian form.

At another crucial moment in Irish history, Georgian architecture became a powerful discourse onto which leading figures attached all manner of political and cultural values—the ideology of progress, the hope of overcoming history, and the desire to assert sovereignty. In the immediate aftermath of Irish inde-pendence in 1922, Georgian buildings and their denizens were largely ignored, the edifices left to decay while their inhabitants either departed back to England or remained in the new nationalist state, nostalgic relics of a faded era. By the 1960s, following what were commonly perceived as decades of stagnation, the leaders of the postcolonial state embarked on a process of internationalizing the economy and modernizing Irish culture. A new generation of leaders rejected Georgian architecture, adopting the standards of international style and modern-ist architecture in order to accommodate and produce a new economic model: corporate, efficient, industrial, and competitive.

Today, in the first decade of the twenty-first century, after more than ten years of neoliberal economics, Ireland has, in the eyes of many, rounded a corner. Jobs are plentiful, construction is booming, new migrants from Africa and Eastern Europe are arriving, and former Irish emigrants are returning home. Irish culture, too, has achieved a new level of international commercial success. On the one hand, contemporary movies and plays find acclaim by portraying bleak tales of family life or political strife from the bad old days of colonialism or the immediate post-independent period. The revelations, in part, suggest that a particular past—of repression or violence—is over, and that the past can now be contemplated safely from the distance of a global, more optimistic, and post-national present. On the other hand, a version of modern Irish culture—its music and dance—is celebrated for its Celtic appeal; that is, for the vague sense of mythic history, premodern folklore, and simplistic spiritual identity for which all things Gaelic are a repository.

Architecturally, Dublin is experiencing similar stylistic trends to other urban areas that have been keen to refashion themselves as up-and-coming global cities: technological, cosmopolitan, and flexible. A Calatrava-designed bridge over the River Liffey was recently commissioned and completed; Daniel Liebskind has just won an architectural competition for redesigning a disused harbor front. Still, the prevalent architectural style in Dublin is obviously Georgian— old Georgian buildings are being renovated with a fervor, and new mock-Georgian suburban homes are gaining new popularity. In the countryside, the decaying Big House is returning as an international hotel and conference center, and in central Dublin, those Georgian squares and structures that survived the 1960s wrecking ball are being restored and jealously guarded in the name of national heritage. A generation that is able to forget the mistakes of the 1960s now looks back to a golden moment, an era when prosperity was limited to a very few people, but when the symbols of wealth were obvious and recognizable, and tries to recast and recapture this glory.

At pivotal moments in Irish history, therefore, architectural style has been used to further ideological ends and signal deliberate historical shifts. Terry Eagleton writes in *Heathcliff and the Great Hunger* that colonial policy in Ireland during the eighteenth and nineteenth century moved back and forth between force and hegemony, violence and persuasion.[1] English policymakers began in Ireland with violence and conquest, but gradually colonial officials sought to establish the structures of a colonial state, shifting their strategy toward a politics of hegemony, and initiating institutions and practices designed to win the consent of the governed. The most dramatic example of this is Ireland's initial Georgian moment, and the reconfiguration of the city by the Wide Streets Commissioners in the late eighteenth and early nineteenth centuries. Appointed by George II, the commissioners were constituted by several acts of Parliament, and operated in the city between 1757 and 1841 (when they were abolished by municipal reforms) and set the tone for sweeping, aggressive, and highly political urban renewal. Empowered to "carry on improvements by making . . . wide streets . . . through many parts that were before narrow, dangerous and inconvenient," these landowners (most of the commissioners were either aristocrats, merchants, or parliamentarians) collected taxes, acquired imminent domain, assessed property valuations, compensated those displaced by clearance, and enforced a series of regulations with regard to the width of pavements, the uniformity of façade, and the cleanliness of roads.[2]

The commissioners' justification for intervening in the spatial layout of Dublin comes through in the language they employed: The words "improvement," "convenient," "trade," "healthfulness," ornament" and "safety" appear frequently in their tracts and in the minutes of their meetings. Their first project was to create a "Wide and Convenient Way . . . from Essex-Bridge to the Castle of Dublin. . . . Whereas the ways, streets, avenues, and passages, leading from Essex Bridge to the Royal Palace . . . are at present narrow, close, and crooked . . . a wide and convenient way . . . will contribute to the ease and safety of passengers, the adorning those parts of the city, and will be of use and benefit to the publick."[3] The resulting fifty-one-foot wide bridge, designed by George Semple, and, in part, modeled on London's Westminster Bridge, facilitated greater movement between the Castle and the military barracks in the Phoenix Park. From the bridge, a new street, Parliament Street, cut its way toward the Castle through a tangle of narrow lanes and alleys. Where it opened onto the Castle, the commissioners planned a new public space, Bedford Square, that would be centered by a new Exchange Building, for which the merchants of the city had long campaigned.

The Exchange was intended to facilitate "the improvement of trade," as well as, in the words of Lord Lieutenant Carlisle, "beautifying the city," and having a "tendency to national improvement."[4] The commissioners chose a neoclassical design by Thomas Cooley for the new edifice. (The merchant members of the Wide Street Commissioners opted for Cooley's plan, as that architect was closely associated with the City of London, whereas the more gentried members of the body pushed for a design by James Gandon, a former pupil of William Chambers, the leading proponent of neoclassicism in Britain and key promoter of the idea that civic architecture led to wealth, prestige, and imperial unity.) Completed in 1779, Cooley's Exchange, James Malton wrote, "is one of the principal ornaments of the city . . . commanding a great length of prospect . . . [that] adds considerably to the approach to the residence of the Viceroy."[5] Cooley's Royal Exchange was but one of the many Georgian civic buildings that served as a focal point for the British administration in Ireland. Opposite the north entrance, the merchants commissioned a statue of George III, replete in Roman military uniform. Three of the entrances to the square, domed structure have richly ornamented Corinthian columns that sustain a classical portico. An interior statue of Charles Lucas, a contemporary Irish politician who campaigned for legislative autonomy from England, has him holding up the Magna Carta, that ur-document of state liberalism. Inside, Ionic pillars hold up the dome. The second storey contained a coffee house, symbol of the emerging public sphere in Ireland, albeit a Protestant one. The merchants who met at the Exchange did not pay mere lip service to the free trade ideals they espoused. They would assemble regularly, according to Malton, as military volunteers, ready to defend the "Advantages rising from a Free Trade. . . . [F]rom the clang of arms, the vibrating Dome caught the generous flame, and re-echoed the enlivening found of Liberty."[6] In the Georgian style of the Royal Exchange, commerce and civic authority come together in the name of a hegemonic edifice: nonviolent, imposing, and rock-solid.

Having completed the widening of Essex Bridge and created Parliament Street, the commissioners turned their attention to the reordering of Dame Street. Dame Street, now one of Dublin's busiest thoroughfares, was, in the 1700s, considered to be "a most narrow and inconvenient street," but a crucial one for trade.[7] Streamlining this particular avenue also facilitated greater movement between the seat of government (the Parliament Building), a military center (Dublin Castle), and an Anglican center of education (Trinity College). Apart from overseeing the widening of Dame Street, an undertaking that also enabled the construction and upgrading of new shop fronts and businesses, the commissioners tightly regulated aspects—height, size, materials—of buildings that would line the new thoroughfare. Architects designed grand, unified façades on terrace blocks to create a sense of order and uniformity. The European style of shops on the ground floor, with glass walls in order to better display commodities, was introduced. Georgian ornament—carved stonework over the doorways, uniform quoins, and a continuous cornice—was insisted upon.

The names of the commissioners, such as D'Olier, Beresford, and Gardiner, are now street names—permanent fixtures in Dublin today. These municipal improvers, however, were not just benevolent leaders, they were also landlords. As such, they were keen to see their holdings in the city developed and turned into commercial and civic hubs. Following the completion of Dame Street, the commissioners turned their attention northward, to opening up Westmoreland (1799) and D'Olier (1800) Streets, and to constructing a new bridge, Carlisle Bridge (1795), between the new southern thoroughfares and the fashionable Sackville Street on the city's north side. During the 1750s, Luke Gardiner, a leading banker and speculator, initiated a housing development on Sackville Street, which included widening the street by one-hundred-fifty feet, in order to accommodate two roadways of fifty feet each, and a central enclosure surrounded with lamps, railings, and obelisks for perambulation. The commissioners also integrated large-scale architectural schemes into their plans, and between 1814 and 1818 Gardiner brought in architect Francis Johnston to build the General Post Office in the center of Sackville Street. But it was slightly to the east of Gardiner's estate that Lord Beresford employed James Gandon to construct a new Custom House, which is now celebrated as the finest example of neoclassical building in Ireland. Gandon then commissioned Edward Smyth, a sculptor, to add classical ornamentation to his building; Smyth designed a large statue of Commerce to sit atop the building's dome, as well as, on its pediment, the four figures of Neptune, Mercury, Plenty, and Industry. Smyth also designed the keystones that represent the Atlantic Ocean and the thirteen principal rivers of Ireland. At either end of the building, the pavilions display carvings of the

Arms of Ireland, a woman and a harp, being enveloped by the lion and the unicorn of Great Britain, which, wrote Malton, "represent the friendly union of Britannica and Hibernia, with the good consequences relating to Ireland."[8]

By 1851, before Haussmann's Paris, Dublin had a rational, symbolic, colonial infrastructure, which communicated its values through the use of Georgian architecture and Baroque planning. The commissioners' vision of the city as a manageable and controllable unit had largely been realized, making Dublin "the second city of the Empire." This rearrangement of physical space served the implementation of several ideologies at once: the efficiency of commerce through greater speed; the enhancement of the military through greater mobility; the consolidation of the state through the building of ceremonial routes and institutional architecture; the creation of new classed neighborhoods; the establishment of private parks; and the regulation of hygiene, taxes, and public movement. The commissioners also increased the scope of the expert and the professional, namely the architect and the engineer, new specialists in urban space administration. They further introduced new styles of classical architecture that were clearly distinguished from older, more indigenous forms and materials. But most important, they provided the streets themselves that encouraged greater mobility, transparency, safety, and order, all euphemisms for modern life. At the moment of its introduction into Ireland, Georgian architecture was not neutral, but rather deeply implicated in the tactics of colonial governance.

The relationship between nationalism and history has always been an ambiguous one. Adherents to nationalist ideology simultaneously look to the past for the putative origins of identity, and to the future with the optimistic hope that a fractured history can be overcome. In this way, nationalism's leaders are often deeply modern, contradictory and insecure, at times pathological in their claims to have solved the paradox between modernization and tradition. It is hardly surprising, therefore, that the legacy of Georgian architecture in Ireland would tap into a wellspring of anxieties and hopes about sovereignty, economic self-sufficiency, and cultural identity in the face of a looming and tantalizing internationalism.

In 1960, Dublin only had one modern office block, Busaras, a post-World War II building complex of glass and steel that also housed the central bus station. By the mid-1970s, there were over three hundred new office buildings, supplying the city with more than ten million square feet of administrative space.[9] The 1960s in Ireland marked a significant official rethinking of the state's economic and cultural priorities, an about-face from the heady but insular post-independent goals of national consolidation. Beginning in the 1960s, a new generation of leaders—architects, planners, writers, historians, politicians—challenged the postcolonial status quo that had dominated the Irish landscape since Independence but that had, so evidently, failed to solve Ireland's perennial problems of emigration, economic and cultural stagnancy, and territorial partition. Space reflects ideological changes, and the dramatic new stark, streamlined buildings of steel, glass, and concrete on the Dublin skyline not only pointed to the bright, industrial future these leaders hoped for, but were a physical, deliberate rejection of Dublin's history, of what had been, but would no longer be, the unfortunate dialectic of British colonialism and the simplistic, even chauvinistic nationalism bred from it.

In 1922, the Irish Free State was formed. Deep-seated hopes and passionate ideologies were on the line with the creation of Ireland's first autonomous state. The postcolonial government would now have to prove that the fight for Irish independence had been worthwhile. The anticolonial struggle had been premised upon the fact that British rule had stifled both the Irish economy and spirit. It was on the shoulders of the postindependent generation to achieve the full national potential that they claimed had so long been denied them. Irish independence carried with it the opportunity for cultural, social, and economic rebirth. In the 1930s, Eamonn De Valera's populist Fianna Fail party embarked on a series of symbolic and real attempts to merge some of the former ideals of Irish nationalism—rural iconography, Catholic rhetoric, and Gaelic naturalism—with the reality of state building. Fianna Fail, for example, crafted a new Constitution in 1937. In this new legal framework, the Catholic Church was accorded a "special position," while the national goals of restoring the Irish language and ending the partition of the country were given aspirational status. The Constitution attempted to regulate the role of women by recognizing their status as "mothers" and their "duties in the home."[10] De Valera's St. Patrick's Day speech is now often satirized for presenting a simplistic, essentialized folkish picture of national life, one that was deliberately naïve and willfully ignorant of the wider world. "That Ireland which we dreamed of," he stated, "would be the home of a people who valued material wealth only as the basis of right living, of a people satisfied with frugal comfort and devoted their leisure to the things of the spirit."[11] (What modern commentators overlook, however, are the very modern qualities of this discourse: its delivery on radio; the fact that it went out on St. Patrick's Day, a day that celebrates global Irishness; and its partaking in then-Western language of myth and primitivism—one that, of course, flowered elsewhere, and to a degree in Ireland, into fascism.)

Not just culturally, but economically too, the postindependence decades were viewed by 1960s modernizers and social critics as being wrongfully autarkic. Postindependence governments built up and supported state industry: Fianna Fail established Aer Rianta, which nationalized the airports, and Bord na Móna, which oversaw the extraction of natural resources. By 1936, De Valera's government had imposed over 1,900 tariffs on imported products. According to one economist, between 1931 and 1936, taxes on these goods quadrupled.[12] Meanwhile, given the traditional lack of native industry, the state bureaucracy continued to expand, employing members of the increasing Catholic middle class. Socially, an influential modern historian reflected on how envy, jealousy, and spite were rampant in the "traditional" days of postindependence Ireland. What all of this amounted to, from the perspective of the early 1960s, was a failed society. Despite the complicated efforts of the postcolonial state to solve the enduring problems of an unmoored nation—cut off from the paternalistic assistance of England, unconfidently trying to make its own way and assert its piecemeal identity in an interwar period that was caught worldwide between nationalism and internationalism—by the 1950s things were as bad as they had ever been. Emigration was higher than ever. The economy, in relation to the boom experience in post-World War II Europe, remained underdeveloped. Partition remained, and the numbers of people speaking Irish continued to decline. Something had to be done. The answer to the ills of a society stuck in traditionalism is, of course, modernity. So, beginning in the 1960s, a host of new writers, planners, economists, and historians launched an ideological and economic campaign to refashion national goals and priorities.

The push for modernization—which included both an embrace of free trade rhetoric and a critique of postindependence nationalism—emerged from a broad spectrum of discourses: economics, popular culture, educational policy (a move towards technical subjects), historiography, planning, and architecture. Sean Lemass, for example, who became Taoiseach (prime minister) in 1959, liked to cite Asian economic growth as a model for what Ireland could achieve: "[T]he swift advance of Japan to be a modern industrial state is a striking example of what can be achieved by standing on other people's shoulders. . . . But this exploitation of foreign brains is made more difficult by the nature of Irish nationalism."[13] His methods were fairly predictable, Keynesian ones: greater state investment and planning (overseen by the United Nations and other supervisory institutions), a series of five-year plans, tax concessions to foreign financiers, and government grants to those companies engaged in manufacture and export. Economic transformations require ideological support, and this came from a number of areas. In 1961, for example, television became nationally available; by the mid-1970s, the vast majority of shows were of British and American origin. In historiography, an up-and-coming writer, David Thornley, representing a new breed of "revisionist historians," suggested that the modern era of economic vitality was the beginning of "delayed peaceful social revolution."[14] The implication was that the earlier, more militant revolution had brought little in the way of social change, and may, in fact, have actually hindered economic and cultural improvement.

Also driving economic liberalization, while supporting its supposedly more professional and scientific spirit, was the language of planning. Writing in 1966, planner Lorraine Donaldson defined development planning as the manipulation of economies "to achieve established objectives," underscoring the emphasis "to shake the Irish loose from the lethargy of the past and move them boldly into the formulation of long-range plans for the nation's future."[15] In 1968, Garrett Fitzgerald, a future prime minister, wrote how the objectivity of planning was "a positive reaction against the divisive effects of ideological commitments of any kind."[16] Architecture too, most notably in the wholesale adoption of International Style for hundreds of new commercial and industrial premises, would be at the forefront of this new attempt to establish a new national project, a more viable, business-oriented, and cosmopolitan one. And in order to make space for the shiny new structures of modernism, albeit a stripped-down corporate version of International Style, much of old Dublin would have to be torn down. In particular, Georgian Dublin, with its crumbling masonry, its premodern infrastructure and inefficient use of space (new planning laws meant that most Georgian buildings were not up to code), and its colonial legacy, fell victim to the developer.

Architectural journals led the charge against historical styles of building. As early as 1954, the *Architectural Survey* was connecting the battle of styles (traditional and native influences versus modernism) to the larger political task of redirecting and rewriting the national narrative. In an editorial of that year, International Style was lauded, as were new technological advances in building and engineering, such as systems building and prefabrication. "The first bogey is the danger of an 'international style' as opposed to the merit of a 'national style.' The whole idea of an architectural 'style' is dangerous. . . . [S]tyle is . . . irrelevant to the appreciation of architecture."[17] By 1959, the year that Sean Lemass' government launched the first of its five-year modernizing drives, the Survey claimed that "[T]he demands for a rigorous economy on the one hand, and of an increasingly educated public taste on the other, have led to a situation where, with few exceptions, the architect is free to devise solutions to his clients' problems in truly contemporary terms, untrammeled by any preconceptions."[18] By 1962, the journal was championing "the magic formulae of twentieth century man—'mechanization, organization and method, automation.'"[19] In 1966, the fiftieth anniversary of the Easter 1916 Rising, *Build* magazine warned that the coming decade would "form a baseline for the future: a baseline of real progress onwards, or an effective terminal point to the extremely modest hopes and inordinately unambitious aspirations of the Irish nation in this century. 1916 began and finished nothing."[20] If 1916 began and finished nothing, the 1960s would rectify the problem. In short, this meant saving the nation from the perils of overzealous, ideologically motivated nationalism that had so retarded economic and social progress. This project found its spatial counterpart in Dublin during the 1960s as a cubic, rational, and concrete architecture debuted en masse.

As with today's globalization, the push for prosperity, progress, and free trade was initiated by the state. Perhaps the first major architectural structure to reflect the new times was to occur was in 1960, when Radio Telifís Éireann (RTE), the state broadcasting company, shifted its headquarters from the General Post Office in O'Connell Street to a twenty-three acre suburban site, south of the city proper. The building, designed by Ronald Tallon in 1961, was an homage to Le Corbusier and Mies: standing on concrete pillars, evocative of Le Corbusier's beloved "pilotis," the long, three-storied building reflects light from its horizontal expanse of window walls; its open floor plan and lack of ornamentation signify a functional, bureaucratic space. The new, peripherally located campus, along with its corporate-style buildings and overwhelming scale, reinforces its formal and professional atmosphere. Gone are the traditional aesthetics of academic buildings—a clustered group of classical style buildings, organized around a public space. "The factory," as UCD was nicknamed, stands as a monument to a different intellectual purpose: function and technology. Science was the first of the faculties to be moved into the new complex. The first building erected, the Administration Building, set the tone for the buildings that followed: standing in the corner of an exposed plaza, a series of cement pillars holds up four glass-curtained stories, each separated from the levels above and below by large slabs of whitewashed concrete. Futuristic concrete walkways originating in other parts of the campus enter the upper sides of the building. The arrival of modernist architecture in Ireland during the 1960s critiqued the achievements of nationalism since independence in 1922; in particular, its inability to grow a viable and prosperous bourgeoisie. But the brave, ahistorical new structures (planar, rational, and devoid of all ornamentation and references to older styles) that were appearing on the urban landscape were equally dismissive of the city's Georgian architecture. A common official view at the time, expressed most succinctly by Neil Blaney, Minister for Local Government, was that Georgian buildings were representative of British conquest on the island: "I was glad to see them go," he said. "They stood for everything I hate."[21]

The construction of the Electrical Supply Board [ESB] building in 1963 and its attendant controversy are a microcosm of many of the tensions that arose out of Ireland's quest for development during these years, as conservationists butted heads with speculators, and the rhetoric of progress clashed with that of tradition. For many years, the headquarters of Ireland's electricity industry had been located in a rundown Georgian house at the corner of Merrion Square and Fitzwilliam Street. A growing population, expanding suburbs, and a hoped-for thriving industry requires energy, and it was not long before the ESB was looking to build a progressive, worldly new administrative headquarters. The company purchased fifteen Georgian homes on Fitzwilliam Street, opened an architectural competition to design the new building, and, incidentally, inaugurated a fierce cultural fracas. Both sides rallied their troops. The Irish Georgian Society, led by a number of respected Anglo-Irish personalities such as Desmond Fitzgerald (the Knight of Glin) and Lord Talbot of Malahide, recruited Sir Albert Richardson, an elderly, renowned scholar on British Georgian architecture, to defend the integrity of the street. On the other side were government ministers determined to impose the new aesthetics onto a reluctant populace. Kevin Boland, Minister for Local Government, liked to refer to the leaders of the conservation movement as "a consortium of belted earls," deriding them, "their ladies and left wing intellectuals" as malingerers "who can afford the time to stand and contemplate in ecstasy the unparalleled manmade beauty" of these "downtrodden 18th century structures."[22] They, too, had their international supporters. Walter Gropius sent them an encouraging telegram, while Sir John Summerson, another English expert, denounced the buildings as "architectural rubbish . . . just one damned house after another."[23] But despite the public outcry, Dublin Corporation, in 1963, granted planning permission for the ESB's new building, designed by Sam Stephenson, the winner of the competition and the latest promoter of the severe "brutalist" international style. The building was four-storied and clad in brown, precast concrete panels, with vertical brick fins between the windows. Its development required the destruction of the longest complete Georgian streetscape in Europe.

The new campuses at UCD and RTE, and Stephenson's ESB building on Fitzwilliam Street were among some of the most dramatic examples of spatial and architectural shifts in Ireland during the 1960s. That decade also saw the completion of Liberty Hall, Ireland's first skyscraper (197 feet tall), in 1967. Other large office blocks sprouted up as well, including O'Connell Bridge House (145 feet high) and a new Bank of Ireland Headquarters in Baggot Street, which, reported *Build* in 1972, did more for Dublin "than the Seagram Building did for New York."[24] The 1960s saw the state actively promote free trade, pursue membership in the European Union, and engage in the politics of reconciliation with the unionist administration in Northern Ireland. International style architecture and modernist planning were the spatialization of these ideological shifts. They both symbolized a new kind of lifestyle, an erasure of the past in favor of a clean, orderly, sophisticated urbanism, one concerned with the quotidian, functional details of capital, rather than the messy complexities of memory and history, the textures and layers of local politics and geographies. In many ways, this marked an attempt to transcend the divisions left over from the civil war: parochialism, sectarianism, underdevelopment, and stagnation. These buildings, and the ideological and physical assault on Georgian architecture that was meant to hasten their arrival, signified an official attempt to represent and create prosperity.

The hopes for economic advancement that were represented in the new buildings of the 1960s were not to be met. By the mid-1970s, a series of crises had interrupted the hope for economic and cultural development. Nationalist and sectarian violence broke out again in the North of Ireland, disrupting the clean trajectory of progress, and stymieing the idea that one could overcome history. Ireland was also caught up in larger international situations. The oil crisis and global recession of the 1970s put an end to building and to the modernizing agenda. The 1970s and 1980s returned to a familiar postcolonial pattern: emigration resurfaced as a mass phenomenon, unemployment hit 20 percent, and many of the international industrial ventures that had settled in Ireland during the 1960s turned tail. Beginning in the 1990s, therefore, a new round of corporate tax cuts were introduced in order to attract foreign capital. With an educated, English-speaking workforce and as a member of the European Union, Ireland was again seen as fertile ground for speculation and for foreign companies. Ireland soon gained a reputation for being a cheap location full of a willing, almost desperate workforce. Computer companies in particular found a lucrative home in Ireland. What all of this amounted to, starting in the early 1990s, were annual growth rates in the double digits, unemployment at 3 or 4 percent, a booming property market, and the growth of a culture industry that continues to attract global audiences; hence Ireland's new nickname, the Celtic Tiger.

Dublin's contemporary urban landscape has again been at the center of these transformations. The city has undergone massive renewal on a scale that seems to continually take residents and commentators by surprise. The International Financial Services Center (IFSC) towers over a new financial district. The building itself stands at the heart of the abandoned docks, in a dank, impoverished area that would not previously have been considered ripe for anything much, much less fervent economic development. Temple Bar, a formerly rundown warehouse and bohemian district, has been dramatically refurbished and become a colorful cultural center, gaining the reputation as Dublin's Left Bank, its thriving pubs, restaurants, and artistic venues testament to Ireland's new celebration of cosmopolitanism. Meanwhile, Dublin acts as a magnet on the rest of the country (and elsewhere), drawing natives and new immigrants to its bustling economy. The result is, of course, endemic modern urban problems: congestion, pollution, and suburbs that sprawl fifty miles into the surrounding countryside.

The 1990s and contemporary Dublin do not seem to have fostered a singular architectural aesthetic; what dominates, instead, is postmodern eclecticism: the aerodynamicism of the Calatrava bridge; the corporate postmodernism of the IFSC; the Victorian "Tudorbethan" of Dublin's rejuvenated medieval quarter, Temple Bar. In the midst of the building boom in Dublin, Georgian architecture has experienced a surprising rebirth. Rows of mock Georgian houses appear where old ones fell to the 1960s wrecking ball, while those that survived are now protected and listed buildings at the heart of gentrification. Meanwhile, in the suburban hinterlands and across rural Ireland, Georgian McMansions spring up, with no historical context surrounding them, save the unmoored aspirations of their owners to conjure up a vague aristocratic feel. The Georgian houses of Ireland's former Anglo-Irish ascendancy, which, in the decades after independence, were left to ruin and had no place in the forward-looking national narrative, are now being converted into lush, grandiose hotels, conference centers, and, most interestingly, golf clubhouses (the demesnes themselves being converted into world-class golf courses). Why the resurgence of Georgian architecture now? What is it about this particular style that taps into a contemporary need to reconnect with a particular facet of Irish history?

Postmodernity, of course, needs history. Theorists such as David Harvey and Neil Smith have drawn our attention to the ephemeral and fragmented qualities of today's global marketplace. That is, a newly thriving regional economy is often inextricable from foreign capital and investment, which always has one eye on a potentially more lucrative country or region. This conflation of qualities produces an insecure workforce, an influx of migrant labor, a rise in property values without an equal rise in income, and, especially in the case of Ireland, so new to wealth, the persistent sense that it could all come crashing down. What helps to lend an air of permanency to all of this is architectural depth. In a prosperous but frighteningly transient economy, an edifice can look like permanence, can evoke security, can reassure. The most obvious architectural choice for new buildings in the 1990s and early twenty-first century Ireland to serve these goals is Georgian neoclassicism. Colonial architecture is entrenched, authoritarian, confident, solid, and rooted in classical reason and paternalism. In the contemporary era, as Dublin attempts to emerge as a global city, architecture looks back to the one other moment in Irish history when Dublin boasted prospering international connections (in literature, Jonathan Swift, Thomas Sheridan, and Goldsmith; in architecture, James Gandon and Francis Johnston; in politics, George Berkeley, Edmund Burke, and Henry Grattan), and was known as the second city of the British Empire. Today's Georgian structures are the aesthetic answer to postcolonial insecurity.

Three architectural phenomena illustrate this complex interplay of cultural aspiration, economics, and historical reference. Perhaps the most dramatic example is the way the Big House, formerly a stark symbol of inequality and separation, has come back into play. Physically, the Big House in the 1700s was a Georgian fortress on the rural Irish landscape. Large and imposing, these Palladian estates concretely resisted dissent, with their columned porches, planar blocks of granite, classical order, and walled surroundings. Contemporary backers of the restoration of Ireland's Big Houses have found obvious ideological and semiotic connections between the 1700s and today. In tourist brochures marketing the golf courses and hotels that have replaced the Big House, advertising employs regal language and lush landscape photography to enhance the historical and visceral connection. The pamphlet "Golfing Around Dublin," put out by Dublin Tourism, welcomes "[k]ing and commoner. [Both] can sit down and exchange stories with total ease. They are bonded, it does not matter that they return to different worlds after the round."[25] *Links of Heaven*, a narrative account of the best courses in Ireland, includes a brief history of the post-World War II game in Ireland: "The transformation has been remarkable. What were once the playgrounds of the gentry are now lovingly managed by the descendants of tenant farmers."[26] Georgian architecture is no longer being demolished. There has been a change in national ideology. The Irish no longer strive to escape the past, but to market it, to use it to add to the newly accumulating wealth, and to right the wrongs of history. The Big House was a symbol of oppression, but now the Irish (or at least those who aim to sell Ireland's image) are using it to advantage, to claim that the nation has overcome a humiliating and painful history of poverty, dispossession, and emigration.

At the same time, the Big House has produced odd spawn: the rural bungalow, and its cousin, the suburban semi-detached. Part of the postcolonial psychology is a lack of national confidence, an internalized legacy wherein one measures cultural and economic achievements according to imposed standards. Traditional culture, historically, was made shameful: the Irish language was seen as primitive and a drag on modernity, rural habits were considered embarrassingly provincial. Colonialism becomes internalized, a form of self-hatred, along with the attendant opposite of over-valuing the imposed culture. The difficult postcolonial period itself, instead of being viewed as a transitional time when a fledgling national government was emerging out of a long dark era, has instead been recast as another shameful Irish failure, the product of innate weaknesses.

An aesthetic expression of this psychological inferiority complex is the mock Georgian home. Mock Georgian is an updating of Georgian style with contemporary materials: plaster columns, plastic-framed windows, graveled driveways, ornamental shutters, pediment porches. The visual effect, to the outsider, is undeniably gaudy; mock Georgian is showy ostentation, an exaggerated reference to an aristocratic style that was, until recently, available only to a few, and one that marked a victory over the Irish themselves. Now reappropriated by the home-owning middle class, this architectural style serves a number of purposes. Plastic, iconic pillars can easily be dismissed as kitsch. But embedded in the mimicry is a hope: the desire for a kind of economic security that would be symbolized by colonial architecture, but one that, too, masks a particular kind of postcolonial insecurity. As well, mock Georgian evokes the cultural sophistication of the original Georgian moment, a period of literary production and civic improvement. Often appearing as additions to the front of homes in urban housing estates, the style is an attempt to achieve individuality from the drab conformity of 1960s-era housing. From the wide array of historical architectural styles available to builders, developers, and individuals in Ireland, Georgian architecture is the one form that appears repeatedly across the urban, suburban, and rural landscape. The reasons for its choice are historical, ideological, and rooted in a complex interplay between economics and psychology. A bridge between the two global moments, the updated Georgian home communicates a paradox of class mobility and class frailty, international aspirations and postcolonial limitations.

Architecture is always political. Ideology achieves spatial form. When economic or political climates change, we see a corresponding shift in the production of physical space. Irish history has been marked by a series of ruptures, transformations, and revivals. Urban space has both created and reflected the particular colonial and postcolonial tensions and struggles that have defined Ireland. The early colonial period witnessed the building of new English towns across Ulster. As colonialism consolidated its hold over the country, Dublin was reconfigured as an imperial space. In the aftermath of independence, Ireland's capital again took center stage in the modernizing quest for prosperity—a goal that would not be achieved, its proponents believed, without a crucial distancing from its colonial heritage. Today's Ireland has seen another round of urban renewal and transformation as it plays host to global capital. At each of these pivotal moments, Georgian architecture has communicated remarkably similar values, made particular by the specific times in which they thrived and reappeared. The symmetry, classical semiotics, and rational order of Georgian architecture imposed external order on the Irish landscape and, generations later, was vilified for being a most visible reminder of British rule. Today, its revival speaks not only to a change in historiography and a reviewing of nationalism, but also, poignantly, to a country's desire to alter its place in the global order and establish, at last, a secure, confident, permanent native middle class.

Notes

1. Terry Eagleton, *Heathcliff and the Great Hunger* (New York: Verso, 1995), 27-103.

2. *An Act for making a wide and convenient way, street, and passage, from Essex-Bridge to the Castle of Dublin, and for other purposes therein mentioned* (Dublin: Printed by the executor of George Abraham Grierson, 1758).

3. *An Act for making a wide and convenient way, street, and passage, from Essex-Bridge to the Castle of Dublin, and for other purposes therein mentioned* (Dublin: Printed by the executor of George Abraham Grierson, 1758).

4. Murray Fraser, "Public Building and Colonial Policy in Dublin, 1760-1800," *Architectural History: Journal of Architectural Historians of Great Britain* 28 (1985): 113.

5. James Malton, *Malton's Dublin* (Dublin: The Dolmen Press, 1987), 57.

6. James Malton, *Malton's Dublin*, 55.

7. Wide Streets Commission, *City of Dublin: Wide and Convenient Ways, Streets and Passages* (Dublin: Wide Streets Commission, 1802).

8. James Malton, *Malton's Dublin*, 57.

9. Frank McDonald, *The Destruction of Dublin* (Dublin: Gill and Macmillan), 4.

10. *Constitution of Ireland* (Dublin: Government of Ireland Publications, 1937).

11. John Water, *An Intelligent Person's Guide to Modern Ireland* (London: Duckworth, 1998), 41.

12. Mary Daly, *Dublin, The Deposed Capital: A Social and Economic History 1860-1914* (Cork: Cork University Press, 1984), 66.

13. Paul Bew and Henry Patterson, *Seán Lemass and the Making of Modern Ireland: 1945-66* (Dublin: Gill and Macmillan, 1982), 122.

14. David Thornely, "Ireland: The End of an Era?" *Studies* 53 (1964): 1-17.

15. Loraine Donaldson, *Development Planning in Ireland* (New York: Frederick A. Praeger Publishers, 1966), 2.

16. Garret Fitzgerald, Planning in Ireland (Dublin: Institute of Public Administration, 1968), 198.

17. Editorial, *Architectural Survey*, 1954.

18. Editorial, *Architectural Survey*, 1959.

19. Editorial, *Architectural Survey*, 1962.

20. Michael Quinn, "1916: Progress Backwards," *Build* (January, 1966).

21. Kevin Kearns, *Georgian Dublin: Ireland's Imperiled Architectural Heritage* (London: David and Charles, 1983), 70.

22. Dáil Éireann, Parliamentary Debates, (11 March 1970) www.oireachtas-debates.gov.ie.

23. Kevin Kearns, *Georgian Dublin*, 59.

24. "Bank of Ireland Headquarters, Dublin: Architect's Account," *Build* (December, 1972).

25. Dublin Tourism, *Golfing Around Dublin: A Visitor's Guide to Golfing in and around Dublin* (Dublin: Dublin Tourism, 2001), 2.

26. Richard Phinney, *Links of Heaven: a Complete Guide to Golf Journeys in Ireland* (New York: Baltray Books, 1996), 3.

Chapter 6

Trying to Be World-Class:
Ottawa and the Presentation of Self

Caroline Andrew

- A responsible and responsive city
- A caring and inclusive city
- A creative city rich in heritage, unique in identity
- A green and environmentally sensitive city
- A city of distinct, livable communities
- An innovative city where prosperity is shared among all
- A healthy and active city

Guess what city has these principles for its strategic plan. Better still, try to think of what city has *not* endorsed these principles, or versions thereof, within its most recent strategic plan. These are Ottawa's—adopted by the city council in June 2002. And they illustrate the problem for Ottawa in determining its niche, and therefore its claim to be world-class: how to define your particular identity while wanting to be exactly like everyone else. This chapter will outline Ottawa's attempt to both decide how it wants to present itself to the world and how it has gone about trying to do this. The chapter will cover developments since the 1980s but focuses primarily on the post-2000 period.

To situate Ottawa, Canada's capital city, it is on the Ottawa River, the boundary between Ontario and Quebec and about two hours drive north-west of Montreal. Ottawa has a population of about 750,000 and, if Gatineau is included as part of the metropolitan area, the overall population is close to one million. As such, it is the fourth largest Canadian city, but well below the first three (Toronto, Montreal, and Vancouver). Ottawa was chosen to be the capital of Canada in 1857 and, in the 1970s, the National Capital Region was defined to include the urban area on the Quebec side of the Ottawa River. The Algonquins were the first settlers in the area, which became a part of the Aboriginal trading system. The next wave of settlement was on the Quebec side, in the early nineteenth century when Philemon Wright settled in what is now Gatineau and began to develop the timber trade. In the 1830s Ottawa began to develop as the site for the construction of the Rideau Canal. The lumber industry dominated the region until federal government employment took over as the major economic force.

Looking at Ottawa immediately raises the question of who are the actors whose communication strategies are the subject of analysis. As Canada's capital the federal government is an obvious participant, as is the City of Ottawa. But this only covers state actors and, in order to understand the ways in which the political, economic, and cultural players interact with the various levels of government, it is useful to make use of the literature, largely most developed within geography by geographers, on "rescaling." These studies analyze the ways in which different scales of political action grow or shrink in importance because of global economic restructuring but also because of political, social, and cultural strategies of actors from civil society and from the state. Authors such as Neil Brenner, Neil Smith, and many others have argued that globalization has opened up new scales of political action, notably the global and the local, but without eliminating the nation state as a significant political actor.

This literature is useful in helping to make sense of the shifts that have taken place in the cast of characters in the Ottawa story over the past thirty years. There are questions of personalities and of strategies, but there are also major socio-economic and cultural changes that have had an influence on determining the opportunities for different sets of actors. The federal government was for the first one hundred years of Ottawa's history the chief governmental actor. And, because of this role, the economic and cultural elites in Ottawa exercised their influence primarily through the federal level. The first federal agency to be specifically concerned with Ottawa's development was the Ottawa Improvement Commission, created in 1899 by the then-prime minister, Sir Wilfrid Laurier.

Laurier was interested in converting Ottawa from the ugly lumber town that he had first encountered in coming to Ottawa in 1874. This kind of personal interest in planning Ottawa on the part of a prime minister was continued by William Lyon Mackenzie King, particularly in the immediate post-war period. King was personally responsible for getting Jacques Gréber, a very well-known French urban planner, to draw up plans for post-war Ottawa. This was a very important moment in the city's history. The war fueled the growth of the federal public service simply continued and increased in the post-war period, as officials constructed a rather timid Canadian version of the construction of the modern welfare state. Gréber's ideas had in fact a real and important impact on the development of Ottawa as a government town. His plans included a greenbelt to contain urban development on the Ontario side of the urban area, development of Gatineau Park on the Quebec side, a network on parkways, the removal of the railway lines from the center of Ottawa, and the relocation of the train station to a suburban location.

The third prime minister to have a lasting impact on the capital was Pierre-Elliott Trudeau. One of the elements of his political strategy to include the Quebec side in the national capital region was the siting of two major museums, the

Museum of Civilization and the National Gallery, built across from each other on the two sides of the Ottawa River. The building of the museums under the political leadership of Trudeau both marks the end of the period of clear federal dominance in planning Ottawa's development. At the same time, Trudeau's efforts also established what are now the major tourist attractions in Ottawa. Figures for 2004 indicate 1,301,094 visits to the Museum of Civilization, 416,649 to the National Gallery and 367,746 to Parliament Hill.[1]

Trudeau announced the building of the two museums in 1982, in the middle of his last mandate as prime minister, with the clear intention of leaving a personal legacy relating both to his personal image as someone who valued culture and to his political strategy of inclusion of the Outaouais in the national capital.[2] Initial cost estimates were calculated on what was politically acceptable and the huge increases in cost were therefore not unexpected. The Museum of Civilization had been called the Museum of Man and the new name was the result of pressure from the women's movement and of political sensitivity to this pressure. The architect for the museum was Douglas Cardinal, a prominent First Nations' architect, and the design of the museum is a reflection of Aboriginal culture. The most spectacular part of the museum is the First Nations' Hall with West Coast Aboriginal totems placed in a site that looks across the Ottawa River both to the art gallery and to Parliament Hill.

The National Gallery of Art was designed by Moshe Safdie, who had made his mark in Canada during Expo 1967 with the residential complex, Habitat. It was situated in Ottawa, next to the Roman Catholic Cathedral and on the point of land overlooking the Ottawa River and in proximity to Parliament Hill. The Interprovincial Bridge, with full pedestrian and bicycle access, links the two museums. The museums were opened in the late 1980s, after Trudeau had left federal politics, but they do remain associated with his vision for the capital. And, in addition to being the major tourist destinations, both are extensively used by local residents.

The shift to greater importance of the city government in determining an Ottawa strategy needs to be seen in the context of a number of factors, including globalization, neoliberalism, federal policies, the development of the high-tech sector in Ottawa, institutional reform, decentralization, Ontario politics, demographic shifts, and Ottawa's unique civil society with its particular political culture and traditions. All these play in to creating greater political opportunities at the local level, although clearly within a context of multiple political scales.

The federal government in the 1980s and 1990s reacted to global pressures and budgetary constraints by cutting its budgets and decentralizing responsibilities to the provinces.[3] The neoliberal tendencies of the Mulroney and Chrétien administrations led to federal policies that facilitated the private sector growth of the high tech industry in Ottawa.[4] This growth was strongly supported by the then-Regional Municipality of Ottawa-Carleton, in part through its encouragement for the creation of OCRI, a partnership between private sector high-tech companies, and the post-secondary education sector. During the 1990s, with federal budget cutting and cuts to the public service and with the high-tech boom (before the downturn post 2001) Ottawa began to see itself as transformed from a government town to a diversified economy based on a vibrant private sector. Municipal Ottawa was very much taken with this vision of the city and, by a logical consequence, with the role that this would entail for the municipal government.

This focus on the local level was strengthened by institutional reforms, first with the creation of a regional government in 1970, the strengthening of this regional government through the 1980s and 1990s and, lastly, the municipal amalgamation of 2001. This took place at the same time as the Ontario government's decentralization policies (or "downloading") whereby many areas of social policy (social housing, much of social welfare, public health, day care) have been effectively transferred to the municipal level. There is debate about the reasons for these decisions on the part of the right-wing populist government of Mike Harris but, whatever the reasons, it did expand the areas of responsibility of municipal governments and therefore also focused the attention of Ottawa's civil society on the municipal level.

These shifts are reflected in the various stories that Ottawa has tried to tell about itself. The first versions of the presentation of self were largely determined by the National Capital Commission's planning activities in the area. The Gréber legacy—with the greenbelt, Gatineau Park, and the parkways—underpinned the idea of the "green capital," Ottawa as a city of parks in immediate proximity to the countryside, with a lifestyle more peaceful than that of Toronto or Montreal and linked to outdoor recreational opportunities, bike paths, and environmental concerns. This has proved to be a very popular image, both with tourists and perhaps even more so with the residents of Ottawa themselves. Indeed, even the National Capital Commission, author of the image, has become concerned with the "green capital" fixation of local citizens who have so bought into this idea that almost any development project is viewed with suspicion. The image aimed at tourists is still strongly linked to parks and the natural physical attractions of the region but here too there is a feeling that the image needs to be varied, with a more urban identity.

The National Capital Commission moved on to new visions although without entirely abandoning the "green capital" image as part of its portfolio of representations of self. One of the new images was that of the capital as the "meeting place" for Canadians. For the commission, this involved thinking about how to better represent the provinces within the capital region, so as to include the concept of Canadian federalism as a necessary part of the representation of Canada as illustrated by, and in, the capital. There are interesting comparisons to be made between the way that this question has been thought about in Australia and in Canada. In the Australian case, the idea was to represent the provinces through the representation of dominant state economic sectors whereas, in the Canadian case, the representation of the provinces tended to be seen as purely political. For example, provincial flags are used as the chief representation of the provinces in the Garden of the Provinces, a rather unattractive park across from the National Library and National Archives. The theme of the meeting place also opened up the potential for the inclusion of a space for the Aboriginal presence in the capital, but this was compromised by the ongoing refusal of the federal government to agree to the development plans proposed by the Assembly of First Nations for Victoria Island.[6] Jean Laponce's analysis of the Ottawa presentation of self, given at the conference on capital cities held in Ottawa in 1990, was that the city should emphasize the theme of the meeting place, but place it in an international context.

> Ottawa might also want to project itself more forcefully on the international scene. Canada is the only major country at the juncture of the two dominant world languages of science: English and French. . . . An arts centre for the locals, a major scientific conference and research centre for the world. Museums opening on the past, a science centre to help shape the future.[7]

While the theme of the meeting place continues to play a role in the debates around Ottawa's self-presentation, themes related to who is meeting in Ottawa have become even more prevalent with the growing importance of identity politics. Indeed the meeting place may not even be the right image as these themes, to use the vocabulary of Robert Putnam, are more about bonding than bridging. John Meisel addressed this question at the 1990 conference on capital cities:

> In Canada, for instance, the efforts of dominant elites, which historically focused on achieving national unity, improving relations between French and English, and methods of mitigating regional economic disparities, are now much more diversified and dispersed. Feminism, multiculturalism, redress of grievances of native populations, helping the handicapped: these are new concerns added to those that preoccupied entire generations. . . . Where previously the dominant groups tended to be male, of British and French origin, and largely coming from middle-class families, the present composition of the movers and shakers is much more diversified. Whatever the salutary consequences of this process—and they are significant—it also results in the political agenda being taken up with sectorial rather than country-wide concerns.[8]

Putting aside the question of whether the portrayal of the former elites is overly positive, the quotation does point to the growing importance of debates around the inclusion of the Aboriginal population, of ethno-cultural diversity, and of women (and the intersections of these groups) in symbolic and built Ottawa. However, these debates over the role of multiculturalism in the capital's self-image emerged after the development of the high-tech story under the leadership of the City of Ottawa and The Ottawa Partnership (TOP) and it is to this story that we now turn.

As has been mentioned, the combination of the cutbacks at the federal level with the development of the high-tech sector led in the late 1990s to considerable enthusiasm on the part of the then regional government for a new definition of Ottawa, one based on private sector economic development. This led to the creation of TOP in 1999, described as "a group of private and public leaders who are committed to advancing the local economy."[9] TOP was very much a project of the then chair of the regional municipality (now the mayor of Ottawa), Bob Chiarelli, in partnership with some of the key local high-tech leaders (particularly Rod Bryden, then with SC Stormont Corporation and Kirk Mandy of Mitel). Funded by the regional government along with the Ontario Ministry of Economic Development and Trade, TPO hired a big American consulting firm, ICF Consulting, to develop its Economic Generators Initiative. The firm developed a clusters-based model organized around what the firm called "the engines that fuel Ottawa's economy"[10]—those that export goods and services and therefore, according to the model, are those that generate new economic wealth. For this reason the report discounted the federal government activity ("government activity is not viewed as economic activity"[11]) and argued for supporting the development of seven specific economic clusters.[12] As well as cluster-specific actions, the consulting firm's report emphasized nine comprehensive flagship initiatives to be undertaken by the whole community to "kick-start" the economic generators initiative.[13.] The first of these was to better "brand" Ottawa. Marketing, in particular "branding," Ottawa as more than a capital city emerged in the cluster working group process as one of the highest priority challenges facing the region.[14.]

The same consultants were given the task of coming up with a "brand" for Ottawa. The results were made public, with great fanfare, at a huge breakfast gathering of the Ottawa civic and high-tech elites. The brand: "Ottawa: Technically Beautiful." Even at the breakfast launch the reaction was less than enthusiastic and the "brand" disappeared after a combination of ridiculing the slogan and irritation about the cost. A *Globe and Mail* article summed it up best: "Technically, Ottawa's slogan is a disaster."[15]

Not only did the specific slogan disappear but the momentum behind the TOP direction lessened. In part, this related to the high-tech turndown and this, in turn, increased the profile of the federal government role in the region. The City of Ottawa has not abandoned this vision of economic development, but the priorities for action have been somewhat altered with the creation of the amalgamated city of Ottawa. The question of the quality of life focuses around public transportation and art and culture (in part influenced by Richard Florida's arguments about the centrality of culture for urban development), commercializing both high-tech and bio-tech research discoveries, developing Ottawa as a global learning center (better linking the post-secondary institutions into the priorities of urban branding) and tourism development. So, although "Technically Beautiful" bombed as a brand for Ottawa, the promotion of clusters within high-tech and bio-tech areas is still very high on the agenda of the city. The idea that Ottawa should not be seen as merely a government town and that its image should include the high-tech and bio-tech sectors has remained, although the priority being given to this effort by the municipal government since the downturn in the high-tech sector has lessened.

The politics of post-amalgamation Ottawa have focused around the city's strategic planning efforts and the city's budget crises which led to major challenges on the part of a broad coalition of civil society movements. The coalition represented an attempt by local civil society to argue that Ottawa had a community tradition of good public services and that these community traditions should not be sacrificed in the era of neoliberal globalization. In terms of the public story of Ottawa, it was an argument for the greater voice for the community and a greater insistence on conceptualizing Ottawa as a place to *live* because of its good urban public services and its quality of life.

This met with some support from the City of Ottawa, although the municipal council was quite clearly divided on the issue of maintaining services versus cutting (or not increasing) taxes. These confrontations—between the city and the public and within the city itself, particularly around the preparation of the 2004 budget—meant that the city got diverted from its own strategic planning process, which it had initiated shortly after amalgamation in 2001. The city had first set up a Smart Growth Summit (with, of course, Richard Florida as one of the speakers) and this led to a Growth Management Strategy, called Ottawa 20/20. This entailed the development of a new Official Plan and, somewhat innovatively, the simultaneous development of four other plans, a Human Services Plan, an Arts and Heritage Plan, an Economic Strategy, and an Environmental Strategy. There was very considerable public consultation on the plans during the period of the fall of 2002 through the summer of 2003. During the summer of 2003 there were public meetings between city staff and interested citizens about how to monitor progress on implementing the plans which led to extensive discussions of a citizen-driven report card process. But suddenly the city announced a major budget crisis for the 2004 budget and suggested a series of cuts to services. The principles of Ottawa 20/20 were put on a shelf and indeed many of the staff that had been charged with the implementation of Ottawa 20/20 were notified that their jobs would be eliminated.[16]

A major political crisis developed, with a broadly based coalition of arts and heritage groups, environmental groups, groups concerned with poverty and homelessness, those concerned with francophone rights, ethno-cultural groups, women's groups, and unions arguing for no service cuts (and even tax increases), and equally strong pressures (although less visible) from taxpayers who had believed the official Ontario government line that amalgamation would save money. The coalition's actions were directed specifically to the 2004 budget and, at the same time, the coalition argued for a stronger voice for civil society at the local level. The coalition achieved only some of its aims for the 2004 budget; some services were saved although cuts were made. However, the coalition did establish, at least partially, its argument that Ottawa was a community that took seriously its responsibilities for those most marginalized in the community and that Ottawa's quality of life should be shared across the entire community.

The fiscal situation of the city was not resolved but a better process for the 2005 budget meant that the city was able to return to the goals of Ottawa 20/20. The newly reorganized[17] Community and Protective Services Department was to lead off for the city in elaborating a strategic framework based on Ottawa 20/20. In its draft framework the department stated that its overall mission was to place priority on people,[18] and went on to say: "This means more than asking for feedback. It involves establishing partnership to identify innovative solutions, providing community leaders with roles that involve decision making, sharing best practices with community organizations and involving community stakeholders in the measurements of results"[19.]

In this context of concern for Ottawa's quality of life, a number of voices are being raised to argue that they should feature more centrally in the story that Ottawa is telling about itself. This links back to the earlier quotation on the impact of pluralism, or identity politics, on capitals in that these voices all relate to the combined impact of globalization and local action. In part, there are common elements to the different stories—all were galvanized by the combination of reacting to the work of the transition team leading up to amalgamation and the ensuing budget crisis of the City of Ottawa. This led to groups making specific demands on the city but also to a more pervasive sense that the citizens needed to take back the city and that getting the discursive upper hand would be an important element in this fight. Harris had sold the amalgamations on being measures that would cut taxes and many people had believed him. Suddenly the city was saying that, far from lowering taxes as had been done in the first year of the amalgamation, major budget cuts and service cuts would be necessary. This shocked the sense of self of many Ottawa residents. Indeed, one of the most effective documents produced by those opposing the city was a study entitled "From Fat Cat to Tabby Cat" which indicated how poorly Ottawa ranked in a number of social spending areas—libraries, parks and recreation. This report had influence because it contradicted the image many residents had of themselves as citizens of a community with a tradition of good urban public services. The argument then became: "this is our Ottawa tradition, but it is a tradition that is being destroyed by the impact of neo-liberalism." This kind of view had coalition potential, uniting at least parts of the anti-globalization movement, federal and provincial Liberals, red Tories, the NDP, plus all the voluntary sector and community service groups.

But, at the same time, as indicated earlier, identity politics developed a number of distinct calls for inclusion. The idea of a tradition of good quality urban services was all very well but it suggested a reference to the past and therefore in some way of an unchanging Ottawa. The vision of a new Ottawa that was in the process of being created led to a variety of groups wanting to explicitly claim a more central place in this new Ottawa. These additions to the Ottawa story are the greater recognition of bilingualism within the capital, the greater recognition of ethno-cultural diversity and of Aboriginality and, finally, the greater recognition of the participation of women.

The francophone community of Ottawa represents about 16 percent of the population of the city. Indeed, there has been a debate about this percentage as, until very recently, new immigrants whose mother tongue was other than English or French but who spoke French rather than English were not considered part of the francophone population.[20] The francophone community has been an important part of the Ottawa scene from the very beginning of the city, and its institutions played a major role in the establishment of civil society and urban services (the General Hospital, the University of Ottawa, the Cathedral). Municipal amalgamation has been a challenge to the francophone community as not only was Vanier, a predominantly francophone municipality, eliminated as a separate entity but, in addition, the percentage of the population that is francophone is less in the new amalgamated City of Ottawa than it was in the former City of Ottawa.

Since amalgamation, the status of French-language services, and the place of bilingualism, has been a subject of political controversy and the francophone community has been very much on the defensive. The mayor, in his preoccupation to limit the controversy, has taken a very passive position in terms of the enhancement of bilingualism. The arguments for a greater recognition of bilingualism are made partly on local grounds (the rights of Ottawa residents to have services in their language, the fact that the greater dispersion of the francophone population across the city implies that there are demands for increased francophone services coming from more areas of the city, the long-standing contribution of francophones to the local community) and partly on global or international grounds (the place of Ottawa as a capital, the importance of bilingualism in a global context, international tourism development).

The francophone, and francophile, communities were deeply disappointed when the Ontario government decided not to honour its election promise and rather than declaring Ottawa bilingual simply endorsed the language policies of the City of Ottawa. This was certainly a symbolic blow to the vision of Ottawa as an internationally focused capital city with official status given to two of the major languages of international communication. Despite this setback, the francophone community continues to organize, determined to gain recognition for their historical contribution of the building of Ottawa and their present and future contributions to making Ottawa a place of greater cultural richness and a more cosmopolitan quality of life. Having the Ottawa story better reflect the noteworthy co-existence of the francophone and anglophone communities is a vital aspect of this recognition.

Ottawa is, at the present time, rapidly becoming a more diverse community in ethno-cultural terms. Traditionally a very white community, it is now the third in Canada in terms of recent immigrant settlement (behind Toronto and Vancouver). But certainly not all parts of the city recognize this, nor want to include it in the presentation Ottawa makes of itself to the outside world. The city government, for example, has been relatively slow to react to the changing sociodemographic reality; in the early stages of the Ottawa 20/20 planning process there was very little consideration of ethno-cultural diversity. Interest in this question did develop in the later stages and those responsible for the Human Services Plan hired a consultant to organize a round table on ethnic-cultural diversity and produce a report. The final version of the Human Services Plan gave considerably more attention to diversity than had the draft plan. More recently, Community and Protective Services, in their Strategic Framework, give the greatest priority to ensuring "equal access to services" and go on to indicate that this involves two areas of focus—"diversity and disability."[21]

Pressures for greater inclusion come from a variety of sources, including the recent immigrant communities themselves, and they also come from human service providers. Indeed in Ottawa, the coalition formed among service providers—Local Agencies Serving Immigrants (LASI)—has been central in pushing for better services and also in pushing to make Ottawa a more welcoming community, a community more conscious of its diversity and of the positive contribution this recent immigration makes to the city.

During the fall of 2004 a group of community agencies, the local universities, and the federal Metropolis project began a series of round tables in City Hall, aimed at looking at areas of municipal responsibility through the lens of the ethno-cultural diversity and inclusion. The objectives of the round tables were to demonstrate the importance of the municipal level of government in issues of diversity, to demonstrate to the municipal government the reality of the changing socio-demography of Ottawa, and to begin redefining the self-portrait of Ottawa to better include ethno-cultural diversity.

Women have also been one of the voices claiming a greater visibility in the public space in Ottawa. This is in part a recurring theme. Suzanne Mackenzie has argued, for example, that the early twentieth century and the 1960s were key moments where debates about the role of women in public space coincided with debates about the structuring of urban space.[22] The current period would appear to be a third moment where both these concerns emerge and, indeed, are interrelated.[23] Manifestations of women's claims on municipal space in Ottawa over the past fifteen years have centered around questions of violence with the creation of the Regional Coordinating Committee, Women's Initiatives for a Safer Environment and the Ottawa Roundtable.[24] More recently, the intersection of women and diversity has been central to the City for All Women Initiative,[25] a partnership project between the City of Ottawa and community-based women's groups. Its central objective: "strengthen the capacity of the full diversity of women and the City of Ottawa to work in partnership so as to create a more inclusive city and promote gender equality."[26] It has done training with women to enable them to better lobby City Hall and it is presently working with the city on developing an equality framework for strategic planning. The project is connected with a variety of Canadian and international networks that work on issues of women and cities and that attempt to strategize around increasing the presence of women in urban public space, both discursively and in terms of real political practice. The argument for inclusion is therefore both local and global.

Our argument up until now has been that Ottawa has been unable, in recent times, to define its vision of itself and to make choices about its claims to be world class. In part this can be explained in terms of rescaling; there are more voices, and more sites, to be included in the presentation. The city, particularly the new city, is new to this game and, with an extremely prudent mayor, seems more concerned to not irritate constituencies than to make clear choices about a niche image. Constructing an image that is too urban will irritate the already irritated rural parts of the city; creating one that is too rural will irritate the suburbs and exclude diversity. This municipal hesitation can also be seen to be the municipality allowing other voices to play a role in defining the city. Civil society—be it the high-tech sector, ethno-cultural groups, francophones—has seized upon the city's inaction to define how their presence in Ottawa helps to define Ottawa.

To end with a story that sums up our argument about Ottawa trying to be world-class, consider the example of the new War Museum. The museum has just opened in the summer of 2005 on a huge site along the Ottawa River, close by one of the bridges linking Ottawa and Gatineau. The old War Museum was a modest building on Sussex Avenue, between the Mint and the new Art Gallery. It had its devoted fans but was relatively invisible in the public Ottawa. The new museum is quite different. It is very large and automobile-friendly and definitely designed to be in the public eye. But what is the message?

The opening chapter in the museum story was the successful campaign, led publicly by historian Jack Granatstein with the veterans' groups, to push for a new war museum and to refuse to have a Holocaust gallery as part of the War Museum. As Granatstein was extremely well known in the Canadian academic community as one of the leaders of the group of historians determined to eliminate the past thirty years of social history—including especially women's history and labor history—his interest in the War Museum was seen as part of this overall campaign. There were suggestions that the War Museum was going to change the vision of Canada and of Canadian history—that it would show that Canada had been formed, and forged, in war and that the virtues of Canada were the military virtues of obedience, loyalty, and masculinity.

Then Granatstein left and the museum was built, designed by Moriyama, a Canadian of Japanese origin. The newspaper articles underlined the fact that his personal background led him to a position of war as tragedy and not as heroic combat. The building itself and the displays in the building seem to fall somewhere between these two—Canadians played an important role in the wars, the wars were extremely important events, and we don't want any more. Maybe, as far as presenting images of urban selfhood, this is in fact a good position. Maybe this is Ottawa: a decent place that tries to muddle through in a complicated world. But it doesn't quite cut it as world-class. It is as we said at the beginning: It is difficult to have a distinctive image when you want to be exactly like everyone else.

Caroline Andrew

Notes

1. Ellen Tsaprailis, "Luring the Endangered Tourist," *Ottawa*, June/July 2005, 44.
2. See Caroline Andrew, Serge Bordeleau, and Alain Guimont, *L'Urbanisation: Une Affaire* (Ottawa: Editions de l'Université d'Ottawa, 1981).
3. See Susan Phillips, ed., *How Ottawa Spends 1995-96: Mid-Life Crises* (Ottawa: Carleton University Press, 1995).
4. Gilles Paquet and Jeffrey Roy, "Prosperity Through Networks: The Bottom-Up Strategy that Might Have Been," in *How Ottawa Spends*, ed. Susan Phillips, 137-58.
5. Trying to cut provincial budgets or trying to take education spending out of the hands of the Toronto or Ottawa school boards.
6. Victoria Island is situated in the middle of the Ottawa River and the Assembly of First Nations has had plans for building on this site for several years. Among the problems that have emerged around this proposal is the fact that there are old industrial buildings on the site that the federal government wants to protect for their heritage value.
7. J.A. Laponce, "Ottawa, Christaller, Horowitz and Parsons," in *Capital Cities/ Les Capitales*, ed. John Taylor, Jean Lengellé, and Caroline Andrew (Ottawa: Carleton University Press, 1993), 416
8. John Meisel, "Capital Cities: What Is a Capital?" in *Capital Cities/ Les Capitales*, ed. John Taylor, Jean Lengellé, and Caroline Andrew, 4.
9. ICF Consulting, *Choosing a Future: A New Economic Vision for Ottawa*, 2000, i.
10. ICF Consulting, *Choosing a Future*.
11. ICF Consulting, *Choosing a Future*, 1-6.
12. The clusters are telecommunications equipment, microelectronics, software and communications services, professional services, tourism, life sciences, photonics. ICF Consulting, *Choosing a Future*, 1-5, 1-6.
13. ICF Consulting, *Choosing a Future*, 5.
14. ICF Consulting, *Choosing a Future*, 5.
15. Steven Chase, "Technically, Ottawa's Slogan Is a Disaster," *Globe and Mail*, 3 August 2001, 1(A).
16. Finally most of these people did not lose their jobs but the uncertainty caused very high levels of stress within the city bureaucracy.
17. Perhaps the major innovation of the amalgamation was the creation of one department, called People's Services, which brought together social services, housing, public health, and parks and recreation. This produced a huge and unwieldy unit but it did put together all the components of a population health approach. It proved too large and led to a reorganization producing a somewhat smaller, although still very large, unit called Community and Protective Services.
18. Community and Protective Services, *Departmental Strategic Framework: Priority on People*, 31 March 31 2005, Draft, 6.
19. Community and Protective Services, *Departmental Strategic Framework: Priority on People*.
20. Linda Cardinal, *La Francophonie Onatarienne: Un Portrait Statistique: Caractéristiques Générales et Régionales* (Ottawa: Université d'Ottawa, 2002), 41.
21. Community and Protective Services, *Departmental Strategic Framework: Priority on People*, p.7.
22. Suzanne Mackenzie, "Building Women, Building Cities: Towards Gender Sensitive Theory in the Environmental Disciplines," in *Life Spaces*, ed. Caroline Andrew and Beth Moore Milroy (Vancouver: University of British Colombia Press, 1988), 13-30.

23. The Regional Coordinating Committee brings together front-line workers in the area of domestic violence prevention. WISE works on public safety. The Round Table was set up to bring to the same table all the major players in the area of policy and programs in the area of domestic violence.

24. I am a participant in this project and therefore the point of view is of a participant observer.

25. City for All Women Initiative, Newsletter, *Women's Eyes on the City*, 5 July 2005.

26. The project is linked to similar initiatives in Toronto, Montreal, and Vancouver through a Canada-wide network, Women and Cities International, which in turn is linked to networks that operate both internationally, through the UN system, and regionally in Australia, in Europe, and in South America.

Chapter 7

Plugola: News for Profit, Entertainment, and Network Consolidation

Carey L. Higgins and Gerald Sussman

Cities are commonly viewed as artifacts of citizens, public policies, commercial enterprise, and physical infrastructures that give them their specific character. The city of Portland, Oregon, for example, has a reputation of being one of the better planned and most livable locales in the United States—a place with a lively downtown business district, restrictions on urban sprawl, progressive land management, vibrant neighborhood associations, a tradition and political culture of citizen engagement and grassroots activism,[1] and a well-read citizenry that values public space and protected environmental habitats. This has come about over several decades through a regional planning approach and forward-looking decisions about urban design—which led to the tearing down of a city highway to build a waterfront park, legislative commitments to environmental protection and an urban growth boundary, and public transit alternatives to automobile use.

A blindspot and serious omission in Portland's urban policy and planning, however, is the failure to look after and take serious action in developing the city's media infrastructure. Although there are a few independent radio stations in Portland, which receive some funding from the Corporation for Public Broadcasting, the television side of the broadcast spectrum in the city is largely the uncontested terrain of private networks and media chains that have shown little accountability in fostering healthy communities, regional political and cultural identity and diversity, or local artistic or broadcasting talent.

Against the backdrop of a city that Putnam and Feldstein[2] described as having steadily expanded the ranks of civic activists since the 1970s—compared to other cities of comparable size whose level of public engagement went into a steep decline—we investigate how Portland's commercial television practices comport with the metropolitan area's public orientation in planning and policy making. In particular, we are interested in television news practices, which, we believe, reflect TV stations' overall broadcast values, and juxtapose such values against those of local urban planning, identity, and civic participation. To what extent do affiliate news stations act as genuinely local agents and resist the commercializing and culturally homogenizing influences of "world city" network programming, support a vigorous public sphere, and inform and encourage an active, place-conscious, engaged citizenry? Is local television news responsive to and respectful of the unique public culture for which Portland is well known?

Newsrooms across the country, Portland being no exception, are being purchased and vertically integrated into corporate media conglomerates. Indeed, each of Portland's six major network affiliates is owned by an out-of-state media chain, not a good starting point for local accountability. These stations all act in accordance with contract provisions that require their identification and compliance with network and parent company interests. Former CBS news anchor Walter Cronkite pointed out that corporate managers with sales and entertainment backgrounds increasingly demand that newsrooms be run on a more cost-efficient model and turn profits similar to those of the entertainment division.[3] This level of integration with network programming and standards has turned Portland's TV stations into little more local than McDonalds or Starbucks franchises.

A growing and particularly egregious reflection of local stations' homogenizing tendencies is the newsroom practice of *plugola*, the cross-marketing of network or parent company assets, such as use of news time to market prime time programs or self-interested types of news (e.g., coverage about Disneyland by Disney-owned ABC News or its news affiliates). Plugola has become a fact of life in local daily newscasts, including those of network affiliates in Portland. The more industrially diversified and vertically integrated a corporation is, the more likely it is for news departments to make use of plugola.[4] And the more that "local" stations resort to naked promotionalism of network and parent interests, the less responsive they are to serving local news audiences. Regarding the perceived function of news, a general manager at the time of Portland's ABC affiliate, KATU, spoke quite frankly: "We're in this for the money. We have shareholders who expect to get a return on their investment."[5] Plainly, news is construed by station management as a business enterprise, not, as in Canada or the United Kingdom, for example, a public service obligation.

Exactly how prevalent is plugola in local news organizations, and how does this accord with the presumed public service function of television news organizations? To determine the extent of cross-marketing tie-ins with local late night newscasts, the authors conducted a study in Portland, a medium-size city with local media outlets representative of an "average" American urban broadcast news environment. We look at the uses and issues of plugola, which include how urban centers preserve their integrity and diversity as public spaces and identifiable communities in the face of tendencies toward informational commodification and cultural homogenization.

Plugola is the outcome and extension of a highly vertically integrated structure of ownership in U.S. media enterprises. Local television newscasts, serving as de facto subsidiaries of the parent company, are important vehicles for network and parent company publicity. We first look at the national picture of how plugola is inserted into the "news." Next, we discuss specifically the uses of plugola in the Portland television news market. Our conclusions offer observations about the impacts of plugola on community building in the Portland metropolitan context. As a critical point of departure, we are concerned with the possible serious disjuncture between the objectives of local TV news affiliates and the informational requirements of a metropolitan area that prides itself in its strong urban and regional identity and, per Putnam and Feldstein, exceptionally high level of civic engagement.

Impacts of Media Deregulation

Over the last decade, as vertically integrated conglomeration of the U.S. television industry has intensified, TV news has changed in content and presentation. Formerly independent newsrooms now find themselves taking a backseat to the entertainment and promotional divisions of their new parent companies, and are often expected to live up to the same income-generating standards.[6] The most important regulatory decision impacting TV news in recent years is the 1996 Telecommunications Act, which drastically cut back ownership restrictions. Since then, the Federal Communications Commission (FCC) has further loosened cross-ownership rules, permitting, as of 2003, television station duopolies (double station ownership) within a single market. Considered unthinkable combinations as recently as ten years ago, cable, network, and local stations can now be owned by the same entity in the same market. It is also now standard for film and television production companies to own network stations.[7] The conflicts within the FCC and Congress over the limits of network market share portend a major battle over efforts to restrain corporations' centralization of media properties and their growing monopolistic control of the airwaves.

Conglomeration and concentration through horizontal (intraindustry) and vertical (interindustry) integration of communications and entertainment businesses has become the norm in American media management.[8] The wave of deregulation in media industries can be directly traced to the elimination of the financial interest and syndication rules in 1995, which returned the right of networks to produce and syndicate programs in-house. An earlier benchmark of national policy in broadcasting was established with the FCC's 1984 divestiture and deregulation of the telephone service monopoly, AT&T, which broke up the company's regulated monopoly over local and long-distance telephony but allowed it to move into other areas of telecommunications, as well as computers and Internet, mobile, wireless, broadcasting, and cable services. This decision set in motion a gold rush of media and telecommunications buyouts, megamergers, cross-ownership, and vertical integration. The more recent anti-regulation disposition by FCC (Republican) majorities has enabled conglomerates, such as Disney, Fox, General Electric, AOL Time Warner, and Viacom, to buy up media assets and produce, transmit, and market programming and auxiliary products in myriad ways through their multimedia outlets. This has encouraged corporate management to push more extensive cross-promotional initiatives and take advantage of the "synergies" resident in unfettered conglomeration.

Payola, the illegal offering of money or other perquisite to radio stations to play music or do programming without disclosing the payment agreement and sponsor, signaled the corrupting possibilities of commercial broadcasting in the 1950s and 1960s. By comparison to the present era, it was an age of innocence.[9] A more aboveground and pervasive offshoot of payola, plugola loosens the restraints on what TV stations now define as newscasts and similar formats and represents a convergence of news with "infotainment" type shows, in which news becomes subsidiary to new and increasingly profitable options for networks or their parent organizations. TV news departments at both owned and affiliate stations have cross-marketed productions through direct advertising and feature "reports" that treat self-promotion as newsworthy.

Network- and locally-produced news stories that plug the network represent one form of plugola.[10] When *Time* magazine put Pokémon on its cover just as the Warner Brothers subsidiary of the same parent company (AOL Time Warner) released *Pokémon: The First Movie*, that's also plugola. And when Peter Jennings on Disney-ABC's *World News Tonight* did a story on Pearl Harbor at the time that another Disney asset, Touchstone Pictures, released its much-hyped movie by the same name, that's another case of plugola. The business innovation of cross-marketing in broadcasting is the result of a tighter integration of network and local TV management nationally and provides time-strapped and under-budgeted local news organizations with a cheap, convenient, and arguably effective way to fill the news hole.

Plugola stories generally appear only on affiliated stations or the parent network, not as news on any other network or station, as they lack significance and also because there is no financial benefit to plugging the competition. Unlike payola, television news organizations have gotten away with this practice, because their management and staff are not seen as having a direct personal financial return from the products being plugged. It is nonetheless considered controversial, as "news" generally is assumed, in journalism schools at least, to be important public information, broadly objective, citizen- and community-focused, and not self-promoting, commercial, or consumption-oriented in character.[11]

Broadcast news is supposed to be a public trust. Yet, as one observer noted, it is common news practice that "anchors flog upcoming segments of their own programs, offer breathless previews of the evening magazine shows, and pass off unadulterated hype, disguised as 'news features,' about coming entertainment offerings."[12] Local and national news programming has simply followed the lead of the mainstream media in indulging in public spectacle. Feeding off of the general debasement of TV news, plugola represents a further erosion of the community's social interest and representation in broadcasting.

Unlike public affairs and events-type news, plugola is intended solely to generate station revenue, and some network and station owners will argue that plugging products and entertainment programs is also news to viewers. Yet every minute rented to plugola is time taken away from reporting political, economic, governmental, and societal stories that help viewers make informed judgments and decisions in their public lives. Plugola breaks down the separation between commercial marketing and public information, between news and entertainment, and between socially responsible news reporting and straightforward corporate profiteering. Inasmuch as Americans turn to and trust local television newscasts more than any other source for news and information,[13] this informal convergence of news and self-promotion gives stations a unique opportunity to exploit what heretofore had been assumed to be a public trust. Critical observers, on the other hand, who have noticed how public officials and federal regulators have long traded on their government service to obtain well-paid lobbying and consulting positions in the corporate sector, would probably see nothing new in plugola practices.

The Rise of Plugola in Local News

"Supply side" rule reform in the "free market" economy has opened media outlets to a free-for-all in the surge for improved earnings. This is not particularly Darwinian in character, a paradigm that suggests that survival is at stake. The television business as a whole has long been one of America's most profitable enterprises. According to an annual report of the Project for Excellence in Journalism, representing the journalism industry, local TV stations enjoyed an estimated 40 percent average profit margin in 2002.[14]

Neoliberalism, the unfettering of markets from regulatory restraints, diminishes the public accountability of broadcasting by allowing bottom line concerns to trump the need for reliable and disinterested public affairs programming. What little regulation exists is driven mainly by the market itself, whose standards degrade over time. Extremely raucous and partisan radio talk shows with successful Arbitron ratings and high advertising revenues sent an early message, leading local TV station owners to intensify the commodification of news content. This requires not only larger audience share (households with TVs tuned to a particular program) but also the correct audience (demographic) targeted by the products advertised and means that advertising and news content have to be synchronized.

One could argue that serious news-seekers, or at least those with the time and the means to do so, need not depend on local or network news. This is exactly how Michael Powell, former chair of the FCC, made the case for "deregulation" (a rhetorical device for market regulation). Indeed, while broadcast television is still the most relied upon source for news, the percentage of people relying on it is decreasing for both network and local newscasts.[15] People now can turn to 24-hour radio and cable news channels, instantaneous access on the Internet, and international broadcast reception via satellite dish and cable TV, in addition to using the ad-alleviating VCR, remote control, and TiVo, to obtain the information they want when they want it.

The problem is that most of the accepted "alternative" news sources are no less governed by commercial and bottom line considerations than network and local news stations and are largely in the hands of the same conglomerates.[16] Moreover, for those seeking real-time information about what's going on in their city or region, there are limited alternatives to the local TV station. Local newspapers don't compete with the television medium in meeting the public's news consumption habits. The "synergy" that management sees in using national and local newscasts to boost ratings and station profits through promotions and cross-promotions is simply a euphemism for monopoly power.

This logically leads to filling news programs with more publicity and less news.[17] Even the advertising zapping capacities of TiVo can not eradicate the commercial content embedded within the news itself. Plugs for products and network programming have been casually assimilated into the content and context of the news, making advertising less distinct, less distracting, and less avoidable than in the past. News plugola is thus a form of hypertext, linking viewers to programs and products that stations insert as value added material, turning urban viewing areas into promotional spaces and reassigning citizens as consumers.

This synergy between news and product consumption can be found in local television newscasts across the country. In New York City, the capital of capital and the largest local U.S. television market, WABC-TV's (owned and operated by ABC/Disney) *Eyewitness News* was once called the worst offender in advertising and plugola counts. During a monitored one-hour newscast, fourteen minutes were devoted to ads and eight to plugola. At the time of the study, WABC was the market's ratings leader, which boosted ad revenue for the station and its financial backers and encouraged its own and local competitors' commercialization.[18] For parent company ABC/Disney, these commercial tie-ins are a win-win situation: the local news holds viewers from prime time who want to see the related news story, while the network gets free promotion.[19]

Plugola can also move beyond direct plugging practices to more complex tie-ins with network programming. A 1998 study uncovered a prime example of the use of tie-ins at the NBC affiliate in Indianapolis. During its local morning newscast, WTHR aired a network-delivered clip about NBC's upcoming *Seinfeld* finale to be aired during that night's *Dateline: NBC*. To further promote the story, a tease for this "news" ran during a commercial break in the newscast. Since the *Dateline* clip itself was a plug for the *Seinfeld* finale, and the airing during the local news was a plug for *Dateline*, the tease in effect was a plug for a plug for the final episode of a network show—all in the service of a spectacular ratings coup for NBC.[20]

Smaller market news programming is especially open to using commercial tie-ins as a way of boosting revenue, and their plugola use is not limited to spectacles like the final episodes of popular, long-running TV shows, such as *Seinfeld*. Even occasional local newscast viewing is enough to make audiences aware of plugola, though not necessarily the full impact of its intrusive commodification of information and culture.[21] Closely related to plugola, another, more clandestine, form of reporting by both local affiliates and networks involves the use of ready-to-air press kits, called video news releases (VNRs), which are commercials set up to look like news stories. They are usually provided by networks for major corporate promotional events or by industry PR departments to market their products.[22]

VNRs offer a simple and cost-free means of filling news slots, and advances in media technology have made their use even more attractive to news stations. In digital format, VNRs have eclipsed video and satellite feeds and enabled their "news" stories to be sent directly to a computer in a specific newsroom for convenient downloading, minimal editing, and airing.[23] Because of their typical lack of identification as such, VNR use is often seen as a serious violation of media ethics.[24] Such misuses contradict traditional assumptions about the news media's civic obligations and further document the colonization of news by commercial imperatives.

The consequences of the commodification of TV news for urban communities is that the informational function of television that was intended to serve the "public interest, convenience, and necessity" has been seriously eroded. Healthy communities need reliable information in order to engage in deliberative public discourses, identify as citizens, and thereby enrich the meaning and practice of democracy.[25] Plugola negates the informational potential of local news by subsuming it under the entertainment and consumer values produced in the dominant media complexes of world cities. Civic education is conflated with the simulacra of escapist drama, pseudo "reality" shows, and celebrity fetishization. News, as an urban infrastructure, like so much of public life, has been surrendered to the aggressive and acquisitive needs of corporate merchants.

Portland Market Plugola

We chose to look at the television news environment in Portland, Oregon, a west coast city that is widely cited as an exceptional example of a citizen-oriented metropolis, with a remarkably high degree of civic engagement and strong sense of local identity.[26] In 2002, CNN and *Money Magazine* ranked Portland as the second most livable city in America, noting, among other things, its long established community focus. Portland is among the leading cities in the percentage of small businesses and is known for its active resistance to big box chain store development such as Wal-Mart. In the cultural domain, the Portland Development Commission (PDC) reports that Portland ranks among the top ten cities for literacy (library use and book purchasing). Another unusual urban characteristic is that the National Public Radio affiliate in Portland is the top-ranked radio news and overall programmer in the metropolitan area.[27]

Portland is also a city that pays a lot of attention to matters of environmental sustainability, based on a commitment to a well-enforced urban growth boundary, policy limits placed on sprawl, and attention to public planning in general. Portland is among the greenest cities in the country, both in percentage of wooded area and the use of green building designs.[28] Such data suggest a strong community orientation in its urban culture, and, in general, popular lifestyles that compared to other American cities are more locally focused and less attached to commercial and consumer trends. Most important, perhaps, as the urbanist Jane Jacobs commented, is the fact that Portlanders have a uniquely strong sense of place.[29]

Portland's local television market is one of the twenty-five largest in the United States, a cluster that the advertising industry frequently cites in its ranking reports. In September 2005, the Nielsen Media Research ranked Portland twenty-third, which placed it in the middle of the major (top fifty) urban media markets.[30] Market size is determined by broadcast signal population, which in Portland's case includes over one million households in its "designated market area" (DMA).[31] Its actual over-the-air signal footprint covers northwest Oregon and southwest Washington, with an extended reach, via translation equipment, beyond the official DMA region.

Ownership characteristics of local stations in the United States vary from location to location. Many, if not owned by networks, are part of regional or national media chains. In the largest markets, such as New York City and Los Angeles, all of the Big Four major network stations (ABC, CBS, NBC, and Fox) are owned and operated (O&O) by the networks themselves. Other urban markets, including Portland, have stations that are affiliated with and run the prime time programming of the networks, but are not directly owned by them. Although Portland's major stations are all part of out-of-state media chains, none is network-owned (See Table 7.1).

Table 7.1 Ownership of Portland's Major Affiliates

Station	Affiliation	Owner	Headquarters	Major Media Holdings
KPTV	Fox	Meredith Corporation	Des Moines, IA	TV, magazines
KGW	NBC	Belo Corporation	Dallas, TX	TV, newspapers, cable
KOIN	CBS	Emmis Communications	Indianapolis, IN	TV, radio, magazines
KATU	ABC	Fisher Communications	Seattle, WA	TV, magazines
KPDX	UPN	Meredith Corporation	Des Moines, IA	TV, magazines
KWBP	WB	Tribune Company	Chicago, IL	TV, newspapers, web

We focused specifically on the plugola that found its way into Portland's late-night (10 pm to 11:30 pm) newscasts during the February ratings ("sweeps") periods of 2003 and 2004,[32] selecting the top-three rated (as determined by Nielsen) news programs. As the Fox affiliate does not have an early evening news program, for consistency we therefore chose the late evening news slot. And as quarterly "sweeps" measure audiences and determine advertising rates for the subsequent fiscal quarter, this period is seen as capturing stations' most competitive behavior.

Two questions guided this portion of the study. First, *What is the extent of network plugola in the newscasts of Portland's affiliate stations?* This search covers stories, graphics, and ad-libbed plugs. The second is, *What types of programs are most commonly plugged during their newscasts?* We mainly looked at story tie-ins to network programming and did not consider sports stories and commercial breaks. Teases for upcoming stories within news blocks ("coming up next . . . stay tuned" pieces), obviously ad-libbed, unscripted anchor chatter, and closing segments were all counted, along with regular, scripted full-length reports.

Of the 162 newscasts analyzed during February sweeps 2003 and 2004, 63 (39 percent) contained at least one instance of network-related plugola. During the 56 studied newscast air dates, 47 (84 percent) included some type of network-related plugola on at least one station. At least two of the stations aired network-related plugola on twenty-one (38 percent) of the same nights. Two nights (4 percent) had at least one instance on all three studied stations.

This indicates that even sporadic viewers were regularly exposed to network program advertisements featured as "news." Those who watched the CBS affiliate daily during both sweeps periods were most likely to be exposed to such ads, with plugs for at least one network program 29 of 53 nights (55 percent) with regularly scheduled newscasts. The Fox affiliate aired similar stories 26 of 54 nights (48 percent), and the NBC affiliate 15 of 55 newscasts (27 percent). These plugs followed one of two patterns: the first involved full-blown, scripted news stories, including video, graphics, sound bites, and the occasional live reporter introduction; the other involved a quick, informal "stay tuned for . . ." the network program airing after the news (see Table 7.2). These items consumed minutes of pseudo-news, while the second pattern typically involved anchor chatter at the end of a newscast, using up only a few seconds of the program.

Table 7.2 Instances of Network Plugola in Portland's Late Local Newscasts

Type of Plugola	KPTV (Fox)	KGW (NBC)	KOIN (CBS)
Scripted Story			
2003	28	2	8
2004	13	8	7
Ad-Libbed Tease			
2003	0	3	12
2004	0	4	11
Scripted Tease			
2003	45	4	4
2004	22	16	9
Total Plugola			
2003	73	9	24
2004	35	28	27

Note: Due to technical problems, the final segments of the February 12 and February 19, 2003 shows on KGW were not available to be analyzed.

One Fox affiliate (KPTV) newscast, with forty minutes of potential news time (total program time minus weather, sports, and commercials), used over five minutes of "hard" news time to plug four different Fox network prime time entertainment shows. Another night, the station dedicated 6.5 minutes to plug a network special, using network produced updates on the Michael Jackson pedophile investigation. Such tie-ins are sometimes introduced by a live local reporter, further integrating, without benefit of contract, the local news staff with network management. On another KPTV newscast, a local investigative reporter discussed a scam that happened to be related to the prime time Fox program, *American Idol.*

The CBS affiliate (KOIN) newscast spent five minutes of news time on two different network specials during one half-hour broadcast, more than one quarter of the total news time allotted to this particular newscast. Another KOIN newscast used an entire segment between commercial breaks to report two "news" stories about the CBS "reality" series *Survivor* and the network's *David Letterman* show. Including teases, this CBS plugola segment used up nearly 6.5 minutes of newscast time. Plugola stories that evening got about two-thirds as much air time as hard news.

Portland's TV stations regularly employ plugola in news programming as a way of promoting parent network programming, almost always (98 percent of the time) tied into entertainment-related programming. The vast majority of the three stations' plugs and related teases promoted hit prime time programs and late night talk shows. Not one of these "news" stories appeared on any of the competitors' newscasts, suggesting that they have no genuine public value and are strictly self-promotional. With such habitual patterns of self-reference, networks have made themselves the news, and local news programming is increasingly used as a promotional platform for network commercial programming and the advertising revenue that flows from it.

Table 7.3 Time Devoted to Scripted Plugola Stories on Portland's Late Local News During Sweeps (in Seconds and Minutes)

Station	Total Plugola Time 2003	Total Plugola Time 2004
KPTV (Fox)	55:10	20:08
KGW (NBC)	01:33	06:27
KOIN (CBS)	11:20	15:37

Note: Due to technical problems, the final segments of the February 12 and February 19, 2003 shows on KGW were not available to be analyzed.

During both sweeps periods, Fox affiliate KPTV was the leader in cross-promotional activity in terms of the number of plugs aired and minutes devoted to plugola during newscasts.[33] This might be expected of an affiliate of the most aggressive media conglomerate, News Corporation, in recent years. Mirroring the copycat tendencies of the networks, the NBC affiliate KGW (with the highest late night newscast ratings), had the least amount of plugola both years but was quickly catching up, from 14 percent of newscasts in 2003 to 30 percent in 2004 and a fourfold increase in minutes (See Table 7.3). Apparently, the requirements of being a loyal affiliate competed with its status as local news leader.

Local news is further integrated into national programming through the use of logos and graphics that associate local stories with network entertainment. The CBS affiliate, KOIN, for example, ran news stories on crime scene investigations (CSI), which employed the logo from the network program of the same name. The Fox affiliate, KPTV, likewise ran graphical tie-ins and theme music from its prime time show, *American Idol*, in some of its news stories. Both stations often ran tie-in content on the scheduled day of the prime time hits, creating marketing links between the news and the networks. More egregious, however, are "news" stories about newly minted mini-celebrities and notorieties from various network programs, such as *Survivor* and *American Idol*. Local newscasters thus serve, without benefit of portfolio, as public relations and marketing agents for the networks.

The stations had other methods of promoting their network's highly rated programs. "Tune in Tuesdays . . ." type plugs made appearances on each of the three stations. This promotional practice was most widely used by the Fox affiliate, which regularly aired story tie-ins related to currently-running prime time series, often the same night the plugged show aired. The CBS and NBC affiliates were more likely to use this type of plug with special non-regularly scheduled programming, such as awards shows or network specials. More frequently, these two stations used shorter ad-libbed "stay tuned for . . ." promos at the end of the newscast.

Tie-ins are not limited to the stories themselves. A new trend in newscasting is to run promotions for promotions (or plugs for plugs), which are known as teases (i.e., previews for promotional-type reports, such as "How do potential contestants compete for a spot on *American Idol*? Stay tuned . . .").[34] With more news time and more commercial breaks in its one-hour newscast, Fox affiliate KPTV led in teases for plugola stories, with 67 over the eight week period. This included 17 during the customarily highest-rated first news block prior to the first commercial break. NBC affiliate KGW used the high-ratings first tease to plug 12 NBC network shows, with 10 of these occurring in its more plugola-friendly 2004 February ratings period. Although it employed no first-tease (highest rated) time during the 2003 sweeps' regularly-scheduled late night newscasts, CBS affiliate KOIN plugged 8 network shows prior to the first commercial break in the 2004 sweeps period. Because higher ratings normally increase advertising revenues, stations bank on these network tie-ins to lock in viewers. Entertainment stories were often teased again later in the news prior to the full story airing, using an additional ten to fifteen seconds of news time as commercials for longer commercials for network shows.

Sometimes, the teases began even before the actual newscast. As part of a multiple-story tease, KPTV did network programming tie-ins six different nights prior to airing their first news story. Four of these plugs aired as the first story in the tease, adding dramatic significance to the network event. KGW picked up on this trend in 2004, teasing plugola stories prior to beginning five newscasts, after airing none of this type of promotion in 2003. KOIN tended to save this type of promotion to tie into their special edition news programs, which were not included in this study.[35]

Further blurring the categorical and temporal distinction between Fox entertainment and local news, KPTV ran a two-minute pre-news "news" story about the movie *X-Men II* just prior to their regular 10 PM newscast. The "news" lead-in followed the prime time airing of the first *X-Men* movie, a plug that easily could have been mistaken for a commercial, inasmuch as the station gave no indication that it was part of the newscast. Both *X-Men* and *X-Men II* were produced by 20th Century Fox, the film division of the News Corporation media empire, which also owns 35 TV stations and has 178 TV affiliates in the United States (2004), including KPTV.

Plugola use does not necessarily correspond to ratings. According to Nielsen reports, KGW newscasts were the market's late-night news leader, though the station ran the least amount of network plugola compared to its competitors.[36] Unlike the WABC example, *supra*, this indicates that tie-ins do not necessarily contribute to or correspond with increased audience share. One study done in 2001 found that the formula for a successful local newscast included more community stories, more enterprise (original investigative) reporting, better story selection and sourcing, longer stories, and more reporters and more time to report stories.[37] Nowhere did the study suggest that audiences seek entertainment news, advertising, or promotions. Rather, it appears, people actually tune into news to get information.

Newsrooms seem to understand this on some level. During the period of our study, the three stations dedicated at least two nights each to the Columbia space shuttle disaster, local flooding, and controversial local gay marriage policy changes, emphasizing hard, albeit very dramatic "breaking" news, with less time spent on scripted plugola. The hard news pattern was not typical, however. And the "local" in local news remains rife with "if it bleeds, it leads" type stories.

Plugola, Privatization, and the Public Sphere

Throughout the United States, viewers increasingly are responding to commercialization of local newscasts by changing the channel or using recording equipment to skip the ads. Since 1997, local late-night newscasts have lost 16 percent of their audience share.[38] Early evening newscasts have lost 18 percent. Studies indicate that community trust in local television news is similarly on the decline,[39] with 42 percent of the general public believing that advertisers influence the news product.[40] While it is uncertain whether plugola disguised as "news" stories contributes to this perception, it is clear that local news audiences are dissatisfied with what they see as "influenced" newscasts. As much as news programming may be doing injustice to public service broadcasting, it is expanding its service on behalf of a different master—the global corporate media organizations that have been unleashed by recent government rule changes from several public accountability restrictions.

American TV stations generally used to adhere to program boundaries and schedules, but all that has changed in today's more integrated, consolidated, convergent, and flexible market economy. Local affiliate stations formally are not owned by the networks, but they often operate as if they were. Portland's KPTV, for example, owned by the Meredith Corporation, brands its newscast as "Fox News." Television programming in general, in the service of market demands, now heavily caters to celebrity "news," so-called reality TV, and a host of other voyeuristic, surveillance, and tabloid formats that intrude on the personal lives of actors and non-actors and turn audiences into fan clubs and peeping toms.

The more these formats attract targeted demographics and provide satisfactory quarterly earnings reports, the more they influence the content of evening. news programs. Television programming and the airwaves appropriated in this fashion do little to help citizens understand such critical societal issues as job creation and security, livable and stable incomes, health care, accessible higher education, affordable housing, racial and gender equity issues, and peaceful international relations. Instead, the commercial stations prime viewers for consumption and draw their attention through exposés of Michael Jackson and other celebrities or high-profile murder trials and other soap opera spectacles. Television "infotainment" promotes what political scientist Lance Bennett sees as "bad news" tendencies toward fragmentation (transmitting a series of seemingly disconnected story events) and personalization (exaggerated dramatization playing on individual personalities rather than conflicting social forces).[41] If television news has never lived up to its potential for informing, educating, and promoting an engaged citizenry, the recent wave of media deregulation and plugola has further corrupted the medium with unremitting sensationalism and promotionalism on an unprecedented scale and steered viewers into defining themselves as hedonistic consumers.[42]

Plugola absorbs precious newscasting time (minutes not already dedicated to direct advertising) to promote its sponsors' agenda and a ratings war. The bottom line and the newsline have merged, effectively collapsing the barrier between news and entertainment. If this tendency continues, intelligent and publicly oriented journalists will either actively resist, at their own peril, or, perhaps more likely, turn away from careers in commercial broadcasting. The business of news distorts its public and community character and the institutional responsibility of news organizations to inform and educate, free of commercial or governmental imperatives, and improve the quality of a democratic civil society.

The flip side of plugola is news censorship, which is another major problem for the newsroom. While parent companies push profit-building practices such as plugola, news that may hurt revenues is not so readily acceptable, especially stories that touch unflatteringly on advertisers, potential business partners, or the parent company. TV journalists have historically been loathe to challenge the corrupting influences of plugola in the news, and for many, censorship begins prior to hitting the air or even story selection.[43] In their propaganda model, published years before media deregulation and mega-mergers hit their stride, Herman and Chomsky warned of the greater threat of censorship in vertically integrated companies.[44]

Numerous cases of management-imposed censorship and news direction have been reported, and despite growing criticism of the corporate media, it continues to occur. One well-known example was the CBS veto of a *60 Minutes* story about Big Tobacco at the same time that the network was courting potential merger partner Westinghouse. Disney-owned ABC was also criticized for not running a story about sex offenders working at Disney World.[45] GE, parent of NBC, vetoed a story about a boycott of GE products.[46] A 2004 documentary film, *Outfoxed*, exposed the politically partisan news spin orders that regularly came down from Fox TV executives to the network's news anchors and talk show hosts.

Networks see exposure of their dirty laundry as potentially financially disastrous. Given the pressures to be company players, many journalists do not even bother to investigate stories that could hurt the parent company's reputation (and financial interests). Career is another consideration. One journalist admitted that as long as reporters are thinking about their livelihoods, investigative journalism is going to suffer. After doing an independent piece on his own corporate employer, a reporter was warned, "You're not going to win any popularity contests writing up stories like this."[47] Once a labeled troublemaker, a journalist is an easy target at a time of job compression.

Directives to avoid reporting on a corporation usually do not come straight from the parent organization. One exception to this is Michael Eisner, CEO of Disney, who made it known explicitly that he prefers that ABC not cover Disney.[48] Rupert Murdoch, head of News Corporation, is widely reported to strictly control his news outlets, print and television, including Fox News, with staunch commitments to politically conservative values. Murdoch hired Roger Ailes, political strategist to Nixon, Reagan, and the elder Bush, to run the Fox News network. Under such leadership, balanced, journalistic freedom is out of the question.

In most cases, however, the lack of investigative reporting in corporate media comes about through journalists' own silence or self-censorship. Though often willing to discuss internal problems and potentially controversial news stories with fellow reporters, journalists usually will not take the same risk with management. This fosters a (self) censored work environment[49] in which reporters, feeling paranoid or second-guessing themselves, bypass stories that might have passed muster with their superiors. Self-gagging inhibitions are always more effective in controlling journalists than direct censorship from the top.[50]

The problem is not only the job insecurity of the reporters, but, more important, how the chilling atmosphere of newsroom/salesroom censorship ultimately destroys the integrity and social value of the "free press." A study by a group of media unions found that almost 80 percent of 400 journalists surveyed believed that journalism standards have declined, and 69 percent said that corporate owners exercise too much influence over news reporting.[51] The Radio and Television News Directors Association has a code of ethics for American journalists, which includes the charge to "provide a full range of information to enable the public to make enlightened decisions."[52] But in a conglomerate-controlled media structure, such a voluntary professional standard seems extremely difficult to carry out. The biggest losers in the controlled newsroom ultimately are readers and audiences as citizens.

Excommunicating the Community

Plugola is an outgrowth of the growing privatization, conglomeration, and vertical integration of the mass media nationwide. It was inevitable that the relative sanctity of the newsroom would be invaded by the onslaught of the media behemoths, and even public broadcasting has not been spared. The FCC relaxation of ownership and production rules, supportive of the "media-industrial complex," has contributed to an unremitting drive toward monopolization, increased commercialization, and continued violations of the public airwaves and the public trust. At the same time, the growing use of plugola is an indication of the decline in the autonomy of news departments and the abdication of stations' obligation to provide disinterested informational and public affairs programming. The bottom-line mentality in TV stations supports McChesney's arguments about media *hypercommercialism*—namely the intensification of market-based values over every aspect of the media business and, more generally, the commodification of public space.[53]

The rush to exploit fresh profit opportunities enabled by government deregulation and the appropriation and diversion of new digital technologies has made more transparent the intrinsic logic and direction of media conglomeration. Through plugola, newscasting acts as a "Trojan horse," drawing viewers more tightly into the circuit of production and consumption—and betraying its false status as an independent information source. It is increasingly evident that, as Herman and Chomsky have argued with reference to foreign policy,[54] local and network television news has become little more than an organ of propaganda in the service of both state and commercial interests. Broadcast space is thus utilized, per Lefebvre,[55] for its social and political utilities, even as its entertainment style helps to conceal its actual ends. Urban areas as concentrations of people (conceived as "consumers") and "footprints" for network affiliate transmissions are the principal spaces in which capital has intensified the commodification of culture and society and reduction of their public character.

Network-affiliate news media integration has direct and dire consequences on the sustainability of cities and urban communities as spaces of identity. Plugola and other contractual practices between networks and affiliates further centralize the network as the main transmission center in news production. This brings about a delocalization of much of the news, which also weakens the "local" identity of affiliate news broadcasters. In the vertically integrated media environment, local journalists are transformed into promotional agents of the network and parent organization, and the potential of news as a local informational and educational medium declines. As a result, the degree of attention to local politics, policy issues, and community events is reduced as network interests and spectacles are given more significance by the newscaster. Local stations have become mere franchises of networks, serving up an audience-ready formulaic McTelevision.

In this study, we have argued that the city of Portland is no less vulnerable than others to the encroachment and commercialization of the public airwaves by national networks and media chains. From a public service perspective, and given that TV station ownership is enormously profitable even without plugola, there is no reason for local broadcasters to require news departments to be run on a promotional and profit-seeking basis or for the primary benefit of corporate owners and management in faraway headquarters. Although it's difficult in this neoliberal era to conceive of socially responsible corporations or even socially accountable regulators, news programming run in this manner is not in the public interest. Newscasts are supposed to be accountable to and help viewers make informed decisions in their lives by providing a wide spectrum of coverage of politics, public affairs, arts and culture, and community initiatives. Instead, what we see is public life and politics being reduced to a form of amusement while the serious side of governance is taken over by corporate elites.

Television is part of the urban informational infrastructure. McChesney and others have written about the corruption of that power, going back to the loss of the radio spectrum to commercial ownership in the 1920s and 1930s. Commercial broadcasting promotes a consumer, not a producer, culture and denies media access by denizens of cities like Portland who might otherwise use the airwaves for exhibition of local arts and politics that better reflects the needs, interests, aesthetics, and achievements of their citizens. It also denies journalists the opportunity to act as public service professionals for which they were trained. TV station owners typically defend their commercial practices by arguing that dissatisfied audiences have other news media options, but they can not defend the degradation of the public status of the broadcast spectrum, a breakdown which the FCC was originally created to correct.

Viewers are not helpless and already are responding with their remotes and off buttons to news and other programming they don't like—although switching off is a far less affirmative way of asserting control than reclaiming the airwaves. Massive public objection to FCC attempts to reduce controls on media ownership in 2004 was one positive collective initiative, and public opposition again resurfaced in 2005 to challenge the conservative politicization of the Public Broadcasting System. Journalists, too, have an obligation to resist self-censorship and go public with corporate malfeasance and misuse of broadcast licenses. To not do so is to be complicit in the violation of a code of professional ethics they are supposed to uphold and to invite the loss of public trust. When journalists are unionized, it is easier for them individually to take a stand, which is a big reason why media corporations so strongly object to broadcasting and newspaper unions.

Media deregulation has led to more advertising clutter and other forms of promotionalism but not higher quality and more informative news programming, and recent FCC rulings and corporate behavior, including that of PBS, have not been encouraging. At the same time, a growing box office demonstration of interest in documentary films suggests that news programming needs to recapture more of the critical edge that some networks, particularly CBS and PBS, had in the years before deregulation. TV news departments need more autonomy from the stations in which they are lodged and require cross-subsidies in order to do their task well. Public broadcasting needs far more state support, as in Britain, to make it competitive with and set a positive example for the commercial media. And the public must become more educated, vigilant, and vocal in expressing dissatisfaction with the broadcasting industry and government regulatory bodies.

The Portland case suggests that even in a city that purports to support viable and vibrant communities, the network news media and their chain-operated local affiliates have the upper hand in the delivery of news and information on the air. In the media sense, "local" refers only to physical place; it has little to do with supporting local culture, talent, identity, or sense of place. The time devoted to "synergy"-minded network self-promotion at the expense of place-based content in Portland's local news affiliate programming demonstrates that this heralded civic-minded city is, with respect to television broadcasting, no exception. TV news content in Portland, run by out-of-state media chains, is about as formulaic, commercially-driven, and "local" as in any other major American city. The fact that both the local television and radio sections of the local PBS affiliate, KOPB, enjoy the highest audience share of any market in the country, is one indication of the strong publicly oriented culture of the city and the regions within its signal reach. But KOPB is not strong enough to protect Portland's and

Oregon's public interest in broadcasting.

Concerned Portlanders, including many now in government who as political activists migrated to the city in the 1960s, have been leading advocates for the kind of public planning and policy making that gives the metropolitan region a vibrant and progressive character. However, the city has had little success in regulating cable television, let alone FCC-licensed broadcasting, toward public service standards. Local government, together with citizen activists, should begin to challenge local news' practices, including the corrupt and abusive system of plugola, and false claims to inform and educate. A combination of citizen and formal political action, together with initiatives from independent-minded journalists (and of course the election of more publicly minded legislators), is the starting point for recovering the airwaves from the clutches of corporate media moguls and executives whose principal identity is with their fellow travelers in the high-rise boardrooms of the broadcast industry. As plugola and other commercial broadcast practices reveal, television news is too important to the future of democratic urban communities and communications to be entrusted to the profit motive.

Notes

1. See R.D. Putnam and L.M. Feldstein, *Better Together: Restoring the American Community* (New York: Simon & Schuster, 2003).

2. Putnam and Feldstein, *Better Together*.

3. N. Hickey, "Money Lust," *Columbia Journalism Review* 37 (July/August 1998): 28-37.

4. D. Williams, "Synergy Bias: Conglomerates and Promotion in the News," *Journal of Broadcasting & Electronic Media* 46 (2002): 453-72.

5. H. Lenhart, "The Race to the Bottom," *Oregon Business* (May 1997): 31.

6. N. Hickey, "Money Lust."

7. The combined impact of these rule changes effectively opened up the market for major corporate takeovers. By 2001, the top 25 station groups controlled 44.5 percent of America's commercial stations, up from 24.6 percent before the passage of the Act just five years before. The national household audience cap has since expanded further in 2004 to 39 percent, compromised down from a high of 45 percent demanded by the FCC but above the 35 percent pushed in Congress. Statistics cited in N. Hickey, "Money Lust." See also J. Pelofsky, "FCC Vote Prelude to Appeal," *Houston Chronicle*, 31 May 2003; Federal Communications Commission, *The Telecommunications Act of 1996: Broadcast Ownership and Dual Network Operations,* Sections 202(c)(1) and 202(e), accessed at http://www.fcc.gov; Federal Communications Commission, "FCC Sets Limits on Media Concentration: A Summary of the Broadcast Ownership Rules Adopted on June 2, 2003," accessed at: www.fcc.gov/ownership/documents.html#brdcastownrlmt.

8. B.H. Bagdikian, *The New Media Monopoly* (Boston: Beacon Press, 2004).

9. H. Martin. "Payola Controversy Heats Up," *Radio Magazine*, accessed online at

http://beradio.com/ar/radio_payola_controversy_heats. Thanks to New York State attorney general Elliot Spitzer, it is now known that pay for play practices are still rife in the recorded music and radio industries. See Jeff Leeds and Louise Story, "Radio Payoffs are Described as Sony Settles. *New York Times*, 26 July 2005.

10. M.P. McAllister, "Television News Plugola and the Last Episode of *Seinfeld*," *Journal of Communication* 52 (2002): 383-401.

11. W.L. Bennett, *News: The Politics of Illusion*, 5th edition (New York: Longman, 2003); R.M. Cohen, "The Corporate Takeover of News: Blunting the Sword." In *Conglomerates and the Media*, ed. E. Barnouw et al. (New York: The New Press, 1997); R.W. McChesney, *Rich Media, Poor Democracy: Communication Politics in Dubious Times* (New York: The New Press, 1999).

12. J. Benson and B. Alden, "The Plugola Problem," *Columbia Journalism Review* 34 (May/June 1995): 17.

13. J. Carroll, "Local TV and Newspapers Remain Most Popular News Sources," accessed online at http://www.gallup.com, 22 December 2004.

14. Pew Project for Excellence in Journalism, *The State of the News Media: 2004*, accessed online at: www.stateofthenewsmedia.org.

15. Pew Research Center, "News Media's Improved Image Proves Short-Lived: The Sagging Stock Market's Big Audience," 4 August 2002, accessed online at http://people-press.org.

16. Ben Bagdikian, *The New Media Monopoly*.

17. Gerald Sussman, *Communication, Technology, and Politics in the Information Age* (Thousand Oaks, CA: Sage Publications, 1997).

18. J. Benson and B. Alden, "The Plugola Problem," *Columbia Journalism Review* 34 (May/June 1995): 17-18.

19. J. Hammer, "A Season of Sleaze in TV News," *Newsweek* 115 (1990): 71.

20. M.P. McAllister, "Television News Plugola and the Last Episode of *Seinfeld*."

21. In one of the more egregious uses of news for hire, an NBC affiliate in Jackson, Mississippi, WLBT-TV, openly advertised a fee of $500 per week and $2,000 per month for a two to two and a half-minute interview conducted by one of its news anchors, with interviewees rounded up by the station's sales department. Howard Kurtz, "Local TV News: Now Part of Sales?" *Washington Post,* 3 November 2003, http://www.washingtonpost.com.

22. W.L. Bennett, *"News: The Politics of Illusion."* See also M. McAllister, "Television News Plugola."

23. K. Sweeney, "Spotlight On: Video News Releases. What's Next for VNRs? The War Is Over, But Stations Are Still Choosy about What to Air," *Public Relations Tactics* (June 2003), accessed online at http://www.prsa.org/_Publications/magazines/

24. One of the more notorious cases of abuse involving VNRs was the delivery of stories to national news networks by the public relations firm, Hill & Knowlton, under contract by the Kuwaiti government, during the 1990-1991 Persian Gulf war. The public was misled into believing that the "news" items were produced by the networks themselves. In 2004, another VNR controversy arose when the Bush administration provided a number of stations with a story, employing an actor posing as a reporter, about the passage of a Medicare prescription bill. It was widely seen as a form of election year government propaganda, with the stations involved complicit in the deception. In September 2005, the General Accountability Office found the administration to have engaged in

illegal "covert propaganda." See Robert Pear, "Buying of News by Bush's Aides is Ruled Illegal," *New York Times*, 30 September 2005, 1.

25. J. Gastil and P. Levine, *The Deliberative Democracy Handbook: Strategies for Effective Civic Engagement in the Twenty-First Century* (San Francisco: Jossey-Bass, 2005).

26. Putnam and Feldstein, *Better Together*. See also C.P. Ozawa, ed. *The Portland Edge: Challenges and Successes in Growing Communities* (Washington, DC: Island Press, 2004).

27. P. Schulberg, "KGW's Barry Is Still an Anchor in Local Waters," *Portland* [Oregon] *Tribune*, 2 August 2005, accessed online at http://www.portlandtribune.com.

28. Portland Development Commission, accessed online at www.pdc.us/bus_serv/ praises/default.asp.

29. Ozawa, *The Portland Edge*, 2.

30. Nielsen Media Research, 11 October 20, http://www.nielsenmedia.com/ DMAs.html.

31. There are 210 markets across the United States, ranging in size from over 7 million households in the largest market, New York City, to less than 5,000 in the smallest, Glendive, Montana. See *Nielsen Media Research Local Universe Estimates: 2005*, accessed online at http://www.nielsenmedia.com/DMAs.html.

32. The study dates included the weeks between January 30 and February 27, 2003 and between February 5 and March 3, 2004. Only newscasts airing during their regularly scheduled time periods were analyzed. Five newscasts not included for analysis: KOIN's February 23, 2003, February 8, 2004, and February 29, 2004; KPTV's February 26, 2004 and February 27, 2004; and KGW's February 29, 2004.

33. KPTV plugola was especially heavy in 2003, with more than three times as many scripted plugs as its competitors. Over 55 minutes were spent plugging network programming in February 2003, all of it scripted and entertainment-related. Over the course of a year, this is the equivalent of nearly 16 newscasts of potential local hard news time devoted entirely to network programming advertisements. Although KPTV news reduced network programming plugs during this same period in 2004, more than 20 minutes of their 2004 plugola was focused on Fox's hit prime time contest show, *American Idol*.

34. M.P. McAllister, "Television News Plugola."

35. As an example, *KOIN6 News* did a promotion for itself (a "special edition") during the airing of the *Grammy Award* credits with a recap of the just-concluded ceremonies in both 2003 and 2004.

36. This is difficult to measure, however, as news plugola may *transfer* ratings advantages to the programs being plugged.

37. T. Rosenstiel, C. Gottlieb, and A. Finlayson, "The Magic Formula: Five Proven Steps to Financial Success in the News," *Columbia Journalism Review* 40 (November 2001): 5-7.

38. Pew Project for Excellence in Journalism, *The State of the News Media: 2004*.

39. Pew Research Center, "News Media's Improved Image Proves Short-Lived."

40. Pew Project for Excellence in Journalism, *The State of the News Media: 2004*.

41. W.L. Bennett, *News: The Politics of Illusion*.

42. The very style of newscasting reflects the influence of advertising, with fast-paced video and audio clips that are designed more toward sponsor preferences and con-

sumption stimulation than for comprehensive high-quality news stories. See especially
R.M. Cohen, "The Corporate Takeover of News: Blunting the Sword."

43. N. Klein, *No Logo* (New York: Picador USA, 1999); See also J. Turow, "Hidden
Conflict and Journalistic Norms: The Case of Self-Coverage," *Journal of Communication*
44 (1994): 29-46.

44. Edward Herman and Noam Chomsky, *Manufacturing Consent: The Political
Economy of the Mass Media* (New York: Pantheon Books, 1988).

45. Examples drawn from W.L. Bennett, *The Politics of Illusion*; N. Klein, *No Logo*.

46. R. Anderson, *Consumer Culture and TV Programming* (Boulder, CO: Westview
Press, 1995).

47. J. Turow, "Hidden Conflict and Journalistic Norms," 38.

48. Examples drawn from W.L. Bennett, *The Politics of Illusion*; N. Klein, *No Logo*.

49. J. Turow, "Hidden conflict."

50. N. Klein, *No Logo*.

51. *Television Week,* 20 July 2004, accessed online at www.tvweek.com.

52. Radio and Television News Directors Association, *RTNDA Code of Ethics*,
2000, accessed online at http://www.rtnda.org/ethics/coe.shtml

53. R.W. McChesney, *Rich Media, Poor Democracy*.

54. Herman and Chomsky, *Manufacturing Consent*.

55. Henri Lefebvre, *The Production of Space* (Cambridge, MA: Blackwell, 1991).

Part III

The City in Context

Chapter 8

Communicating Urban Values Through Megasport Events: The Case of Australia's "High Performance" Cities

Paul Tranter and Mark Lowes

It is a truism among many politicians and business interests that major sports teams and megaevents are major engines of economic growth. Civic leaders argue that it makes good economic and cultural "common sense" to invest public resources in showcase sporting events, which are presumed to be essential in projecting a world-class image of their city. Motorsport events, especially those run on city street circuits, have become a preferred method of image-making for cities around the world.

The general population typically supports major motorsport events in city locations, although for many residents the location of the events is a critical consideration in their level of support.[1] For their part, urban leaders widely regard hosting a city-based motorsport event as a successful event-tourism strategy, one that can boost the image of cities involved, contribute to the local economy, and, especially, cultivate a "winner" image for the politicians who champion such spectacles.

Despite the widespread acceptance of motorsport in Australian society, we argue that it is crucial for researchers to systematically investigate the environmental and public health impacts of motorsport events held in major urban public spaces. Currently there is a paucity of sustained critical analysis along these lines. Indeed, with a few exceptions, there has been very little critical scholarship that examines the role of motorsport in the broader context of urban space.[2] What critical scholarship there is on the subject is often devoted to exploring the economic costs of hosting megasports events. While much of this literature casts doubt on the claims that hosting, for example, the Olympics pays off for cities in economic terms, this question of economic risks and benefits is not our focus here. Instead, our aim in this chapter is to explore the question of whether the strategy of staging major motorsport events makes sense in terms of public and environmental health.

Sustainable sport, notes Lenskyj, is a relatively new concept in both sport and environmental circles.[3] There is little scholarly research on the complex relationship between sport and the environment generally, and virtually nil with respect to research concerning the impact of motorsport events on the natural urban environment of their host cities. This is a problem we hope to at least begin to address with this chapter.

In doing so, we want to be clear about our aims. We are not "anti-sport" or even "anti-spectacle." Major sports events have a range of symbolic (and actual) impacts as well their supposed impact on the status or prestige of their city. They can operate to support or undermine policies on sustainable cities. Different types of sports events will have hugely differing impacts on and symbolism for cities in terms of their sustainability. Furthermore, sport is undoubtedly an integral component of Australian society. It is part of Australia's cultural identity. It seems understandable then, that sporting events would be given pride of place in our major cities. At the same time, if city, state and national governments are serious about a policy agenda which ranks public health and sustainable environments above the profits of private companies, then we believe there are grounds for being selective about the types of sporting events that are allowed to be staged in a city's significant public spaces.

Staging any major event in a city's major public spaces involves some disruption to the normal running of the city. This includes traffic congestion, disruption of access to certain locations, and an increase in pollution and litter associated with a concentration of large numbers of people.[4] However, certain events—including motorsport events—have significantly greater negative environmental and public health impacts and messages than other events.

The particular characteristics of motorsport spectacles as they are currently conducted in Australian cities may intensify any impacts that the sport has on environmental and public health. For example, unlike France, Australia continues to allow tobacco sponsorship to occur with motorsport. Motorsport in Australia has also been allowed in locations that increase both its physical and symbolic consequences on public health. Melbourne's Grand Prix is unusual by world Formula One racing standards in being a street circuit located in a high-density urban area. Canberra's V8 Supercar motorsport events were also unusual in that national monuments such as Parliament House were used as a backdrop for the events and their associated advertising. Other major motorsport spectacles in major Australian cities include the various motor racing events that have been held in parkland in central Adelaide (including Grand Prix Formula One events and V8 Supercar events), as well as the Gold Coast Indy event on public streets in Surfer's Paradise, which has recently also incorporated V8 Supercar events. (The motor racing formula of V8 Supercars is a formula that is unique to Australia, and is exclusively for Holden Commodore and Ford Falcon V8-engined cars that are similar in appearance to cars of the same name available to members of the public for use on public roads.)

In short, in Australia, motorsport events have come to occupy a central place in urban cultural and material life. In this chapter, therefore, we investigate the public health and environmental consequences of these motorsport events. What we will discover is that these events' location in significant public spaces is a major factor in understanding their cultural, political, and environmental impacts on their host cities.

Environmental Impacts of Sport

The notion of sustainable cities speaks to the recognition that the kind of environments that future generations will inherit are directly affected by the kinds of decisions made by contemporary planners and policymakers. One of these decisions involves the attraction and promotion of major sporting events.

For instance, the International Olympic Committee (IOC) amended its Charter in 1991 to include language that ensures that Olympic Games were held under conditions that demonstrated a responsible concern for environmental issues. Among other initiatives, the IOC introduced an environmental requirement for bidding cities, issued an environmental policy, and created a Commission on Sport and the Environment. Writing in 1993, IOC Executive Board member Richard Pound argued that:

> It is natural that the International Olympic Committee, as leader of a worldwide humanistic Movement, should be concerned with the integration of the activities of the Olympic movement with the wellbeing of the world in which we live. Indeed, the Olympic Movement is predicated on holistic principles of balance between body and mind, between action and contemplation, between sport and culture. It would be inconceivable for the IOC to divorce itself from recognition of the desirable balance between the needs of the present and those of the future. Expressed in more concrete terms, the IOC must seek a balance between the needs of our generation and those of the next and succeeding generations. It is, after all, the youth of the world who will inherit the earth which we leave them.[5]

Subsequently, the Sydney Olympic Bid Committee recognized in its *Environmental Guidelines* document that Olympic host cities have "a great opportunity to promote the principles of sustainable urban development." In this sense, hosting the Olympic Games can be used as "a catalyst for the transition to ecologically sustainable cities, by going beyond formal compliance with current environmental requirements."[6]

This concern for the environment in Australia extends far beyond Olympic bids. As Helen Lenskyj has argued, Australia in fact has a long tradition of conservation awareness and activism. A signal moment of this was the founding in 1963 of the Australian branch of the World Wildlife Federation—one of the first formal steps toward Australian involvement in the international environmental movement. "Living on an island," she writes, "with a fragile ecological balance, unique flora and fauna, and regular extremes of weather—droughts, floods, and bushfires—Australians can hardly afford to ignore the environment."[7]

This history of environmental activism has recently been extended to the relationship between sport and the sustainability of Australian cities and their public spaces. The Australian Conservation Foundation (ACF), for example, has developed a policy on sport in Australia. Though this does not specifically mention motorsport, it does recognize that different sporting events have different environmental impacts. It divides sporting activity into three areas by reason of their environmental impacts:

1. Sports that are currently largely ecologically sustainable, but can still be improved in some form;
2. Sports that are currently not ecologically sustainable, but which may be significantly improved in sustainability because their core activity is not inherently unsustainable;
3. Sports that can never be ecologically sustainable, nor made significantly more sustainable, due to the inherent nature of their core activity.[8]

The ACF policy document goes on to recommend that certain sporting activities should be encouraged in preference to those "that require external processed sources of energy . . . or require significant modification to environmental conditions and processes," those that "generate significant ecological impacts through the manufacturing of new equipment necessary for that activity" or those that "require the construction of specific facilities and infrastructure." It also argues that sports that "promote environmental improvements in sectors such as transportation" should be encouraged.

Given the ACF policy on sport, it is unlikely that most motorsport events (particularly those currently staged in Australia's urban street circuits) would rate highly in terms of their ecological sustainability. The inherent nature of motorsport's core activities usually involves considerable pollution and use of energy: in the manufacture of the equipment needed for the sport, including the vehicles themselves; in the construction (and subsequent removal) of the race infrastructure in city street circuits; and in the operation of the vehicles during the events. Furthermore, when motorsport events are held in street circuits, they can also disrupt ecologically supportive activities such as walking and cycling as well as (at least in the case of Albert Park in Melbourne) participation in other sports.

Symbolic Importance of Public Space in Cities

Locating motorsport events in significant urban public places can magnify any environmental messages or impacts of motorsport in two ways. First, the total local impact of the motor racing events (for example, through pollution or disruption to healthy modes of transport) is greater in city street circuits than in dedicated racing circuits away from urban areas, because of the greater density of human activity. Second, the symbolic characteristics of locations with special significance and meaning can enhance the impacts on health by adding legitimacy to the events and their sponsors, thus helping to promote products or activities that either undermine or support sustainability.

A city's public spaces are of remarkable symbolic and ideological importance since they are the primary sites of its public culture.[9] When any activity is given priority in a city's public spaces, this suggests that this activity is an acknowledged part of the local culture. Staging major motorsport events in important public places adds to the public legitimacy of the sport, and of all its attendant commercial sponsors, including motor vehicle producers, alcoholic beverage companies, and, for some events, even the tobacco industry. Beyond the specific concerns about lending public legitimacy to industries of questionable public health and environmental value, turning important public spaces over to a motorsport event—with its omnipresent advertising billboards—has the effect of advancing a city culture that favors the consumer over the citizen as the central point of city life. During the event, key public spaces become the backdrop for an advertising and marketing spectacle, a process that commodifies civic space and promotes the interests of hegemonic commercial interests while potentially undermining important public health or environmental goals.

In short, when a city's most significant public spaces are handed over to the motorsport industry and its key sponsorship interests, these spaces are imbued with the discourses of consumption and the relentless promotion of "the good life" that motorsport culture celebrates. This serves to "naturalize" these vested commercial interests as self-evident, as part of the general "common sense" of society and, therefore, as something to be taken for granted. Promotional messages that celebrate "life in the fast lane"—fast cars, hyper-masculinity, smoking, and drinking—are privileged. Those messages that might call attention to the negative aspects of privatizing public spaces are downplayed, marginalized or excluded all together. This is a point to which we will return later.

Given such concerns, and we have yet to mention the time and resources host cities must devote to setting up and removing race infrastructure, what explains the enthusiasm of local officials for hold such mega-events in significant public spaces? The short answer is that the events hold material and symbolic significance for places eager to re-image themselves and to reinvigorate their local economies. Not only do these events promise to project images of the city's signature spaces to national and global audiences, but there are also the promises of increased tourism and consumption revenues during the event itself. For this reason, the pursuit of hallmark events of sporting or other kinds—which in Australia has become a particularly vigorous contest since the early nineties' election of the brashly entrepreneurial Kennett government in the State of Victoria—is now a common part of a battery of place-competition strategies deployed by cities jostling for position in the global fray.

While major motorsports spectacles in city streets are seen as an important aspect of image making for the city involved, they can also be seen as an important promotional tool for the sport of motor racing. An excellent example of this is the motorsport event held in the Parliamentary Zone in Canberra. While it was claimed that the V8 Supercar event provided an opportunity to promote Canberra to the rest of the nation, and to showcase the national icons to the rest of the world, this argument can be reversed. Parliament House provides powerful national symbolism to help sell Australian cars and other products, and to help promote car racing. It seems likely that the organizers of the race (as well as the various sponsors) were aware of the way in which sponsors benefited from the race venue. Evidence for this can be found in the television coverage of the 2002 race. One commentator was explicit about how the location of the race gave status and national prominence to car racing:

> It's fantastic kudos for the V8 Series—to have a V8 race around the Houses of Parliament—that doesn't happen anywhere else in the world. It's a great circuit. It's hard on cars, but its great publicity for the V8 series.

In other words, it was not so much that the motor race showcased Canberra, but that the Parliamentary Zone gave status to motorsport—and its associated corporate interests.

Symbolic Environmental Messages from Motorsport

There is potential for motorsport to provide positive environmental messages.[10] For example, motor racing personalities could promote environmentally responsible behaviors such as planting trees and recycling beer bottles and cans. If, today, such opportunities for promoting environmentally and socially supportive behaviors through motorsport are as yet poorly developed, an awareness of the environmental impact of motorsport is nonetheless developing within the motorsport fraternity. For example, GreenMotorsport.com was set up to promote the concept of "environmental racing," where "zero carbon electric race cars" are operated and fossil fuel generators are discouraged in the racing paddock. In Britain, a series of "green motorsport" racing events was established in 2003.[11] And back in Australia, some motor racing personalities have attempted to reduce the environmental impact of motor racing. In fact, two famous motor racing drivers have given their support to the non-profit Formula Green Foundation, which aims to encourage organizations (starting with motor racing) to plan for an environmentally sustainable future. One initiative of this is to plant several thousand trees at the Mount Panorama Circuit in Bathurst (central western New South Wales) to offset the likely levels of carbon dioxide produced by racing drivers and spectators.[12]

However, such messages may be counteracted by the various negative messages that come from motor sport, particularly in its current forms in Australia. Also, while planting trees is a commendable environmental initiative, it is not sufficient to reverse the actual and symbolic impacts of motor racing on public and environmental health. More to the point, an increased level of carbon dioxide is only one of the environmental impacts of motorsport and motor vehicles.

While it may be possible to improve the environmental image of motor racing, this may even have long term negative impacts, particularly if it simply contributes to the glorification (or at least the legitimation of) motor vehicles.

In short, there is a growing awareness of the health damaging impacts of the automobile.[13] Not only does motorsport contribute to the glorification of an environmentally and socially unhealthy form of transport, it also celebrates a range of driving behaviors that are defined in the road safety literature as "driving violations" when practiced on public roads. These behaviors include high speed driving, tailgating, and dangerous overtaking. In normal on-road driving, all of these behaviors are related to higher accident levels.[14]

Concerns about the way in which racing car drivers act as destructive health and environmental role models also connect to both sponsorship issues and driving behaviours: the winners of car races, decorated with the names of alcohol and tobacco companies become role models for young boys who identify with the "guts and glory" images they provide. Furthermore, U.S. research indicates that racing drivers may be poor role models in terms of their own safety record on public roads.[15]

Motorsport also glorifies fast and powerful cars. If this encourages Australian drivers to purchase faster and more powerful cars, then this will obviously have negative consequences on the environment and on road safety. More powerful cars use more energy and create more pollution than cars with more modest performance. Also, not only do drivers who take more risks purchase more powerful cars, but high vehicle performance leads independently to higher levels of risk taking.[16]

In short, motorsport on street circuits in urban areas sends particular messages about road safety. Watching racing cars (especially if they are V8 Supercars that are similar in appearance to Australian road cars) drive on city streets at speeds of 160 km/h *above* the speed limit undermines the road safety message "there's no such thing as safe speeding." Motor races on public street circuits may reinforce the view of some drivers that current speed limits are too low. This also has important public health implications, if it increases public opposition to measures to reduce urban speed limits.

This is a point recently echoed by Ian Johnston, a professor in the Monash University Accident Research Unit, who recently argued that road safety policymakers should carefully consider the impact of car advertisements and motor racing spectacles that glorify speed, as well as car advertisements that use links with motorsport to sell cars through a glorification of speed. It is difficult, he argued, for road safety messages regarding the dangers of speeding to be successful when competing with powerful and well-funded advertising campaigns—campaigns which use speed as a selling feature for motor vehicles.[17]

Apart from toxic messages about road safety, the speed, power, and excitement of motorsport are also used as marketing tools for tobacco and alcohol. These two drugs have widely recognized and well-researched negative health impacts.[18] Some international sporting events are granted exemptions from the ban on tobacco advertising in Australia. Most of these events are motorsport events, including the Australian Formula One Grand Prix at Albert Park in Melbourne, the Australian Motorcycle Grand Prix at Phillip Island, the Australian Indy Car Championship at the Gold Coast, and the Rally Australia event in Western Australia. By allowing the continuation of tobacco sponsorship in international motor racing events, Australian governments also allow motorsport to undermine public health.

Research in the United States shows that motor racing has also become a high priority for brewing companies, who use motorsport sponsorship to "condition the psyches of their young targets, reshaping their social environments to actively but unobtrusively associate beer, cars, and speed."[19] Breweries seek links with sport as this offers them a macho vehicle (literally in the case of motorsport) to appeal to young males.[20] Like their American counterparts, Australian brewing companies appreciate the value of sponsorship of motor sport. The major sponsor for the Australian Grand Prix is a brewing company. An important sponsor for Australian V8 Supercar racing is another brewing company, which promotes a full-strength beer as the "Official Beer of V8 Supercars." Large signs advertising this beer are located on racing circuits, including the street circuit in Australia's Parliamentary Zone, where these signs appeared with Australia's Parliament House as a backdrop.

Alcohol sponsorship of Australian motorsport provides a tacit message associating full-strength beer with power and fast driving—an especially noxious form of lifestyle advertising. Given the popularity of motorsport for many teenagers (especially males), this is a highly questionable message for young people about to reach drinking age and driving age. Given that alcohol is the second biggest cause of drug-related death in Australia (after tobacco),[21] it is difficult to justify any activity that promotes alcohol use. It is even more difficult to justify extending government support for such activities.

Direct Consequences of Motorsport

As well as the various messages associated with motor sport, there is also evidence of direct impacts on environmental and public health. While some of these impacts may be positive, available evidence suggests that the total impact of motorsport on health and on the environment is negative. Motorsport is credited with assisting in the development of "safety features" of modern cars (e.g., better occupant protection) as well as contributing to the development of engine technology to reduce emissions. However, advances in such features of motor vehicles can still occur independently of motor sport, and it is not necessary to stage motorsport events in city street circuits for such advances to occur. The negative impacts of motorsport include air and noise pollution, disruption to medical services, increased road accidents, and the loss of freedom for pedestrians and cyclists. If equity and ecological sustainability are considerations, a better approach than protecting car occupants would be to make car travel less attractive to motorists. Staging motor racing events in city street circuits may simply add to the culture of the glorification of motor vehicles in urban areas.

There are dangers to the racing drivers and to nearby spectators from the pollution created by motor racing vehicles.[22] Exhaust fumes are a particular problem on city street circuits, where fumes are trapped within enclosed concrete race course. Another important source of pollution from racing cars is the particles of rubber from skidding tires, which produce fine black dust containing carcinogens. This dust may persist for some time after a motor racing event.[23]

Noise pollution is another environmental issue in motorsport. The noise from Formula One racing cars is similar to the noise level experienced when standing next to a jet plane taking off. The low frequency noise of racing cars also penetrates buildings more easily than high frequency noise. This problem is heightened when motor racing is held on street circuits in areas of high population density. One of the world's most extreme examples of this is in Albert Park in Melbourne, where more than 100,000 people live within three kilometers of the Grand Prix circuit and 30,000 live within one kilometer.

Motorsport events may also be linked to increased accident levels on public roads.[24] Williams and O'Neill examined the driving records of 447 licensed race car drivers in three states in the United States.[25] The racing drivers, who all held national competition licences, were more likely than other drivers to have been involved in crashes or have speeding and other driving record violations. Road accidents in South Australia around the time of the first Formula One Grand Prix in Adelaide were found to be significantly higher than average, even allowing for other factors such as increased traffic levels and weather conditions.[26] It was estimated that between $3.2m and $5.8m in accident costs could be "attributable to the glorification of speed and daring brought about by the media attention to the Grand Prix."[27] Another study found that accident rates are higher on roads that are known by motorists to be motor racing circuits at particular times of the year: "risks will be taken by motorists testing their skill as potential racing car drivers."[28]

Finally, high profile motorsport events held in urban locations can compromise opportunities for healthy activities or forms of transport. For example, motor sports events in urban parkland contribute to the long-term degradation of the quality of such parks, and interfere with other sporting activities normally occurring in them. In some cases, such as in Albert Park, active sport and informal recreation can be disrupted for months while the infrastructure for motor racing events is constructed and later removed. Major urban parkland such as Albert Park has the health-supporting role of providing a tranquil area of escape from the pressures of urban life to a place of peace and relaxation providing contact with nature. The Grand Prix event in Melbourne is incompatible with such a role, and contributes to the long-term degradation of the natural quality of an important public park. Pedestrians and cyclists can also be further marginalized by major motorsport events in urban areas, when pedestrian and cyclist access is disrupted.

Taken together, it seems clear that the geography of motorsport in Australia is a significant factor in the impact of this sport on the sustainability of Australian cities. Allowing motorsport events to be held in significant public places indicates that particular values are dominating Australian society. The glorification of motorsport through its location in significant public spaces indicates that our society privileges speed, power, private profit, energy-wasting activity, and spectacular consumption. Such glorification undermines the values of sustainability, equity, democracy, and the promotion of public health.

The Canadian sociologist Jean Harvey poses a useful question for us to consider: is the city a place to live or is it a showcase?[29] When motorsport events are located in symbolically important urban public places, this leads to the loss of these as "public" space. They become, for a time, privatized spaces, subject to the demands of the marketplace, and this occurs for much longer periods than for the period of the race itself. For several months each year, places such as Albert Park lose much of their role as urban parks, and become construction sites before they become racing circuits. And when the race begins, these important public spaces become a week-long backdrop for activities and messages that undermine the city's public and environmental health. To this end, Jean Harvey's question is apropos: do we preserve the truly public quality of urban public spaces for the well being of our citizens, or do we promote world-class sports entertainment spectacles in these spaces to attract tourist consumers (as is the prevailing philosophy among business and political elites)? Policymakers' answers to these questions will reveal much about their priorities.

As it stands, the location of some of Australia's most spectacular motorsport events indicates that state and federal governments are willing to support the staging of environmentally damaging events in significant places, places that have been imbued with a special meaning. This special meaning has been developed either through a deliberate planning process (the Parliamentary Zone), through the historical development of tourism (the Gold Coast), or through the long-term use of parkland as public recreational and sporting space within cities (e.g., Albert Park).

If we accept the argument that the location of motorsport spectacles in Australian cities boosts the image of the sport of motor racing and reinforces all of its negative impacts, then there may be an important lesson here in terms of making our cities healthier and more sustainable. If motorsport spectacles in a city's public spaces can be moved to purpose built racing circuits away from urban areas, these major events can be replaced with other events (including other sporting events) that are largely ecologically sustainable and help promote activities that have positive environmental and public health messages. Examples of such activities include major international bicycle racing events or walking or running racing events in city street circuits. Not only would these have minimal environmental impacts compared with motorsport events, but they would also be helping to raise the public profile and acceptance of active and sustainable modes of transport.

Notes

1. E. Fredline and B. Faulkner, "Variations in Residents" Reactions to Major Motorsports Events: Why Residents Perceive the Impacts of Events Differently," *Event Management* 7 (2001): 115-25.

2. An exception here is Lowes' work which examines the conflict that arose between a Vancouver, Canada, community and the civic and corporate boosters who wanted to move the Molson Indy Vancouver motorsport event to their neighborhood park. See Mark Lowes, *Indy Dreams and Urban Nightmares: Speed Merchants, Spectacle, and the Struggle over Public Space in the World-Class City* (Toronto: University of Toronto Press, 2002).

3. Helen Lenskyj, *Inside the Olympic Industry* (Albany: SUNY Press, 2000).

4. K. Robertson, "Downtown Redevelopment Strategies in the United States: An End-Of-the-Century Assessment," *Journal of the American Planning Association* 61, no. 4 (1995): 429-37.

5. Richard Pound, "The IOC and the Environment," *Olympic Message* 35 (March 1993).

6. Sydney Olympic Bid Committee. "Environmental Guidelines for the Summer Olympic Games," http://www.greenpeace.org.au/olympics/reports/enviroguide.pdf.

7. Helen Lenskyj, "Sport and Corporate Environmentalism," *International Review for the Sociology of Sport* 33, no. 4 (1998): 341-54.

8. Australian Conservation Foundation, ACF Policy Statement: SPORT, http://www.acfonline.org.au/asp/pages/document.asp?IdDoc=743.

9. Sharon Zukin, *The Cultures of Cities* (London: Blackwell, 1995).

10. Paul Tranter, "Motor Racing in Australia: Health Damaging or Health Promoting?" *Australian Journal of Primary Health* 9, no. 1 (2003): 50-58; Procar Australia, "Formula Green: Brock and Brabham target help for environment," accessed online at http://www.procar.com.au/newsitem.asp?news_id=1159&event_id=38.

11. Green Motorsport, "GreenMotorsport.com—The Home of Environmentally Friendly Motorsport on the Web," http://www.btinternet.com/~keneth.foat/greenmotorsport.

12. Procar Australia, "Formula Green: Brock and Brabham Target Help for Environment," http://www.procar.com.au/newsitem.asp?news_id=1159&event_id=38.

13. C. Dora, "A Different Route to Health: Implications of Transport Policies," *British Medical Journal* 318 (1999): 1686-1689; F. Godlee, "Transport: A Public Health Issue," *British Medical Journal* 304, no. 6818 (1992): 48-50; A. Haines, T. McMichael, R. Anderson, and J. Houghton, "Fossil Fuels, Transport and Public Health," *British Medical Journal* 321 (2002): 1168-69; C. Mason, "Transport and Health: En Route to a Healthier Australia?" *The Medical Journal of Australia* 172, no. 5 (2000): 230-32.

14. M. Horswill, "How to Have a Car Crash," Public Lecture 27 February 2001, Department of Psychology, University of Reading; D., Parker, J.T., Reason, A.S.R. Manstead, and S.G. Stradling, "Driving Errors, Driving Violations and Accident Involvement," *Ergonomics* 38, no. 5 (1995): 1036-48; D. Parker and S. Stradling, *Influencing Driver Attitudes and Behaviour: Road Safety Research Report No. 17* (2001) (London, Department of the Environment, Transport and the Regions (DETR).

15. A.F. Williams, and B.O'Neill, "On-the-Road Driving Records of Licensed Race Drivers," *Accident Analysis and Prevention* 6 (1974): 263-70.

16. M.S. Horswill, and M.E. Coster, "The Effect of Vehicle Characteristics on Driver's Risk-Taking Behaviour," *Ergonomics* 45, no. 2 (2002): 85-104.

17. I. Johnston, "Educating Drivers About Speed," in Australian College of Road Safety *Road Safety Workshop on Speed* (National Museum, Canberra, 2003).

18. T.N. Chikritzhs, H.A. Jonas, T.R., Stockwell, P.F. Heale, and P.M. Dietze, "Mortality and Life-Years Lost Due to Alcohol: A Comparison of Acute and Chronic Causes," *The Medical Journal of Australia* 174, no. 6 (2001): 281-84; D.J. Collins, and H.M. Lapsley, *The Social Costs of Drug Abuse in Australia 1988 and 1992,* accessed online at http://www.health.gov.au/pubhlth/publicat/document/mono30.pdf; Y.F. Tai, J.B. Saunders, and D.S. Celermajer, "Collateral Damage from Alcohol Abuse: The Enormous Cost to Australia," *The Medical Journal of Australia* 168, no. 1 (1998): 6-7; M. Teesson, W. Hall, M. Lynskey, and L. Degemhardt, "Alcohol and Drug-Use Disorders in Australia: Implications of the National Survey of Mental Health and Wellbeing," *The Australian and New Zealand Journal of Psychiatry* 34, no. 2 (2000): 206-13.

19. D.R. Buchanan, and J. Lev, *Beer and Fast Cars: How Brewers Target Blue-collar Youth through Motor Sport Sponsorships* (Washington, DC: AAA Foundation for Traffic Safety, 1988), 2; see also Jim Wright, *Fixin' to Git* (London: Duke University Press, 2002).

20. J. Crompton, "Sponsorship of Sport by Tobacco and Alcohol Companies: A Review of the Issues," *Journal of Sport and Social Issues* 17 (1993): 148-67.

21. R.P. Mattick, and T. Jarvis, *An Outline for the Management of Alcohol Problems: Quality Assurance Project* (Canberra, AGPS, 1993).

22. D. Graham-Rowe, "Too Hot to Handle—It's Not Just the Speed That Makes Motor Racing Dangerous," *New Scientist* 170, no. 2293 (2001): 13; C. Urie, *Doctors' Working Group Report on the Health Impact of the Albert Park Grand Prix* (Melbourne, 1994), http://www.save-albert-park.org.au/sapweb/pDW1.html.

23. C. Urie, *Doctors' Working Group Report.*

24. G. Bannerman, *Racetrack in the Park—Success or Failure: An Accident Analysis of the Realigned Public Roads in Albert Park Reserve, May 1995 - December 1999* (Melbourne, 2000); A. Fisher, J. Hatch, and B. Paix, "Road Accidents and the Grand Prix," in *The Adelaide Grand Prix: the Impact of a Special Event*, ed. T.J. Mules, 151-68 (Adelaide: Centre for South Australian Economic Studies, 1986); A.F. Williams, and B. O'Neill, "On-The-Road Driving Records," 263-70.

25. Williams, and B. O'Neill, "On-the-Road Driving Records," 263-70.

26. A. Fisher, J. Hatch, and B. Paix, "Road Accidents and the Grand Prix," 151.

27. J.P.A. Burns, J. Hatch, and T.J. Mules, eds. *The Adelaide Grand Prix: The Impact of a Special Event* (Adelaide, Centre for South Australian Economic Studies, 1986), 27.

28. C. Urie, *Doctors Working Group Report.*

29. Jean Harvey, "Sports and Recreation: Entertainment or Social Right?" *Horizons* 5, no. 1 (2002), 26-28.

Chapter 9

From "Dangerous Classes" to "Quiet Rebels": Politics of the Urban Subaltern in the Global South

Asef Bayat[1]

Notwithstanding some overestimated claims of the globalization thesis (such as the waning role of the nation-states, the breakdown of borders, the homogeneity of lifestyles, cultures, political systems, and so on),[2] it is generally agreed that the economics of globalization, comprised of a global market "discipline," flexible accumulation, and "financial deepening," has had a profound impact on the post-colonial societies.[3] One major consequence of the new global restructuring in the developing countries has been a double process of, on the one hand, integration and, on the other, social exclusion and informalization.

The historic shift in the periphery from socialist and populist regimes to liberal economic policies, through the Structural Adjustment Program, has led to the erosion of much of the social contract, collective responsibility, and welfare state structures. Thus, millions of people in the global South who depended on state provisions must now rely on their own to survive. Deregulation of prices on housing, rent, and utilities jeopardize many poor people's security of tenure, subjecting them to the risk of homelessness. Reduction of spending on social programs has meant reduced access to decent education, health care, urban development, and government housing. Gradual removal of subsidies on bread, bus fares, or petrol has affected radically the living standards of millions of vulnerable groups. In the meantime, in a drive for privatization, public sectors have either been sold out or "reformed," which in either case has caused massive layoffs without a clear prospect of boosting the economy and creating viable jobs. According to the World Bank, in the early 1990s, during the transition to market economies in post-socialist, adjusting Latin American and Middle Eastern countries, formal employment fell by 5-15 percent.[4] In Africa the number of unemployed grew by 10 percent more every year throughout the 1980s, while labor absorption in the formal wage sector kept declining.[5] By the late 1990s, a staggering 1 billion workers, representing one-third of the world's labor force, most

177

of them in the South, were either unemployed or underemployed.[6] A large number of once-educated, well-to-do middle classes (government employees and students), public sector workers, as well as segments of the peasantry have been pushed to the ranks of the urban poor in labor and housing markets.

Thus, accompanied with the development of highly affluent groups, the new structuring has given rise to the growth of a marginalized and deinstitutionalized subaltern in Third World cities. There are now an increasing number of unemployed, partially employed, casual labor, street subsistence workers, street children, and members of the underworld—groups that are interchangeably referred to as "urban marginals," "urban disenfranchised" and the "urban poor." Such socially excluded and informal groups are by no means new historical phenomena. However, the recent global restructuring seems to have intensified and extended their operation. Only in the recent 1998 financial crisis at least two million people lost their jobs in South Korea, three million in Thailand, and a staggering ten million in Indonesia.[7] What is novel about this era is the marginalization of large segments of the middle classes. Slum dwelling, casual work, and street hawking are no longer the characteristics of the traditional poor, but have spread also among educated young people with higher status, aspirations, and social skills.

How do these growing urban disenfranchised in the Third World respond to the larger social processes that affect their lives, if and when they do? Those who promote globalization suggest that the trickle-down of an eventual national economic growth will in the long run compensate for the inevitable sacrifices that the poor make in the transitional phase. In the meantime, social funds and NGOs are encouraged to create jobs and assist in social programs to alleviate hardship and avert possible social unrest. Indeed, some view the upsurge of the (NGOs) in the South since the 1980s as a manifestation of organized activism and grassroots institutions for social development. However, granting that the development NGOs vary considerably, their potential for independent and democratic organization of development for the poor has generally been overestimated. Advocates simply tend to expect too much from the development NGOs, and by doing so underestimate their structural constraints (e.g., organizational rationale, unaccountability, and professional middle-class leadership) for a meaningful development strategy.[8] My own work on Middle Eastern development NGOs supports this conclusion. The professionalization of the NGOs tends to diminish the mobilizational feature of grassroots activism, at the same time it establishes new forms of clientelism.[9]

Many on the left point to a number of "reactive movements" (identity politics), which, they say, challenge globalization by appropriating technologies that this phenomenon is offering. While Melucci's "new social movements" focus exclusively on the "highly differentiated" western societies, other sociologists like Manuel Castells and Ankie Hoogvelt, taking a southern perspective, suggest religious, ethnic, and feminist movements as well as the Latin American post-development ideas as the backbone of the anti-globalization trend.[10] Identity movements do take up some of the challenges of globalization in post-colonial societies. However, they reflect more the sentiments of middle-class intellectuals than the actual everyday practices of the ordinary people. What do the grassroots think or do? What form of politics, if any at all, do the urban marginalized groups espouse? This chapter attempts to address these questions. Critically navigating through the prevailing models, including culture of poverty, survival strategy, urban social movements, and everyday resistance, I would suggest that the new global restructuring is reproducing subjectivities (marginalized and deinstitutionalized groups such as the unemployed, casual labor, street subsistence workers, and street children), social space and thus terrain of political struggles that current theoretical perspectives cannot on their own account for. I propose an alternative outlook—"quiet encroachment"—that, I think, might be more pertinent to examine the activism of the marginalized groups in the cities of the global South. Quiet encroachment refers to non-collective but prolonged direct action by individuals and families to acquire the basic necessities of their lives (land for shelter, urban collective consumption, informal jobs, business opportunities, and public space) in a quiet and unassuming, but nonetheless illegal fashion. Although this perspective has emerged out of my observation of urban processes in the Middle East, nevertheless it might have relevance to other Third World cities.

Prevailing Perspectives

The sociological examination of urban "marginality" dates back to nineteenth-century Europe. Problems associated with urbanization (urban crime, inner-city conditions, unemployment, migration, cultural duality, and so on) acquired scientific treatment from the social science community. George Simmel's "The Stranger" dealt with sociopsychological traits of new urban settlers, and Durkheim was particularly keen on their "anomie." Such a conceptualization later informed the work of the Chicago School of Sociology and Urban Study in the USA during the 1920s and 1930s when Chicago acted as the laboratory to examine the social being of many ethnic migrants who flowed into this city. For scholars in the Chicago School, many immigrants were "marginals"—a trait that was embedded in their social structure. Marginal personality was a manifestation of cultural hybridity, living on the margin of two cultures without being a full member of either.[11]

Unlike the Chicago School functionalists, mainstream Marxism, however, did not take the issue seriously. Relative to the centrality of working as the agent of social transformation, Marxist theory either ignored or described the urban poor as "lumpenproletariat," a term that included "nonproletarian" urban groups. This nomenclature gave rise, as Hall Draper, a close reader of Marx's work, notes, to "endless misunderstanding and mistranslation."[12] For Marx, lumpenproletariat was a political economy category. It referred to propertyless people who did not produce—"nonworking proletariat," obsolete social elements such as beggars, thieves, thugs, and criminals who were in general poor but lived on the labor of other working people. Due to such economic existence, they were said to follow a politics of non-commitment which in the end may work against the interests of the producing classes.[13] It is this uncertain politics that renders lumpenproletariat, for both Marx and Engels, the "social scum," "refuse of all classes," the "dangerous classes." Although Marx theorized them later in terms of the "reserve army of labor," thus a segment of the working class, nevertheless controversy continued as to the relevance of this concept in the current capitalist structuring as it does not leave much chance for these people to be re-employed. Some suggested that far from being on "reserve," the urban disenfranchised were integrated into the capitalist relations.[14] Even with Frantz Fanon's passionate defense of lumpenproletariat as the revolutionary force in the colonies, the Communist parties in the Third World did not go beyond looking at the urban disenfranchised as the "tolling masses" who might have the potential for alliance with the working class.[15]

However, the continuous prominence of the "informals" (which in many developing economies clearly outweighed the industrial working class) and their assumed threat to political stability in the developing countries brought back them to academic analysis. Against the descriptive term of "informals" and the derogatory one of "lumpenproletariat," some opted for the notion of "proto-proletariat" while others preferred "urban poor"—concepts that recognized some degree of agency.[16]

Yet, the more serious studies on the social conditions and the politics of the urban subaltern in the Third World emerged as a major field for U.S. social scientists during the 1960s. Modernization and urban migration in the developing countries had caused a dramatic expansion of impoverished urban settlements; and the growing urban "underclass" was thought to provide a breeding ground for the spread of radical guerrilla movements, which in the midst of the Cold War were perceived to jeopardize the political interest of the United States and those of the local elites. The Chinese Revolution of 1949, the Cuban Revolution of 1959, and the growing guerrilla movements in parts of the Third World were taken as convincing proof by political observers. Latin America, however, acted as a laboratory for the much debated theories about the social and political behavior of the urban underclass. Studies by Samuel Huntington and Joan Nelson, among others, reflected the concerns of the time.[17] Here the prevailing attention of scholarship focused on the poor's "political threat" to the existing order. Scholars, mostly political scientists, were preoccupied with the question of whether the migrant poor constituted a destabilizing force, but such preoccupations often overlooked the dynamics of the poor's everyday life. Many viewed the politics of the poor in the binary terms of the revolutionary/passive dichotomy, consequently limiting the possibility of looking at the matter in a different light. Essentialism informed both sides of the controversy. The ensuing debates were galvanized into four identifiable perspectives: the "passive poor," "survival strategy," "urban territorial movement," and "everyday resistance" models.

The Passive Poor

While some observers working in the functionalist paradigm still viewed the urban poor as essentially disruptive and imbued with the sentiments of anomie, many still considered the poor as a politically passive group struggling simply to make ends meet. Oscar Lewis's theory of the "culture of poverty," based upon ethnographies among the urban poor in Puerto Rico and Mexico offered a scientific legitimacy to such notion.[18] Highlighting certain cultural/psychological essentials as components of a culture of poverty—fatalism, rootlessness, unadaptability, traditionalism, criminality, lack of ambition, hopelessness, and so on—Lewis unintentionally extended the notion of the "passive poor." With an underlying emphasis on identifying the "marginal man" as cultural type, the "culture of poverty" remained a dominant perspective for many years, informing much of anti-poverty discourse and policies in the United States as well as the perception of Third World elites toward the poor.

The conceptual weaknesses of "culture of poverty," despite Lewis's empathy with the poor, became clear before long. Simply, Lewis essentialized the culture of the poor, since his "culture of poverty" was only one type of culture among many. Lewis's generalization disregarded the varying ways in which the poor in different cultures handle poverty. Critiques such as Worsley charged Lewis as a middle-class scholar who blamed the poor for their poverty and passivity.[19] Interestingly, Lewis's conceptualization shared many traits with those of the Chicago School urban sociologists such as Robert Park, Everett Stonequist, and even the thinkers of the earlier generation like Simmel. Noted urban researcher Janice Perlman's powerful critique of *The Myth of Marginality*, together with Manuel Castells' critical contributions, undermined this outlook in academia, if not among officialdom.[20] They demonstrated the myth of marginality as an instrument of social control of the poor, and the marginalized poor as a product of capitalist social structure.

The Surviving Poor

As such the "survival strategy" did not directly deal with the politics of the poor, but a relevant, implicit conceptual assumption underlies this perspective. The survival strategy model goes one step forward, implying that although the poor are powerless, nevertheless they do not sit around waiting for their fate to determine their lives. Rather they are active in their own way to ensure their survival. Thus, to counter unemployment or price increases, they often resort to theft, begging, prostitution, or the reorientation of their consumption pattern; to respond to famine and war, they choose to leave their home places even if emigration is discouraged by the authorities. In this thinking, the poor are seen to survive and live their lives; however, their survival is at a cost to themselves or their fellow humans.[21] While resort to coping mechanisms in real life seems quite widespread among the poor in many cultures, nevertheless, an overemphasis on the language of survival strategy may contribute to maintaining the image of the poor as victims, denying them any agency.[22] The fact is that the poor also strive to resist and make advances in their lives when the opportunity arises. Beyond that, evidence in many parts of the world does indicate that they also create opportunities for advancement—they organize and get involved in contentious politics. The notion "empowerment," developed by John Friedman, an urban planning professor from UCLA, is just one indication of such opportunity-creating tendency of the poor.[23] It describes poor people's self-organization for collective survival through the institution of the household as the central element for the production of livelihood, the principle of moral economy (trust, reciprocity, voluntarism) and the utilization of their "social power" (free time, social skill, networking. associations and instruments of production).

The Political Poor

Critiques of "passive poor" and "culture of poverty" models opened the way for the development of an outlook in which the urban subaltern emerged as political actors—the "urban territorial movement" standpoint. Perlman, Castells, and some other scholars of Latin America insisted that the poor were not marginal, but integrated into society. Rather, they argued, the poor were "marginalized"—economically exploited, politically repressed, socially stigmatized, and culturally excluded from a closed social system. Not only did the poor participate in party politics, elections and mainstream economic activities, more importantly, they established their own territorial social movements. Thus community associations, barrios, consumer organizations, soup kitchens, squatter support groups, church activities, and the like were understood as manifesting organized and territorially based movements of the poor who strive for "social transformation"[24] (according to Castells), "emancipation"[25] (according to Schuurman and Van Naerssen), or an alternative to the tyranny of modernity, in the words of John Friedmann.[26] In their immediate day-to-day activities, the poor struggle for a share in urban services, or "collective consumption."

The territorial character of these movements results from the mode of existence of the agents—the urban poor. Although quite differentiated (in terms of income, status, occupation, and production relations), the urban poor nevertheless are thought to share a common place of residence, community. Shared space and the needs associated with common property, then, offer these people the possibility of "spatial solidarity."[27] The attempts to highlight contentious politics as well as noncontentious cooperation among the urban poor undercut drastically both the "culture of poverty" and "survivalist" arguments, granting a significant agency to the urban disenfranchised. However, the "urban movement perspective" appears largely to be a Latin American model rooted in the sociopolitical conditions of this region. Not surprisingly, it is a perspective that has been offered primarily by the scholars working on Latin America.[28] Local soup kitchens, neighborhood associations, church groups or street trade unionism are hardly common phenomena in, say, the Middle East, Asia, or Africa (with the exception of countries like India and South Africa). In the Middle East, for instance, the prevalence of authoritarian states (of despotic, populist, or dictatorial kinds), which are wary of civil associations, together with the strength of family and kinship relations, render primary solidarities more pertinent than secondary associations and social movements.[29] While collective entities such as the charity organizations and mosque associations do exist, they rarely lead to political mobilization of the popular classes. Although associations based upon neighborly relations, home people or traditional credit systems are quite common, nevertheless, social networks which extend beyond kinship and ethnicity remain largely casual, unstructured, and paternalistic.[30]

Some scholars tend to present the Islamist movements in the region as the Middle Eastern model of urban social movements. A few functional resemblances notwithstanding, the fact remains that the identity of Islamism does not derive from its particular concern for the urban disenfranchised. Islamism in general has broader aims and objectives. Unlike the Catholic Church, in particular the Liberation Theology Movement, the Islamist movements tend to mobilize often not the poor but largely the educated middle classes, which they view as the main agents of political change.[31] So, it is mainly in exceptional circumstances (e.g., crises and revolutionary situations) that some degree of mobilization and contentious politics are encouraged, as in revolutionary Iran and the crisis-stricken Algeria. It is true that the Islamist Rifah Party in Turkey mobilized slum dwellers, but this was so primarily because Turkey's free electoral system had granted the urban marginals voting power and thus bargaining leverage which the Islamists as a legitimate political party could utilize.

Still, it must be realized that the prevalence of urban movements in Latin America varies considerably. For example, due to the multiplicity of competing interest groups (government, private interests, and others) the poor have had more opportunity for collective action in Peru than in Brazil, where the extremity of constraints forced the poor to "seek their betterment through the paternalistic, individualistic channels of favors and exchange of interests."[32] In Chile, in the episodes of political openness and radical groupings, the poor have been organized more extensively.

The Resisting Poor

The dearth of conventional collective action—in particular contentious protests among the subaltern groups (the poor, peasants, and women) in the developing countries—together with a disillusionment with dominant socialist parties, pushed many radical observers to "discover" and highlight different types of activism, however small-scale, local, or even individualistic. Such a quest, meanwhile, both contributed to and benefited from the upsurge of theoretical paradigms, during the 1980s, associated with poststructuralism which rendered micro-politics and "everyday resistance" a popular perspective. The departure of urban political scientist James Scott from a structuralist position in studying the behavior of the peasantry in Asia into a more ethnographic method of focusing on individual reactions of peasants contributed considerably to this shift of paradigm.[33] In the meantime. Foucault's "decentered" notion of power together with a revival of neo-Gramscian politics of culture (hegemony) offered a key theoretical backing for micro-politics and thus the "resistance" paradigm.

The notion of "resistance" came to stress that power and counter-power were riot in binary opposition, but in a decoupled, complex, ambivalent and perpetual "dance of control."[34] It based itself on the idea that "wherever there is power there is resistance": although the latter consisted largely of small-scale, everyday, tiny activities which the agents could afford to articulate given their political constraints. Such a perception of resistance penetrated not only the peasant studies which until then had remained *atheoretical*, but a variety of fields including labor studies, identity politics, ethnicity, women's studies, education, and studies of the urban subaltern.

Thus multiple research discussed how relating stories about miracles "gives voice to popular resistance";[35] how disenfranchised women resisted patriarchy by relating folk-tales, songs, or by pretending to be possessed or crazy;[36] how the extension of familyhood among the urban poor represented an "avenue of political participation."[37] The relationships between Filipino bar girls and western men were discussed not simply in terms of total domination, but in complex and contingent fashion;[38] and the veiling of Muslim working women is represented not in simple terms of submission, but in ambivalent terms of protest and cooptation—hence an "accommodating protest."[39] Indeed, on occasions, both veiling and unveiling were simultaneously considered as symbols of resistance!

Undoubtedly such an attempt to grant agency to the subjects that until then were depicted as "passive poor," "submissive women," "apolitical peasant," and "oppressed worker" was a positive improvement. The resistance paradigm helps to uncover the complexity of power relations in society, in general, and the politics of the subaltern, in particular. It tells us that we may not expect a universalized form of struggle; that totalizing pictures often distort variations in people's perceptions about change: that the local should be recognized as a significant site of struggle as well as a unit of analysis; that organized collective action may not be possible everywhere, and thus alternative forms of struggles must be discovered and acknowledged: that organized protest as such may not necessarily be privileged in the situations where suppression rules. The value of a more flexible, small-scale, and bureaucratic activism should, therefore, be acknowledged.[40] These are some of the issues that critiques of poststructuralist advocates of "resistance" ignore.[41]

Yet a number of conceptual and political problems also emerge from this paradigm. The immediate trouble is how to conceptualize resistance, its relation to power, domination, and submission. James Scott seems to be clear as to what he means by the term:

Class resistance includes any act(s) by members) of a subordinate class that is or are intended either to mitigate or deny claims (for example, rents, taxes, prestige) made on that class by superordinate classes (for example, landlords, large farmers. the state) or to advance its own claims (for example. work, land, charity respect) vis-à-vis these superordinate classes.[42]

However, the phrase "any act" blocks delineation between the qualitatively diverse forms of activities that Scott lists. Are we not to distinguish between large-scale collective action and individual acts, say, of tax dodging? Do reciting poetry in private, however subversive sounding, and armed struggle have identical value? Should we not expect unequal effectiveness and implications from such different acts? Scott was aware of this, and so agreed with those who had made distinctions between different types of resistance—for example, "real resistance" referring to organized, systematic, preplanned, or selfless acts with revolutionary consequences, and "token resistance" pointing to unorganized incidental acts without any revolutionary consequences, and which are accommodated in the power structure.[43] Yet, he insisted that "token resistance" is no less real than "real resistance." Scott's followers, however, continued to make further distinctions. For instance, Nathan Brown, a political scientist specializing in Egyptian peasant politics, identifies three forms of politics: atomistic (politics of individuals and small groups with obscure content), communal (a group effort to disrupt the system, like slowing down production and so on), and revolt (just short of revolution to negate the system).[44]

Beyond this, many resistance writers tend to confuse awareness about oppression with acts of resistance against it. The fact that poor women sing songs about their plight or ridicule men in their private gatherings indicates their understanding of gender dynamics. This, however, does not mean that they are involved in acts of resistance: nor the miracle stories of the poor urbanites who imagine the saints to come and punish the strong. Such an understanding of "resistance" fails to capture the extremely complex interplay of conflict and consent, and ideas and action operating within the systems of power. Indeed, the link between consciousness and action remains a major sociological dilemma.[45]

Scott makes it clear that resistance is an intentional act. In Weberian tradition, he takes the meaning of action as a crucial element. This intentionality, while significant in itself, obviously leaves out many types of individual and collective activities whose intended and unintended consequences do not correspond. In Cairo or Tehran, for example, many poor families tap electricity and running water illegally from the municipality despite their awareness of their illegal behavior. Yet, they do not steal urban services in order to express their defiance vis-à-vis the authorities. Rather, they do it because they feel the necessity of those services for a decent life; because they find no other way to acquire them. But these very mundane acts when continued are followed by significant changes in the urban structure, social policy, and in the actors' own lives. Hence, the significance of the unintended consequences of agents' daily activities. In fact, many authors in the resistance paradigm have simply abandoned intent and meaning, focusing instead eclectically on both intended and unintended practices as manifestation of "resistance."

There is still a further question. Does resistance mean defending an already achieved gain (in Scott's terms denying claims made by dominant groups over the subordinate ones) or making fresh demands (to "advance its own claims"), what I like to call "encroachment." In much of the resistance literature this distinction is missing. Although one might imagine moments of overlap, the two strategies, however, follow different political consequences; this is so in particular when we view them in relation to the strategies of dominant power. Lenin's *What Is to Be Done* is devoted to the discussion of these two strategies, termed "economism/trade unionism" and "social democratic/party politics."[46]

Whatever one may think about the Leninist/vanguardist paradigm, it was one that corresponded to a particular theory of the state and power (a capitalist state to be seized by a mass movement led by the working-class party). In addition, it was clear where this strategy wanted to take the working class (to establish a socialist state). Now, what is the perception of the state in the "resistance" paradigm? What is the strategic aim in this perspective? Where does the resistance paradigm want to take its agents/subjects, beyond "prevent[ing] the wont and promis[ing] something better"?[47]

Much of the literature of resistance is based upon a notion of power that Foucault has articulated, that power is everywhere, that it "circulates." and is never "localized here and there, never in anybody's hands."[48] Such a formulation is surely instructive in transcending the myth of powerlessness of the ordinary and in recognizing their agency. Yet, this "decentered" notion of power, shared by many poststructuralist resistance" writers, underestimates state power, notably its class dimension, since it fails to see that although power circulates, it does so unevenly—in some places it is far weightier, more concentrated and "thicker," so to speak, than in others. In other words, like it or not, the state does matter and one needs to take that into account when discussing the potentials of urban subaltern activism. While Foucault insists that resistance is real when it occurs outside and independent from the systems of power, the perception of power which informs the "resistance" literature leaves little room for an analysis of the state as a system of power. It is, therefore, not accidental that a theory of the state and the possibility of cooptation is absent in almost all accounts of "resistance." Consequently, the acts of resistance, cherished so dearly, float around aimlessly in an unknown, uncertain and ambivalent universe of power relations, with an end result of an unsettled and tense accommodation with the existing power arrangement.

Lack of a clear concept of resistance, moreover, leads writers in this genre to often overestimate and read too much into the acts of the agents. The result is that almost any act of the subjects potentially becomes one of "resistance." Determined to discover the "inevitable" acts of resistance, poststructuralist writers often come to "replace their subject."[49] While they attempt to challenge the essentialism of such perspectives as "passive poor," "submissive Muslim women," and "inactive masses," they tend to fall into the trap of essentialism in reverse—

by reading too much into the ordinary behavior, interpreting it as necessarily conscious or contentious acts of defiance. This is so because they overlook the crucial fact that these acts occur mostly within the prevailing systems of power.

For example, some of the lower class's activities in the Middle East, which some authors read as "resistance," "intimate politics" of defiance, or "avenues of participation," may actually contribute to the stability and legitimacy of the state.[50] The fact that people are able to help themselves and extend their networks surely shows their daily activism and struggles. However, by doing so the actors may hardly win any space from the state (or other sources of power, like capital and patriarchy)—they are not necessarily challenging domination. In fact, governments often encourage self-help and local initiatives so long as they do not become oppositional. They do so in order to shift some of their burdens of social welfare provision and responsibilities onto the individual citizens. The proliferation of many NGOs in the global South represents a good indicator. In short, much of the resistance literature confuses what one might consider as coping strategies (when the survival of the agents is secured at the cost of themselves or that of fellow humans) and effective participation or subversion of domination.

There is a last question. If the poor are always able to resist in many ways (by discourse or actions, individual or collective, overt or covert) the systems of domination, then what is the need to assist them? If they are already politically able citizens, why should we expect the state or any other agency to empower them? Misreading the behavior of the poor may, in fact, frustrate our moral responsibility toward the vulnerable. As Michael Brown notes, when you "elevate the small injuries of childhood to the same moral status as the suffering of the truly oppressed," you are committing "a savage leveling that diminishes rather than intensifies our sensitivities to injustice."[51]

The Quiet Encroachment of the Ordinary

Given the shortcomings of the prevailing perspectives—that is, the essentialism of the "passive poor," reductionism of the "surviving poor," Latino-centrist of the "political poor" and conceptual perplexity of "resistance literature"—I want to assess the politics of the urban marginals in the developing world from a different angle, in terms of "the quiet encroachment of the ordinary." I believe that this notion might overcome some of those inadequacies, and capture better the essence of urban subaltern politics in the conditions of globalization.[52]

The notion of "quiet encroachment" describes the silent, protracted but pervasive advancement of the ordinary people on the propertied and powerful in order to survive and improve their lives. This is marked by quiet, largely atomized and prolonged mobilization with episodic collective action—open and fleeting struggles without clear leadership, ideology, or structured organization. While the quiet encroachment cannot be considered as a "social movement" as such, it is also distinct from survival strategies or "everyday resistance" in that, first, the struggles and gains of the agents are not at the cost of fellow poor or themselves, but of the state, the rich, and the powerful. Thus, in order to light their shelter, the urban poor tap electricity not from their neighbors, but from the municipal power poles; or to raise their living standards, they would not prevent their children from attending school in order to work, but rather squeeze the timing of their formal job, in order to carry on their secondary work in the informal sector.

In addition, these struggles are seen not necessarily as defensive merely in the realm of resistance, but cumulatively encroaching, meaning that the actors tend to expand their space by winning new positions to move on. This type of quiet and gradual grassroots activism tends to contest many fundamental aspects of the state prerogatives, including the meaning of order, control of public space, of public and private goods, and the relevance of modernity.

I am referring to the life-long struggles of the floating social clusters—the migrants, refugees, unemployed, squatters, street vendors, street children, and other marginalized groups, whose growth has been accelerated by the process of economic globalization. I have in mind the long processes in which millions of men and women embark on long migratory journeys, scattering in remote and often alien environs, acquiring work, shelter, land, and living amenities. The rural migrants encroach on the cities and their collective consumption, the refugees and international migrants on host states and their provisions, the squatters on public and private lands or ready-made homes, and the unemployed, as street subsistence workers, on the public space and business opportunity created by shopkeepers. And all of them tend to challenge the notions of order, modern city, and urban governance espoused by the Third World political elites.

The concrete forms of encroachments vary considerably. Post-revolution Iran saw an unprecedented colonization, mostly by the poor, of public and private urban land, apartments, hotels, street sidewalks, and public utilities. Between 1980 and 1992, despite the government's opposition, the land area of Tehran expanded from 200 to 600 km^2, and well over one hundred mostly informal communities were created in and around greater Tehran.[53] The actors of the massive informal economy extended beyond the typical marginal poor to include also the new "lumpen middle class," the educated salary-earners whose public sector position rapidly declined during the 1980s. In a more dramatic case, millions of rural migrants, the urban poor and the middle-class poor have quietly claimed cemeteries, roof tops and state/public lands on the outskirts of Cairo, creating well over 100 spontaneous communities which house over 5 million people. Once settled, encroachments still continue in many directions. Against formal terms and conditions, the residents then add rooms, balconies, and extra space in and on buildings. Those who have formally been given housing in public projects built by the state, illegally redesign and rearrange their space to suite their needs by erecting partitions, and by adding and inventing new space.[54] Often whole communities emerge as a result of intense struggles and negotiations between the poor and the authorities in their daily lives.[55]

At the same time, the encroachers have forced the authorities to extend urban services to their neighborhoods by otherwise tapping them illegally, using them free of charge. However, once utilities are installed many simply refuse to pay for their use. Some 40 percent of poor residents of Hayy Assaloum, a south Beirut informal community, refuse to pay their electricity bills. The cost of unpaid water charges in the Egyptian city of Alexandria amounts to US $3 million a year. Similar stories are reported in urban Chile and South Africa, where the poor have periodically refused to pay for urban public services after struggling to acquire them, often against the authorities' will. Hundreds of thousands of street vendors in Cairo, Istanbul, and Tehran have occupied the streets in the main commercial centers, infringing on favorable business opportunities the shopkeepers have generated. Thousands of inhabitants in these cities subsist on tips from parking cars in streets which they control and organize in such elaborate ways as to create maximum parking space. Finally, as in many Third World cities such as those in South Korea, the encroachment of the street vendors on copyrights of labels and trademarks has caused inevitable protests by the multinational companies.

These actors carry out their activities not as a deliberate political act; rather, they are driven by the force of necessity—the necessity to survive and improve a dignified life. Necessity is the notion that justifies their often unlawful acts as moral and even "natural" ways to maintain a life with dignity. Yet, these very simple and seemingly mundane practices tend to shift them into the realm of contentious politics. The contenders get engaged in collective action and see their actions and themselves as political chiefly when they are confronted by those who threaten their gains. Hence a key attribute of the quiet encroachment is that while advances are made quietly, individually and gradually, the defense of their gains is often, although not always, collective and audible.

Driven by the force of necessity (effects of economic restructuring, agricultural failure. physical hardship, war and displacement), they set out on their ventures rather individually, often organized around kinship ties, and without much clamor. They even deliberately avoid collective effort, large-scale operations, commotion, and publicity. At times the squatters, for instance, prevent others from joining them in specific areas; and vendors discourage their counterparts from settling in the same vicinity. Many even hesitate to share information about their strategies of acquiring urban services with similar groups. Yet as these seemingly desperate individuals and families pursue similar paths, their sheer cumulative scores turn them into an eventual social force. This is another feature of the quiet encroachment.

But why individual and quiet direct action, instead of collective demand-making? Unlike the factory workers, students, or professionals, these people represent groups in flux and structurally operate largely outside institutional mechanisms through which they can express grievance and enforce demands. They lack an organizational power of disruption—the possibility or going on strike, for example. They may participate in street demonstrations or riots as part of a general expression of popular discontent, but only when these methods enjoy a reasonable currency and legitimacy (as in immediate post-revolutionary Iran, Beirut during the civil war, or after the fall of Suharto in Indonesia in 1998), and when they are mobilized by outside leaders: Thus, urban land take-overs may be led by left-wing activists: and the unemployed and street vendors may be invited to form unions (as in Iran after the revolution, Lima, or in India). This, however, represents an uncommon phenomenon since more often than not mobilization for collective demand-making is prevented by political repression in many developing countries where these struggles often take place. Conse-quently, in place of protest or publicity, these groups move directly to fulfill their needs by themselves, albeit individually and discretely. In short, theirs is not a politics of protest, but of redress, a struggle for an immediate outcome through individual direct action.

What do these men and women aim for? They seem to pursue two major goals. The first is the redistribution of social goods and opportunities in the form of the (unlawful and direct) acquisition of collective consumption (land, shelter, piped water, electricity, roads), public space (street pavements, intersections, street parking places), opportunities (favorable business conditions, locations, and labels), and other life chances essential for survival and minimal standards.

The other goal is attaining autonomy, both cultural and political, from the regulations, institutions and discipline imposed by the state and modern institu-tions. In a quest for an informal life, the poor tend to function as much as possi-ble outside the boundaries of the state and modern bureaucratic institutions, bas-ing their relationships on reciprocity, trust and negotiation rather than on the modern notions of individual self-interest, fixed rules, and contracts. Thus, they may opt for jobs in self-employed activities rather than working under the disci-pline of the modern workplace; resorting to informal dispute resolution rather than reporting to police; getting married through local informal procedures (in the Middle East under local sheikhs) rather than by governmental offices; bor-rowing money from informal credit associations rather than modern banks. This is so not because these people are essentially non- or anti-modern, but because the conditions of their existence compel them to seek an informal mode of life. For modernity is a costly affair; not everyone can afford to be modern. Since it requires the capacity to conform to the types of behavior and mode of life (ad-herence to strict disciplines of time, space, contracts, and so on) which most vulnerable people simply cannot afford. So, while the disenfranchised wish to watch color television, enjoy clean tap water, and possess security of tenure, they are weary of paying their tax bills or reporting to work at specified times.

But how far can the urban subaltern exercise autonomy in the conditions of globalization, amid expanding integration? The point is that not only do the poor seek autonomy; they also need security from state surveillance. For an informal life in the conditions of modernity is also an insecure life. To illustrate, street vendors may feel free from the discipline of modern working institutions, but they suffer from police harassment for lacking business permits. The struggle of the poor to consolidate their communities, attain schools, clinics, or sewers would inevitably integrate them into the prevailing systems of power (that is, the state and modern bureaucratic institutions) which they wish to avoid. In their quest for security, the poor then are in constant negotiation and vacillation between autonomy and integration. Yet, they continue to pursue autonomy in any possible space available within the integrating structures and processes.

Becoming Political

If the encroachment begins with little political meaning attached to it, if illegal acts are often justified on moral grounds, then how does it turn into a collective/political struggle? So long as the actors carry on with their everyday advances without being confronted seriously by any authority, they are likely to treat their advance as an ordinary everyday exercise. However, once their gains are threatened, they tend to become conscious of their doings and the value of their gains, often defending them in collective and audible fashion. Examples may be the mobilization of the squatters in Tehran in 1976, street vendors in the 1980s and street riots by the squatters in several cities in the early 1990s. Alternatively, the actors may retain their gains through quiet non-compliance without necessarily engaging in collective resistance. Instead of collectively standing by their businesses, the mobile street vendors in Cairo or Istanbul simply retreat into the back streets once the municipality police arrive, but immediately resume their work as soon as they are gone again. At any rate, the struggle of the actors against the authorities are not about winning a gain, but are primarily about defending and furthering the already won gains. But they almost invariably involve the state power.

The state's position vis-à-vis this type of activism is affected, first, by the extent of its capacity to exercise surveillance, and, second, by the dual nature of quiet encroachment (infringing on property and power, and, at the same time, being a self-help activity). Third World states seem to be more tolerant of quiet encroachment than those in the industrialized countries such as the United States, where similar activities, albeit very limited, also take place. The industrial states are by far better equipped with ideological, technological, and institutional apparatuses for applying surveillance over their populations. In other words, people have more room for autonomy under the vulnerable and "soft states" of the South than in the advanced industrialized countries, where tax evasion, infringement into private property, and encroachment on state domains are considered serious offenses.

On the other hand, quiet encroachment, although it is an infringement on public property and power, may in many ways benefit the Third World governments, for it is a mechanism through which the poor come to help themselves. It is no surprise then that these governments express often contradictory reactions toward these kinds of activities. The "soft" and vulnerable states, especially at times of crises, tend in practice to allow the encroachment when the latter still appears limited. On their part, the encroachers attempt constantly to appear limited and tolerable while in fact expanding so much that resistance against them becomes formidable. They do so by resorting to tactical retreats, becoming invisible, bribing officials, or concentrating on particular and less strategic areas (for instance, squatting in remote areas or vending in less visible locations).

However, once their real expansion and impact are revealed, when the cumulative growth of the actors and their doings passes beyond a tolerable point, the state crackdown becomes expected. Yet in most cases, the crackdowns fail to yield much result, since they are usually launched too late when the encroachers have already spread, becoming visible and passing the point of no return. Indeed, the description by officials of these processes as "cancerous" brings home the dynamics of such movements.

The sources of conflict between the actors and the state are not difficult to determine. First, the often "informal" and free-of-charge distribution of public goods exerts heavy pressure on the resources which the state controls. Besides, the rich—the real estate owners, merchants, and shopkeepers—also lose properties, brands, and business opportunities. The alliance of the state and the propertied groups adds a class dimension to the conflict. On the other hand, the actors" drive for autonomy in everyday life creates a serious void in the domination of the modern state. Autonomous life renders the modern states, in particular the populist versions, rather irrelevant. Moreover, autonomy and informality (of agents, activities, and spaces) deprive the states of the necessary knowledge to exert surveillance. Unregulated jobs, unregistered peoples and places, nameless streets and alleyways and policeless neighborhoods mean that these entities remain hidden from the governments' books. To be able to control, the states need to make them transparent. Indeed, programs of squatter upgrading may be seen in terms of this strategy of opening up the unknown in order to be able to control it. Conflict between these encroachers and the state, therefore, is inevitable.

Nowhere is this conflict more evident than the "streets," this public space par excellence. Since the "streets" serve as the only locus of collective expression for, but by no means limited to, those who generally lack an institutional setting to express discontent, including squatters, the unemployed, the street subsistence workers, street children, members of the underworld, and housewives. Whereas factory workers or college students, for instance, may cause disruption by going on strike, the unemployed or street vendors can voice grievances only in the public spaces, the streets. Indeed for many of these disenfranchised, the streets are the main, perhaps the only, place where they can perform their daily functions—to assemble, make friends, earn a living, spend their leisure time, and express discontent. In addition, the streets are also the public places where the state has the most evident presence, which is expressed in police patrols, traffic regulations and spatial divisions, in short, in public ordering. The dynamics of the power relationship between the encroachers and the authorities is what I have termed "street politics." By "street politics," I mean a set of conflicts and the attendant implications between a collective populace and the authorities, which are shaped and expressed episodically in the physical and social space of the "streets"—from alleyways to the more visible street sidewalks, public parks, and public sports places. Street politics signifies an articulation of discontent by clusters of different social agents largely outside modern institutions, without a coherent ideology or evident leadership.[56]

Two key factors render the streets an arena of politics. First is the use of public space as a site of contestation between the actors and the authorities. In this sense, what makes the streets a political site is the active or participative (as opposed to passive) use of public space. This is so because these sites (sidewalks, public parks, intersections, and so on) are increasingly becoming the domain of the state power which regulates their use, making them "orderly." It expects the users to operate in them passively. An active use challenges the authority of the state and those social groups that benefit from such order.

The second element shaping street politics is the operation of what I have called the "passive network" among the people who use and operate in the public space. By "passive network" I mean an instantaneous communication among atomized individuals, which is established by a tacit recognition of their common identity, and which is mediated through space. When a woman enters a party full of male guests, she would instantaneously notice another woman in that party. Vendors in a street are most likely to recognize one another even if they never meet or talk. Now when a threat occurs to the women in the party or the vendors in the street, they are likely to get together even if they do not know each other or have not planned to do so in advance. The significance of this concept lies in the possibility of imagining mobilization of atomized individuals, such as the quiet encroachers, who are largely deprived of organizations and deliberate networking. "Passive network" implies that individuals may be mobilized to act collectively without active or deliberately constructed networks. Street as a public space has this intrinsic feature that makes it possible for people to get mobilized through establishing passive networks. Once the individual actors, the encroachers, are confronted by a threat, their passive network is likely to turn into active communication and cooperation. That is how an eviction threat or police raid may immediately bring together squatters, or street vendors, who did not even know one another. Of course, the shift from passive network to collective resistance is never a given. Actors might feel that tactical retreat would yield a far better result than confrontation, a tendency so common in today's Cairo streets, but which was uncommon in revolutionary Iran where on-the-spot collective resistance prevailed.[57]

Quiet Encroachment and the
Prospects for Collective Urban Struggle

I suggested at the outset that a major consequence of the new global restructuring has been a double process of integration, on the one hand, and social exclusion and informalization, on the other. Both processes tend to generate discontent on the part of many urban grassroots in the Third World.

First, there are many among the urban disenfranchised who find it difficult to function, live, and work within the modernizing economic and cultural systems characterized by market discipline, contracts, exchange value, speed, and bureaucratic rationale. These people attempt to exit from such social and economic arrangements, seeking alternative and more familiar, or informal, institutions and relations. Second, globalization also has a tendency to informalize through the programs of structural adjustment, rendering many people unemployed or pushing them to seek refuge in informal production, trade, housing, and transportation. Transnational street vendors (circulating, for instance, between the new Central Asian republics and Istanbul, or between Jamaica and Miami) are a latest product of this age. In short, the new global restructuring tends to intensify the growth of subjectivities, social space, and terrain of political struggles that are coming to characterize the cities of the developing world.

Although the prevailing perspectives (survival strategy, urban social movements, and everyday resistance) provide useful angles to view the activism of the urban subaltern, they do, however, suffer from some major drawbacks. The latter are reflected in the essentialism of the "passive poor," reductionism of the "surviving poor," Latino-centrism of the "political poor" and conceptual perplexity of "resistance literature." I suggested that the "quiet encroachment" perspective might offer a way out of those conceptual problems. Looking from this perspective, the poor struggle not only for survival. They strive in a life-long process to improve their lot through often individualistic and quiet encroachment on the public goods and on the power and property of the elite groups. In this process, the poor do not directly challenge the effect of globalization. Rather, in their quest for security, they get involved in constant negotiations with globalization to maintain or seek autonomy in any space remained unaffected. At the same time, in this process, the unintended consequences of their daily encroachments and negotiations beget significant social changes in urban structures and processes, in demography, and in public policy. We discussed earlier how crucial such a strategy is in the lives of the urban grassroots. Yet the question remains as to how far this quiet encroachment can take these actors?

Given their existential constraints (poor skills and education, or meager income, connection, and organization), quiet encroachment serves as a viable enabling strategy for the marginalized groups to survive and better their lot. However, this non-movement is neither able to cause broader political transformation, nor does it aim for it. The larger national social movements have the capacity for such a transformation. Yet, compared to global/national mobilization, these localized struggles are both meaningful and manageable for the actors—meaningful in that they can make sense of the purpose and have an idea of the consequences of these actions; and manageable in that they, rather than some remote national leaders, set the agenda, project the aims and control the outcome. In this sense for the poor, the local is privileged over the global/national.

It is true that urban grassroots succeed relatively in extending their life chances often through lifetime struggles, nevertheless crucial social spaces remain out of their control. The poor may be able to take over a plot of land to build shelters, may tap running water or electricity illegally from the main street or neighbors; they may secure a job on the street corner by selling things and may be able to bribe or dodge the municipality police every now and then. But how can they get schools, health services, public parks, paved roads, and security—the social goods which are tied to larger structures and processes, the national states and global economy? In other words, the largely atomistic and localist strategies of the disenfranchised, despite their advantages, render a search for social justice in the broader, national sense poorly served. The disenfranchised are unlikely to become a more effective player in a larger sense unless they become mobilized on a collective basis, and their struggles are linked to broader social movements and civil society organizations.[58] Yet, it is crucial to remember that until this is realized and its results are tested, quiet encroachment remains a most viable enabling strategy which the urban grassroots pursue irrespective of what we, social scientists, think of it.

Notes

1. This article was originally presented at the World Congress of Sociology Montreal 1998, in a panel on Globalization and Collective Action. I would like to thank Professor Jan Nederveen Pieterse for organizing the panel, and for his valuable comments and criticisms. I am also grateful for the comments made by the anonymous reviewers of *International Sociology*.

2. For a critique of the exaggerated version of the globalization thesis, see David Gordon, "The Global Economy: New Edifice or Crumbling Foundations?" *New Left Review*, 1988, 168: 24-64.

3. Ankie Hoogvelt, *Globalization and the Postcolonial World* (Baltimore, MD: Johns Hopkins University Press, 1997).

4. World Bank, *World Development Report 1995* (Oxford: Oxford University Press, 1995).

5. J. Vandemoortele, "The African Employment Crisis of the 1990s," in *The Employment Crisis in Africa*, ed. C. Grey-Johnson (Harare: African Association for Public Administration and Management, 1990).

6. Central Intelligence Agency, *World Fact Book* (Washington, DC: CIA, 1992).

7. International Labor Organization, *World Employment Report, 1998-1999* (Geneva: ILO, 1999); David McNally, "Globlization on Trial: Crisis and Class Struggle in East Asia," *Monthly Review* 50 (1998): 1-13.

8. Neil Webster, "The Role of NGDOs in Indian Development: Some Lessons from West Bengal and Karnataka," *The European Journal of Development Research* 7 (1995): 407-33.

9. Asef Bayat, "Globalizing Social Movements? Comparing Middle Eastern Islamist Movements and Latin American Liberation Theology," unpublished paper, Cairo.

10. A. Melucci, "A Strange Kind of Newness: What's 'New' in New Social Movements?" in *New Social Movements*, ed. E. Larana et al. (Philadelphia, PA: Temple University Press, 1994).

11. Everett Stonequist, "The Problem of the Marginal Man," *American Journal of Sociology* 41 (1935): 1-12; Robert Park, "Human Migration and Marginal Man," *American Journal of Sociology* 33 (1928): 881-93.

12. Hall Draper, *Karl Marx's Theory of Revolution* (New York: Monthly Review Press, 1978).

13. Hall Draper, *Karl Marx's Theory of Revolution*.

14. Peter Worsley, *The Three Worlds* (London: Weidenfeld and Nicolson, 1984).

15. Frantz Fannon, *The Wretched of the Earth* (Harmondsworth, UK: Penguin, 1967).

16. T.G. McGee, "The Persistence of Proto-Proletariat: Occupational Structures and Planning for the Future of Third World Cities," in *Comparative Politics: Rationality, Culture, Structure*, ed. M. Linchbach and A. Zuckerman (Cambridge: Cambridge University Press, 1997); R. Cohen, "Cities in Developing Societies," in *Introduction to the Sociology of Developing Societies*, ed. H. Alavi and T. Shanin (London: Macmillan, 1982); Peter Worsley *The Three Worlds*.

17. S. Huntington, *Political Order in Changing Society* (Ithaca, NY: Yale University Press, 1968); Joan Nelson, "The Urban Poor: Disruption or Political Integration in Third World Cities," *World Politics* 22, (1970): 393-414; S. Huntington and J. Nelson, *No Easy Choice: Political Participation in Developing Countries* (Cambridge, MA: Harvard University Press, 1976).

18. Oscar Lewis, *Five Families: Mexican Case Studies in the Culture of Poverty* (New York: Basic Books, 1959); Oscar Lewis, *The Children of Sanchez: Autobiography of a Mexican Family* (New York: Random House, 1961); Oscar Lewis, *La Vida: A Puerto Rican Family in the Culture of Poverty* (New York: Random House, 1966).

19. Peter Worsley, *The Three Worlds,* 190-94. For a broader critique of the culture of poverty thesis, see A. Leeds, "The Concept of the "Culture of Poverty": Conceptual, Logical, and Empirical Problems with Perspectives from Brazil and Peru," in *The Culture of Poverty: A Critique,* ed. E.B. Leacock (New York: Simon and Schuster, 1971), and C. Valentine, *Culture and Poverty: Critique and Counter Proposals* (Chicago: University of Chicago Press, 1968).

20. J. Pearlman, *Myth of Marginality* (Berkeley: University of California Press, 1976); Manuel Castells, *The City and the Grassroots* (Berkeley: University of California Press, 1983).

21. James Scott, "Everyday Forms of Peasant Resistance," *The Journal of Peasant Studies* 13 (1986): 5-35.

22. Ernesto Escobar, *Encountering Development* (Princeton, NJ: Princeton University Press, 1995).

23. John Friedman, *Empowerment: The Politics of Alternative Development* (London: Blackwell, 1992); John Friedman, "Rethinking Poverty: Empowerment and Citizen Rights," *International Social Science Journal* 148 (1996): 161-72.

24. Castells, *The City and the Grassroots*.

25. F. Schuurman and T. Van Naerssen, *Urban Social Movements in the Third World* (London: Croom Helm, 1989).

26. John Friedman, "The Dialectic of Reason," *International Journal of Urban and Regional Research* 13 (1989): 217-44.

27. Bernard Hourcade, "Conseillisme, Class Sociale, et Space Urbain: Les Squatters du sud de Tehran, 1978-1981," in *Urban Crisis and Social Movements in the Middle East*, ed. K. Brown et al. (Paris: Editions L'Harmattan, 1989).

28. For example, see M. Stiefel and M. Wolfe, *A Voice for the Excluded: Popular Participation in Development* (London: Zed Books, 1994).

29. Asef Bayat, "Activism and Social Development in the Middle East," discussion paper prepared for World Social Summit, Geneva, August 2000.

30. Asef Bayat, "Cairo's Poor: Dilemmas of Survival and Solidarity," *Middle East Report*, 202 (1997): 2-6; Asef Bayat, "Activism and Social Development in the Middle East."

31. Asef Bayat, "Globalizing Social Movements? Comparing Middle Eastern Islamist Movements and Latin American Liberation Theology," unpublished paper, Cairo.

32. A. Leeds and E. Leeds, "Accounting for Behavioral Differences: Three Political Systems and the Responses of Squatters in Brazil, Peru, and Chile," in *The City in Comparative Perspective*, ed. J. Walton and L. Magotti (London: John Wiley, 1976), 211.

33. James Scott, *Weapons of the Weak: Everyday Forms of Peasant Resistance* (New Haven, CT: Yale University Press, 1985).

34. Steve Pile, "Opposition, Political Identities, and Spaces of Resistance," in *Geographies of Resistance*, ed. S. Pile and M. Keith (London: Routledge, 1997), 2.

35. E.B. Reeves, "Power, Resistance, and the Cult of Muslim Saints in a Northern Egyptian Town," *American Ethnologist* 22 (1995): 306-22.

36. Lila Abu-Lughod, "The Romance of Resistance: Tracing Transformations of Power Through Bedouin Women," *American Ethnologist* 17 (1990): 41-55.

37. Diane Singerman, *Avenues of Participation: Family, Politics, and Networks in Urban Quarters of Cairo* (Princeton, NJ: Princeton University Press, 1995).

38. Steve Pile, "Opposition, Political Identities, and Spaces of Resistance."

39. A. Macleod, *Accommodating Protest: Working Women, the New Veiling, and Change in Cairo* (New York: Columbia University Press, 1991).

40. This is something that Piven and Cloward wished the America's poor people's movements had. See F. Piven and R. Cloward, *Poor People's Movements: Why They Succeed, How They Fail* (New York: Vintage, 1979).

41. Mike Cole and Dave Hill, "Games of Despair and Rhetorics of Resistance: Postmodernism, Education, and Reaction," *Journal of Sociology of Education* 16 (1995): 133-50.

42. James Scott, *Weapons of the Weak*, 290.

43. James Scott, *Weapons of the Weak*, 292.

44. Nathan Brown, *Peasant Politics in Modern Egypt: The Struggles vs. the State* (New Haven, CT: Yale University Press, 1990).

45. Anthony Giddens, *Sociology* (Oxford: Polity Press, 2000).

46. V.I. Lenin, *What Is to Be Done* (Peking: Foreign Language Press, 1973).

47. Scott, *Weapons*, 350.

48. Michel Foucault, *Knowledge/Power* (New York: Pantheon, 1972).

49. D. McAdam, S. Tarrow, and C. Tilly, "Towards an Integrated Perspective on Social Movements and Revolution," in *Comparative Politics: Rationality, Culture, and Structure*, ed. M.J. Linchbach and A. Zuckerman (Cambridge: Cambridge University Press, 1997).

50. Diane Singerman, *Avenues of Participation* (Princeton, NJ: Princeton University Press, 1995); Homa Hoodfar, *From Marriage to Market* (Berkeley: University of California Press, 1997).

51. Michael Brown, "On Resisting Resistance," *American Anthropologist* 98 (1998): 730.

52. I have elaborated on this perspective in detail in my book *Street Politics: Poor People's Movements in Iran* (New York: Columbia University Press, 1997). Here, I only briefly discuss some major points.

53. Asef Bayat, *Street Politics* (New York: Columbia University Press, 1997), 79.

54. Asef Bayat, "Cairo's Poor"; Farha Ghannam, "Relocation and Use of Urban Space," *Middle East Report* 202 (1997): 17-20.

55. P. Kuppinger, "Giza Spaces," *Middle East Report* 202 (1997): 14-16.

56. Asef Bayat, *Street Politics*.

57. Bayat, *Street Politics*.

58. For an example of such a broader alliance in Peru, see Pedro Arevalo, "Huaycan Self-Managing Urban Community: May Hope be Realized," *Environment and Urbanization* 9 (1997): 59-79.

Chapter 10

The Empire at Ground Zero

Vincent Mosco

This chapter examines the relationship between a global city, a national empire, and an attack on both. Much has been written about the attacks of September 11 and the place of ground zero in the life of New York City, the United States and the world. But surprisingly little has been said about the history of ground zero in the development of an American empire at the end of World War II and the centrality of empire in the reconstruction of the site. Specifically this chapter argues that the World Trade Center (WTC) was built to establish Lower Manhattan as the capital of a post-industrial America and the icon of a world economy increasingly based on the production, distribution and exchange of data, information, and knowledge. It maintains that social class and empire are central to understanding the planning and development of the site as well as its redevelopment in the wake of the attacks.

The chapter begins with a consideration of the theory and ideology of post-industrialism, how it animated plans to create the WTC, and how it was used to press forward with construction even in the face of powerful opposition. The Rockefeller family led the project, drawing fully on its historic ties to the foreign policy establishment and to its leadership in the political, economic, and cultural life of New York City. In spite of its powerful economic and political clout, crystallized in the modernist ideology of post-industrial empire, the forces that would create the WTC faced significant opposition that was rooted in the politics of social class and specifically in the battles over the political economy of post-war New York City and post-war America. It was not a question, as some have argued, of pitting the future, the information age, against the past or the age of industry. Rather, both sides in the struggle over the WTC offered visions for the future, but they were radically different and incommensurable. The chapter describes these alternative futures and the battles to realize them. It then turns to consider the short-lived victory of the WTC's proponents, why the site never realized its potential and actually failed before the buildings themselves fell. Finally, it takes up the effort to reconstitute the site, particularly the interplay of politics and myth that are propelling the inevitable recreation of the original failed development, the attempt to realize an empire at ground zero.

At the end of World War II the United States was poised to replace Great Britain as the dominant power in the world. Europe lay in ruins and the Soviet Union, which would eventually present a formidable military challenge, was devastated by 20,000,000 military and civilian deaths. Arguably the greatest impediment to American empire was internal. In order to extend its imperial hegemony the United States would need to deepen it by solidifying the empire at home. Indeed, success in the war at home was a precondition for success abroad but it would be difficult to achieve because of the very triumphalism that victory in war brought about. Victory fed impatience among a people that had endured the Great Depression and a world war. It was long past time to deliver on the promises of prosperity and freedom that helped people make it through two horrendous decades. The nationwide outbreak of strikes and labor unrest at the end of the war served as a warning that working-class America would not be easily pacified. Government and business responded in two ways, both of which would enlist the working class in the extension of empire. The first was a new form of Fordism that would extend the social contract. In return for labor peace and support for American foreign expansion, including the battle against socialist and communist trade unions at home and abroad, workers would be guaranteed secure, full-time employment and modest social services, particularly in education. If this was the velvet glove of prosperity offered to achieve labor peace, the iron fist was the attack on anything approaching socialist and communist movements at home.[1] These movements grew throughout the 1930s and 1940s, boosted by support for America's ally in World War II, the Soviet Union, and had an enormous impact on American culture.[2] But they could no longer be tolerated both because of the perceived Soviet threat and because the concerted attack on socialism would provide the discipline to control the working class, limiting its demands for consumer goods and restraining the push for political and social democracy, whether defined as expanded civil rights for minorities or national health care for all Americans. Foreign expansion would help fuel prosperity at home and further justify the war at home.

In addition to its military power, the United States was armed with the potent new ideology of post-industrialism which served as an important departure from the traditional vision of a Fordist society built on manufacturing. Combining a near religious faith in communication and information technology with a similar belief in the inevitable triumph over poverty and working class life, the United States pressed forward with a vision of an epochal shift from factory to office, from reliance on manufacturing to services, and from power based on control over money to power rooted in the effective use of information. Post-industrialism is typically presented only as a potent theoretical formulation. As such, it has been an important contributor to debates in the social sciences which began in earnest shortly after World War II when scholars started to notice growth in the number of jobs outside the manufacturing sector. In the early years, the academic emphasis was on developing measures to track the growth of the information sector as an economic force. Machlup was among the leaders in charting the expansion of the data and information components of the economy and Porat built on this work to document the shift from an economy based on the primary (agriculture) and secondary (manufacturing) sectors to one led by services (tertiary) and information (quaternary) occupations.[3] But neither Machlup nor Porat addressed the political, social, and cultural implications of this transformation with anything approaching the theoretical sophistication of Daniel Bell.[4]

According to Bell, we were not merely experiencing a growth in data and information, nor merely a shift in the major occupational categories. He believed that the post-World War II world was undergoing a fundamental transformation in the nature of capitalist society. Capitalism had been governed for two centuries by industrialists and their financiers who comprised the capitalist class. Now, with the rise of a society dependent on technology and particularly on the production and distribution of information, a new class of leaders, a genuine knowledge class of well-trained scientific-technical workers was rising to prominence and ultimately to the leadership of a post-industrial capitalism. Inherited wealth and power would shrink in significance and a genuine meritocracy would rule. Such a society would not necessarily be more democratic, but it did mean that power would be grounded in knowledge and not in family inheritance. The ranks of knowledge workers would literally power and manage the economy, leading to steady economic growth and the decline of historic ideologies. Political battles over public policy would diminish as technical algorithms and other knowledge-based measures, would govern. There would no doubt be tensions in such a society; but these would be technical and not ideological, differences in detail but certainly not class struggles. The only potential for serious division lay outside the economic and political spheres, in, as Bell would argue in his next, far darker, book, the cultural sphere.[5] The only significant internal threat to post-industrial society was a culture sinking deeper and deeper into a consumer hedonism and into irrational beliefs. The conjunction of two seeming opposites—materialism and counter-culture—would threaten the foundation of post-industrialism because they challenged both the delayed gratification and support for technical rationality that were required to maintain it.

It did not take long for others to conclude that hedonistic culture or not, post-industrialism itself was not good for many people. For Herbert Schiller, post-industrialism meant the rise of transnational media and communication businesses that would pump out support for American values, including its military and imperial ambitions, and eliminate alternatives through increasingly concentrated market power.[6] According to Harry Braverman, for the vast majority of workers in the service, retail, and the knowledge professions, labor would be as regimented and ultimately de-skilled, as it had been in assembly line manufacturing. Indeed, given the immateriality of knowledge work, it would be easier than it was in the industrial era to separate conception from execution, and to concentrate the power of conception (e.g., design and management) in a dominant class.[7]

Post-industrialism is not just a theory; it is also a prophetic vision that would be used to justify the war at home against the American working class. In fact, even before post-industrialism was formulated into a conceptual tool for understanding the post-war world, it was used by leaders in business and government to justify profound transformations in American life. Specifically, it was used to eliminate proposals to modernize the manufacturing sector in major cities and it also legitimized massive urban redevelopment plans that would push the working class out of coveted areas in cities and replace them with businesses catering to white collar employment and expensive housing for the new post-industrial elites. The Rockefeller family was in the forefront of pressing post-industrialism "on the ground" and especially in reconstructing New York City as the capital of post-industrialism and in building its dominant architectural icon, World Trade Center. They and their associates led a white collar army in what amounted to the Battle of New York City.

The first skirmish in this battle took place in the early 1950s at the northern end of Manhattan Island, a distance from the primary battle that would be fought over ground zero some years later. But lessons learned from the fight over Morningside Heights would serve the warriors who would build a World Trade Center and transform Lower Manhattan, and, ultimately much of the global political economy. The Heights contained Columbia University and several other of what the Rockefellers called "the institutions" precious to New York intellectual and cultural life and vital for the creation of a post-industrial society. Indeed, Columbia would later on turn out to be the site where Daniel Bell codified post-industrialism into a dominant social scientific theory. The Rockefellers, led by banker David and politician Nelson, supported the schools, cultural centers, and churches in the Heights. All of the Rockefeller brothers except one attended elementary and high school in the Heights. The entire family was personally committed to what was dubbed this "Acropolis of America."[8]

At the end of World War II, more than their financial support would be required as a new challenge or threat appeared at the Heights. This threat which was summarized in a memo written to David by an ally on the city's planning commission. Titled "The Present Crisis," the memo is clinical in its description: "the white population decreased 12 percent, while the non-white population increased 71 percent. . . . Again, let me repeat, if these minority groups come into the Heights in the usual way, it will benefit them little, if any, for the usual course of events will bring with it the same disastrous change in conditions which have resulted elsewhere; but the effects on the institutions will be catastrophic. All of these have appealed to me as reasons why the institutions and the City should combine to take steps necessary to guide local change along constructive lines."[9] In essence as commentators noted, it was necessary "to create a barricade, conveniently shielding the Acropolis of America from Harlem."[10]

Fearing an influx of mainly working-class Hispanics and African-Americans, the Rockefeller team responded in a powerful way. It leveled ten acres of working-class housing, replacing them with a *cordon sanitaire* of luxury housing that would ring "the institutions" of Morningside Heights protecting them from the "catastrophic" consequences of having to share the community with the working class. The latter fought back to prevent their removal in a community-wide Save Our Homes campaign organized in 1951, but to no avail. Community groups were labeled "communist-backed" in the press, making them enemies in the global fight against the Red Menace.[11] This first major skirmish in the Battle of New York City ended as the president of Barnard College, then an elite women's college associated with Columbia, accepted a one million dollar contribution from the Rockefellers and then took a crow bar and slammed it into one of the tenements scheduled for demolition, in a symbolic act of purifying a neighborhood of its working class. Armed with the ideology of post-industrialism, the Rockefellers and their coalition of developers, financiers, and planners, including the legendary Robert Moses, took the lessons learned from Morningside Heights and applied them again, only more spectacularly, in Lower Manhattan to build the capital of post-industrialism.

Rockefeller family wealth shifted in the twentieth century from the oil that built the family fortune and the old manufacturing economy to banking and the finance capital that would build the bridge to a post-industrial future. The center of its financial power was the Chase Manhattan bank whose headquarters in Lower Manhattan stood alone amidst the structures representing the "old" economy. The bank's modern lines made visible the deep differences between the vision of Chase people and those working at the aging buildings of Wall Street, which provided the financial foundation for the manufacturing age. Unlike midtown Manhattan which was home to the headquarters of media giants, pop culture palaces, and other new economy institutions, including the family's own Rockefeller Center with its Radio City Music Hall and the studios of NBC, Chase alone in Lower Manhattan embodied the shift to a post-industrial society. The family, led by David as arguably the leading power broker in New York business and political circles, planned to change all that by turning Lower Manhattan into the center of global finance, trade, and communication. Even as he bristled at suggestions that he has "imperial tendencies," David boasted about private meetings with Pinochet, Saddam Hussein, Jaurzelski of Poland, Botha of South Africa, Zhou Enlai, and Krushchev, among other dictators.[12]

To assist, Chase Manhattan named a leader in the foreign policy establishment as its CEO. John J. McLoy was instrumental in the decision to drop the atomic bomb on Japan and became the first head of the World Bank. David Rockefeller was the bank's chief planner, but empire needed a top foreign policy adviser even for the war at home. Later, as governor of New York, Nelson Rockefeller would fine tune the precedent by appointing Henry Kissinger as his adviser for international affairs. Such powerful figures were necessary because there was powerful opposition in Lower Manhattan. The district was also home to more than just the icons of Wall Street. It also contained a vibrant working class, many small businesses based in industrial districts specializing in printing, electronics and other craft trades, and the associated playgrounds and entertainments that catered to the numerous ethnic communities. Lower Manhattan meant not only old manufacturing but also Old Europe which supporters of post-industrialism were committed to topple. A substantial effort would be required to win this more significant campaign in the Battle of New York City.

The immediate area that is now known as ground zero was called Radio Row, an agglomeration of electronics businesses that had occupied the area for forty years and employed about 30,000 people. It did not have the look of a post-industrial district but was successful in the electronics trade, providing one of the numerous craft-based industrial districts that made New York the model for what has become a fashion among urban planning scholars and policymakers—a set of overlapping specialized manufacturing districts that produce economies based on networks of business and family ties. It is no exaggeration to suggest that New York was home to a "Third Italy" economy before that district in north central Italy marked by customized manufacturing that separated it from Italy's heavy industrial north and the rural south became a model for economic development. Before it was dashed in an onslaught of post-industrialism, New York, and particularly the lower half of Manhattan, was home to the "second industrial divide" that Piore and Sabel, along with many followers, went to Italy to study, model, and marvel at.[13] Indeed in one of the supreme ironies of post-industrialism, one of the leading historians of New York City has speculated that had it not been wiped out by the World Trade Center, Radio Row might have provided the city with the foundation to develop what would eventually become Silicon Valley.[14] This would not have been out of the question for the city that gave birth to the telecommunications and broadcasting industries and the headquarters of AT&T and RCA. Or as one of Radio Row's business leaders put it at the time, "This is a worldwide center for electronics for the home, and now they are going to destroy it so that the real estate interests can take over."[15] Next door to Radio Row was the harbor that had made the city a transportation and trade hub for over a century, providing a major feature of what one commentator called "the infrastructure of blue-collar New York."[16]

Numerous attempts were made to build on this manufacturing infrastructure but most of these were ignored. These offered genuine visions of an alternative to the post-industrial future, and would be taken up by regions such as the Third Italy which recognized the value of maintaining a mix of manufacturing and service work. For example, in 1955, John Griffin, a City University professor, rattled the city's elites, in part because his research received Rockefeller Foundation support, by publishing a study that criticized city planners for failing to provide support for manufacturing companies beginning to leave the city. Griffin called for the revitalization of blue-collar industry, particularly in Lower Manhattan, where new and second generation immigrants lived and depended on manufacturing jobs. Challenging the reigning elite wisdom that industrial clearance and office construction were the solutions, a strategy that meant moving the working class out of Manhattan to find jobs in the outer boroughs and the suburbs rather than bringing the jobs to them, Griffin set out a plan for industrial renewal in Lower Manhattan, including the development of industrial cooperatives.[17] Furthermore, a series of studies produced by a group of Harvard University researchers, particularly Hoover and Vernon's *Anatomy of a Metropolis*, demonstrated the strength of the city's flexible manufacturing base and further argued that the city would not benefit from what amounted to the office monoculture that elites had in store for much of Manhattan.[18] In sum, with an unparalleled communication and transportation infrastructure, New York might have challenged Silicon Valley for supremacy. But the destruction of Radio Row, to build a post-industrial economy, put an end to one of the keys to creating a high-tech base in the city.

Business and community organizations in the surrounding area fiercely opposed the World Trade Center project. They made use of tactics that today's anti-globalization protestors would recognize. One 1962 protest featured business leader Oscar Nadel lying in a coffin alongside a mannequin dressed up as Mr. Small Businessman and parading in a mock funeral procession to protest the imminent death of Radio Row. They were joined by activist intellectuals like Jane Jacobs whose book *The Death and Life of Great American Cities* won widespread acclaim for opposing the monumentalism of projects such as this in favor of cities that grew organically from its streets and communities, the very streets and communities that the twin towers project would destroy. She was prominent in stopping the construction of a Lower Manhattan expressway that would have run through what would become SoHo, severing with it the likelihood of the community becoming what most would agree is one of the great success stories in urban rehabilitation.[19] Alongside these opponents stood some of the city's more powerful business leaders, include those in real estate who feared that construction of the WTC would significantly depress the market for commercial real estate throughout the city. These were led by Lawrence Wien who owned the Empire State Building and led a group that took out advertisements in New York's newspapers describing with eerie prescience, accompanied by a now remarkable image, the likelihood that an aircraft would strike the proposed towers and bring them down.[20]

To combat the opposition, proponents used many of the tactics of empire starting with the selective use of intelligence. In order to convince people that tearing down Radio Row and replacing it with the twin towers made economic sense, proponents commissioned a study from the well known consulting analysts McKinsey and Company. However, the study reported that most business had little need for a central structure to house foreign divisions because all business was becoming international and dispersing globally. Corporations were starting their own international divisions and had little need for a World Trade Center. Consequently, the plan would likely result in financial disaster with serious occupancy problems and little interest in the services that such a center might provide. Instead of taking the McKinsey findings seriously, however, the Downtown Lower Manhattan Association refused to publish the report and paid McKinsey only $5,000 out of a $30,000 contract. It also forced the company to produce a freshly spun favorable conclusion—after one WTC supporter took aside a McKinsey research and, in the words of the supporter, "we stuck a steel rod up his fanny." Furthermore, just to be sure, supporters commissioned a new company to produce the kind of report they wanted.[21]

Moreover, like empires throughout history, the trade center forces made use of supra-legal and even downright illegal institutions to win the day. The former was exemplified in the Port Authority of New York and New Jersey, one of the early public-private hybrids that enjoyed the power of a government agency (especially to expropriate land) without the need to answer to voters. The Port Authority was supposed to maintain the ports, bridges, and tunnels that made up the New York and New Jersey transportation infrastructure. A product of modernist urban planning, the Authority was also supposed to be insulated from daily political pressures, and from voters, which would better enable it to operate efficiently.[22] Instead, the agency was used to control the construction of a trade center that, in a post-industrial age, was supposed to supercede physical transportation networks with the electronic networks of the digital age. In fact, the leadership of the Authority was keen to invest in the WTC partly because it had accumulated a massive surplus from its network of tolls and did not want to get involved in the politically messy business of investing in mass transit. Rather, it would be easier to use its privileged political position to condemn land and invest in a real estate deal that would strengthen its ties to an important force in the business community and possibly increase the flow of revenue to the Authority.

Turning its back on the primary reason for its creation, the Authority led the charge through the political back rooms and the courts, making effective use of its supra-legal authority to win final approval for the WTC. It answered critics who argued that the agency had no right to get involved in big real estate deals when it should be working on the transportation infrastructure by maintaining that constructing the hub of a services economy would ultimately help the port system by increasing its business. The Authority's unique status meant that the WTC project did not have to meet standard environmental and safety reviews which also sped the approval process. But it also created problems down the road because design features meant to maximize office space and less than rigorous fire protection measures also sped the collapse of the towers. But only some of the project's opponents were thinking of possible disaster when the project was approved in 1968 with the Port Authority as the site's owner able to lease development rights to private companies.

Empires often depend on supra-legal authority to carry out their rule. They also often depend on extra-legal forces. In this case, Trade Center backers were not reluctant to draw on connections to the mafia, ultimately employing mob-controlled construction companies to control local unions and to skim money from contracts that were to be applied to such essentials as fire-proofing of the towers. The quality of fire-proofing was questioned throughout the construction of the buildings and would become a key flaw that hastened the collapse of the buildings. But the head of the company responsible for fire-proofing the buildings was not around to face the music because he was found murdered in the parking lot of one of the towers, the apparent victim of a rival mob family.[23]

Empires have historically also used compradors or loyal local agents to carry out orders. This is no different when building an empire at home. In the case of New York, the architect Minoru Yamasaki served this role well. His was a critical role because leading architects were not interested in the project. In order to serve as the capital of post-industrialism, nothing short of the largest buildings in the world would do. Furthermore, developers wanted to maximize return on the dollar and so aimed to squeeze twelve million square feet of office space into the structures. Top architects would not take such a commission because the restrictions would permit the construction of little more than two extremely tall boxes that would require radical and untested building techniques to work. Yamasaki was a middling architect whose only large project had resulted in disaster. He had designed the Pruitt-Igoe low-income housing project in St. Louis which is still held up worldwide as a model of how to destroy a community through public housing. One urban historian has called it "arguably the most infamous public housing project ever built in the United States."[24] In 1956, the development crammed 33 eleven-story structures on a small site and it all was unceremoniously blown up in a 1972 demolition project that signaled the end of this type of public housing in the United States. This is hardly the kind of project that would recommend an architect for one of the most significant commercial real estate developments in history, but Yamasaki was pliable and so eager to please his superiors that he surprised even members of his own firm with his willingness to give up practically all of his design principles to meet the demands to maximize rental space.[25]

The fight over ground zero went on into the late 1960s and was not resolved until proponents offered the City of New York, which was not convinced that the project would bring promised benefits to the city, a sweetened deal. The Port Authority would literally extend Manhattan Island with dirt dug out of the ground to build the towers and then assist in the creation of a luxury housing development to be called Battery Park City. The towers would not only be built, they would be coupled to a brand new upscale community to help replace the area's working class and the docks. The prospects of gentrifying the area by creating housing that the towers' white collar work force might occupy was enough to convince the city to accept the deal. To attract residents, a state-of-the-art park was built on the Battery Park waterfront, at a time when most of New York's parks were suffering from neglect, and one of the city's premier public high schools, reserved for the best of the city's students, was moved into the district and placed in a brand new building costing $300 million, at a time when New York's public schools were also suffering from years of dereliction. It was hard to turn down so magical an offer as a village rising out of what was once only the water of the Hudson River.

Power politics certainly had a great deal to do with why the Trade Center was constructed. The story of how Nelson Rockefeller stacked the Port Authority with family and party loyalists after his election as governor in 1958 is a classic case study in brute political power.[26] But it was always encased in a supportive mythology as well. Much of this had to do with purifying and cleansing the perceived blight of Lower Manhattan and, specifically, Radio Row. For the Trade Center's primary architect Minoru Yamasaki, it was simple and downright Manichean. On the one hand was his design of the towers evoking in his mind "the transcendental aspirations of a medieval cathedral." On the other was Radio Row, in his words, "quite a blighted section, with radio and electronics shops in old structures, clothing stores, bars and many other businesses that could be relocated without much anguish." With thoughts of translucent towers filled with people running the digital world, he concluded: "There was not a single building worth saving."[27]

There is something here reminiscent of Margaret Wertheim's discussion of the dual spaces of the medieval era, as cathedrals were built to purify the real but flawed space of daily life by making room for a spiritual space that would cleanse the blight of the banal, quotidian with a transcendent, indeed sublime, structure.[28] But there is a difference. The medieval cathedral could cleanse and purify the soul but acknowledged a world, however corrupt and sinful, outside its doors. Supporters of the post-industrial myth were not interested in either business or architecture sharing space with different forms. Post-industrial business would purify Fordism by eliminating its need to exist, at least eliminating that need in the major cities of the world's richest nations. Post-industrial design would do the same by purifying, i.e., destroying, the spaces that got in its way. Not everyone lined up on the side of the "posts." For example, architecture critics did not quite get the cathedral metaphor in the Trade Center design. Perhaps because Yamasaki had to bow to the pressures of his financial backers and increase the height of the towers from his proposed 90 stories to over 100, critics lambasted the designs as "graceless," a "fearful instrument of urbicide," and, as for the bit of ornamentation at the base which seemed to copy the uptown tower owned by a leading automobile manufacturer, it was viewed as "General Motors Gothic."[29] The running joke was that the towers were actually recycled shipping boxes for the Chrysler and Empire State Buildings. Even today, after the attacks that re-purified the WTC, architecture critics continue to assail the structures with one referring to their design as "one of the more conspicuous architectural mistakes of the twentieth century."[30]

As a result of the extreme commercial demands, the twin towers project risked disaster from the start because it used too little steel and concrete, inadequate fireproofing and sprinkler systems, and weak structural supports for the office floors whose innovative trusses had never been tested in any furnace. This would maximize office space and keep costs down, but at great risk. Fire department officials warned about the danger for years and the structural soundness of the buildings was also the subject of extensive debate. In essence, the engineering team chose a radical departure from standard skyscraper construction that would make the buildings as light as possible and maximize the amount of useable office space. In order to accomplish this, engineers had to substantially reduce the structural steel and other durable materials, like masonry and cement that would normally provide skyscrapers with stability. They also introduced significant design changes that again traded away stability for more office space. Eager to combat published fears that an airliner crashing into the buildings would bring them down, the Port Authority claimed that an engineering study demonstrated that the towers could withstand a jetliner moving at over 600 miles an hour. In fact, no such study had been done. The only calculations that appear to have been carried out were on a jet going about one-third that speed and no estimate was made of what would happen in the likely event that such a crash would lead to major fire damage. As the project's chief engineer said after 9/11, "should I have made the project more stalwart? And in retrospect, the only answer you can come up with is, yes, you should have. . . . Had it been more stalwart, surely 1, 2, 50, 100, 1,000 people might have gotten out."[31]

As it turned out, the original fears of McKinsey and Company were correct and there were so few international businesses wishing to join the post-industrial society at the towers that Governor Rockefeller had to move in state government agencies and convince other levels of government to do likewise. Eventually anyone could rent space at highly subsidized rents. This was the practice throughout the 1970s when economic problems, which would eventually bankrupt the city, significantly depressed the commercial real estate market. Fifty floors of one tower were occupied by New York state offices, and the Port Authority occupied some of the other tower. As one analyst concluded, "The Trade Center never had enough tenants in international trade to be worthy of its name."[32] The general glut of available office space would continue even as the construction, sparked by subsidies and tax abatements, also continued throughout the 1980s. Between 1988 and 1995 New York City lost 57,000 jobs in banking alone and by the mid-1990s, 60 million square feet of office space lay empty in the downtown area.[33] Meanwhile, the towers and Battery Park City received the most real estate tax relief of any area in New York City over about the last decade of the towers' life. From 1993 to 2001, city budget documents reveal, real estate tax abatements to the WTC totaled $595.5 million or $66.2 million per year and Battery Park City enjoyed $788.3 million in abatements or $87.6 million a year. Over this period, these two adjacent sites enjoyed the most substantial tax abatements of any areas in New York City.[34]

Things got better as Lower Manhattan benefited from the dot-com boom and a high tech district known as Silicon Alley emerged in the late 1990s to occupy some of the office space vacated by financial services and related firms after the major economic restructuring of the early 1990s. New Internet companies filled office buildings left vacant by financial services firms that relocated and replaced workers with new technologies. Once again, New York City, out of bankruptcy but also out of manufacturing alternatives, enjoyed a post-industrial economic allure. Indeed, Silicon Alley embodied a cyber version of the phoenix myth: in this case the city reborn from the ashes of its industrial past. Even so, it also propelled a transformation of urban politics and power as corporate-controlled bodies like Business Improvement Districts remade public spaces into private enclaves and rewrote the rules of policing, civic activity and public spectacle. Moreover, much of the private new entrepreneurial spirit, now celebrated and castigated in books like *Digital Hustlers*, was made possible by government financial subsidies that opened prime rental space at well below market prices and helped to retrofit older buildings with the technologies necessary to run an aspiring dot-com firm.[35]

Centered at 55 Broad Street, a block from Wall, Silicon Alley succeeded for a time in incubating new businesses, particularly dot-com firms associated with the advertising (Doubleclick) and media businesses (AOL-Time Warner's Parenttime.com). For a time, the growth of Silicon Alley revived Lower Manhattan, bringing as many as 100,000 new jobs into the area and its appendages, through 5,000 new media firms. By 1997, journalists were calling it a "juggernaut."[36] But by 2001, Silicon Alley practically vaporized in the dot-com bust leaving the new media industry in New York to the familiar conglomerates like AOL-Time Warner and IBM which could withstand the bust better than any of the many small firms that gave the city its hip attitude in the 1990s.[37] With the dot-coms disappearing and the economy declining in the first nine months of 2001, the office glut returned and visionaries now turned to biotechnology to provide the next boost to the city economy, repeating a story spreading in cities whose dot-com hopes were turning into vaporware.[38] On the day before the towers fell, there was 8.9 million square feet of vacant office space available in Lower Manhattan alone. The goal of turning Lower Manhattan into an office monoculture was failing even before two jetliners struck the twin towers. In the months that followed, in spite of losing 13.45 million square feet in the attack, the amount of available downtown space actually grew, the result of a declining economy and fears of new attacks. Empire did everything it could to support its post-industrial icons until the attacks, what Ulrich Beck dubbed "globalization's Chernobyl," called into grave doubt prospects for post-industrialism itself.[39]

But empire is persistent. The steel from the towers was hastily shipped off to Third World recyclers before an adequate investigation might raise serious questions. The early investigation of what was essentially a massive crime scene was so poorly funded that engineers examining the steel had to do so by taking vacation days from their regular jobs and battling with recyclers eager to haul the steel onto ships bound mainly for Asia. The Federal Emergency Management Agency (FEMA), which had initial authority over the investigation and funded it, behaved like a classic imperial bureaucracy. It refused to provide an investigative team of twenty-six of the country's leading engineers with detailed blueprints of the buildings that collapsed and refused to permit engineers to interview witnesses or even to call for photographs and videos of the towers that might aid in the investigation.[40] As much as government wanted to know what happened, it feared the answers it might find and the embarrassment these answers might create for city, state, and federal officials. For example, why did the city place the mayor's emergency headquarters in a building on the ground zero site and large quantities of diesel fuel that likely led to the collapse of a building near the twin towers? Why did the state allow construction of a building without adequate fire proofing or even fire testing of the new materials used in construction? And why did the federal government permit hauling off vital evidence from the WTC crime scene, before a serious investigation could take place?

The Port Authority is once again being used to rebuild on the site with expectations for the same amount of office space. Shortly after the attacks, there were many proposals for what to do with the site. The leading view was to make the entire site a memorial. After all, it contains the remains of thousands of people who died in the fiercest foreign attack on the United States. In his farewell address to the city former Mayor Giuliani promised to push for a "soaring, monumental" memorial on the WTC site.[41] But that idea was quickly dashed in favor of a modest memorial surrounded by new office towers. Moreover, memorials are supposed to be about learning from the past and, as local authorities appear to be repeating past mistakes, or replicating postindustrial myths about an "informational city," not much learning seems to be taking place. A complete memorial would including rethinking the site and adjoining neighborhoods. It would include revisiting Jane Jacobs' call for diversifying the local economy and its social class composition. Or even, as one historian has suggested, a combination of Jacobs' philosophy with a dose of her nemesis Robert Moses. For all of his near obsession with megaprojects that undermined local neighborhoods, Moses had a keen sense of how public investment in the transportation infrastructure and in recreation facilities spread the benefits widely. That he and others were able to accomplish so much of this during the Great Depression is also a model for how government can rebuild on a massive scale even when the national economy is severely eroded.[42]

Rather than any such reconsideration, the current plan is to rebuild the same amount of office space even though it was very difficult to fill the original towers and most agree that it will be even more difficult now that it means convincing people to come to work at ground zero. As commentator Frank Rich has put it, "What sane person would want to work in a skyscraper destined to be the most tempting target for an aerial assault in the Western World?"[43] So it came as no great surprise to observers that Goldman Sachs, one of the most prominent and largest of Lower Manhattan's employers, decided to pull the plug on a forty-story tower which would have been the most significant new investment by any financial firm anywhere in the vicinity of the site since September 11. Citing security concerns and a general lack of coordination in planning for the site, the company's decision devastated city officials. The centerpiece of the rebuilding is a new tower about as tall as one of the fallen buildings but capped by a 400 foot illuminated tower that will raise the overall height of the building to reach the symbolically significant height of 1776 feet. The initial design called for an elaborate curved structure set close to the streets but shortly before it was to receive final approval, police and security experts raised serious concerns about the building's safety and vulnerability. As a result, the design team hurriedly put together a new plan that would set the building back 90 feet rather than 25 feet from the street and, more importantly, create a twenty story largely windowless concrete and metal base that could repel an explosion. This tower, the largest of several planned for the site will contain 2.6 million square feet of office space. Writing in the *New York Times*, Nicolai Ouroussoff captures the imperial foreboding embodied in the new design:

> The darkness at ground zero just got a little darker. If there is anyone still clinging to the expectation that the Freedom Tower will become a monument of the

highest American ideals, the current design should finally shake them out of
that delusion. Somber, oppressive and clumsily conceived, the project is a
monument to a society that has turned its back on any notion of cultural openness. It is exactly the kind of nightmare that government officials repeatedly as-
serted would never happen here: an impregnable tower braced against the outside world.

Daring to make the comparison with the aesthetics of an era some would rather
forget, Ouroussoff concludes that "it is, sadly, fascinating in the way that Albert
Speer's architectural nightmares were fascinating—as expressions of the values
of a particular time and era. The Freedom Tower embodies, in its way, a world
shaped by fear."[44]
        As if to act out the fear embodied in the new design, about the same
time the new building plans were being unveiled, the authorities overseeing the
site engaged in a fear-inspired act of preemptive censorship. Responding to
pressures to incorporate culture at the site, they planned to include two museums, a large International Freedom Center and a smaller Drawing Center, to
display works of art. But these have come under attack after a local newspaper
raised fears that the former would raise questions about America's past including its treatment of Native Americans and African Americans. The newspaper
also revealed that the Drawing Center, now housed in SoHo, had displayed art
linking President Bush to Osama Bin Laden and portraying terror suspects as
victims of American torture. Responding immediately to the newspaper story,
Governor Pataki was adamant: "*The Daily News* did a good service by pointing
out some of these things. We do not want that at Ground Zero; I do not want that
at Ground Zero and to the extent that I have the power, it's not going to happen." Comparing the site to the beaches of Normandy and the attack on Pearl
Harbor, the governor went on: "We will not tolerate anything on that site that
denigrates America, denigrates New York or freedom or denigrates the sacrifice
and courage that the heroes showed on Sept. 11." Making certain that these
words would not be interpreted as idol rhetoric, Pataki ordered the ground zero
development organization to "contact the cultural institutions on the memorial
site. . . and get from them an absolute guarantee that as they proceed, it will be
with total respect for the sanctity of that site." Asked what would happen if they
did not comply, he made it clear: "I'm hopeful they are able to do that, and if
not, then they shouldn't be there." A few days later this fear was given aesthetic
life in the design revealed for the new Freedom Tower.[45]
        While many agreed with the governor and praised his stand in defense of a
ground zero sealed off from both terrorist attack and political debate, other
voices persist in being heard. Arguably the most interesting emanates from
Lower Manhattan itself where the speaker of the New York State Assembly
Sheldon Silver, a man who has represented the people of Lower Manhattan
since the 1970s, killed a plan hatched by the governor and New York's mayor
and supported by business elites in the city and throughout the United States.
The plan called for building a new stadium in Manhattan's upper west side for

the New York Jets football team and to use the new stadium as the lynchpin in a bid for the 2012 summer Olympic Games. Silver argued that governments at all levels have done very little to support the redevelopment of Lower Manhattan including the ground zero site and that before public funds were spent on a stadium for a professional football team on a site miles from Lower Manhattan, the neighborhoods and businesses devastated by the attacks should receive more than the inadequate support provided so far. Opposing the forces supporting an Olympic bid (and in effect killing the bid) and those lobbying for a new home for the Jets, not only took great courage, it also embodied a spirit that has pervaded the culture of Lower Manhattan for many years but which is under attack today. It is the spirit of opposition and resistance to what passes for political correctness and a willingness to raise hard question about a seemingly impregnable and imperial monoculture. Silver and his supporters were vilified and blamed for the loss of the Olympic bid. But he persisted and along with those in Lower Manhattan who still await genuine assistance and not just plans for new fortresses, continue to represent a vibrant if embattled opposition.[46]

Their actions are a genuine memorial to the dead at ground zero. Certainly they are far more substantial that the official memorial planned for the site which would contain practically no reminder of what happened that day. Rather it proposes to re-purify the site with trees, grass, and pools of water, the "easy listening music" version of a memorial. Impressed by its own power, empire does not learn, nor is it aware of the great irony its actions have created. The steel from these icons of post-industrialism was quickly shipped abroad from the very docks that post-industrialism was supposed to render useless, even as the jobs promised by post-industrialism are shipped abroad thanks to the technologies that were expected to create a "digital sublime" at ground zero and instead created what one guide called "banal monoliths" that have been reduced to dust.[47] Now the defenders of freedom at ground zero call for censoring the voices of those who would exercise their freedom by raising discomforting questions under the Freedom Tower.

Notes

1. Elizabeth Fones-Wolf, *Selling Free Enterprise: The Business Assault on Labor and Liberalism 1945-1960* (Urbana: University of Illinois, 1994).

2. Michael Denning, *The Cultural Front: The Laboring of American Culture in the Twentieth Century* (New York: Verso, 1997).

3. Fritz Machlup, *The Production and Distribution of Knowledge in the United States* (Princeton, NJ: Princeton University Press, 1962); Marc Uri Porat, *The Information Economy* (Washington, DC: Office of Telecommunications, Department of Commerce, 1977).

4. Daniel Bell, *The Coming of a Post-Industrial Society: A Venture in Social Forecasting* (New York: Basic Books, 1973).

5. Daniel Bell, *The Cultural Contradictions of Capitalism* (New York: Basic Books, 1976).

6. Herbert I. Schiller, *The Mind Managers* (Boston: Beacon, 1973).

7. Harry Braverman, *Labor and Monopoly Capital* (New York: Monthly Review, 1973).

8. James Glanz and Eric Lipton, *City in the Sky: The Rise and Fall of the World Trade Center* (New York: Henry Holt, 2003), 16.

9. Glanz and Lipton, *City in the Sky*, 17.

10. Glanz and Lipton, *City in the Sky*, 18.

11. Glanz and Lipton, *City in the Sky*, 19.

12. Glanz and Lipton, *City in the Sky*, 31.

13. Michael J. Piore and Charles F. Sabel, *The Second Industrial Design: Possibilities for Prosperity* (New York: Basic Books, 1986); Michael H. Best, *The New Competition: Institutions of Industrial Restructuring* (Cambridge, MA: Harvard University Press, 1990).

14. Mike Wallace, *A New Deal for New York* (New York: Bell and Weiland/Gotham Center Books, 2002).

15. Glanz and Lipton, *City in the Sky*, 68.

16. Robert Fitch, *The Assassination of New York* (New York: Verso, 1993).

17. John I. Griffin, *Industrial Location* (New York: CUNY, 1956).

18. Edgar M. Hoover and Raymond Vernon, *Anatomy of a Metropolis* (New York: Doubleday, 1962).

19. Jane Jacobs, *The Death and Life of Great American Cities* (New York: Vintage, 1961).

20. See for example "The Mountain Comes to Manhattan," *New York Times*, 2 May 1968.

21. Glanz and Lipton, *City in the Sky*, 34.

22. Jameson W. Doig, *Empire on the Hudson: Entrepreneurial Vision and Political Power at the Port of New York Authority* (New York: Columbia University Press, 2002).

23. Glanz and Lipton, *City in the Sky*, 198-199.

24. Alexander von Hoffman, "Why They Built the Pruitt-Igoe Project," http://www.soc.iastate.edu/sapp/PruittIgoe.html.

25. Glanz and Lipton, *City in the Sky*, 98-117.

26. Eric Darton, *Divided We Stand: A Biography of New York's World Trade Center* (New York: Basic Books, 1999), 82.

27. James Glanz and Eric Lipton, "The Height of Ambition," *The New York Times Magazine*, 8 September 2002, 38.

28. Margaret Wertheim, *The Pearly Gates of Cyberspace* (New York: Norton, 1999).

29. Glanz and Lipton, *City in the Sky*, 116.

30. Paul Goldberger, "Eyes on the Prize," *The New Yorker*, 10 March 2003, 78.

31. Glanz and Lipton, "The Height of Ambition."

32. Paul Goldberger, "Groundwork," *The New Yorker*, 20 May 1991.

33. Wallace, *A New Deal for New York*, 15-16.

34. City of New York, Office of Management and Budget, *Statement of the Mayor*, New York, April 25. 2001, 39.

35. T.R. Longcore and P.W. Rees, "Information Technology and Downtown Restructuring: The Case of New York City's Financial District," *Urban Geography* 17, no. 4 (1996): 354-72.

36. D.W. Chen, "New Media Industry Becoming Juggernaut," *New York Times*, 23 October 1997, 12(B).

37. Casey Kait and Stephen Weiss, *Digital Hustlers: Living Large and Falling Hard in Silicon Alley* (New York: HarperCollins, 2001).

38. Harold Varmus, "The DNA of a New Industry," *New York Times*, 24 September 2002, 27(A).

39. Ulrich Beck, "Globalisation's Chernobyl," *Financial Times* (London), 6 November 2001.

40. Glanz and Lipton, *City in the Sky*, 330.

41. Diane Cardwell, "In Final Address, Giuliani Envisions Soaring Memorial," *New York Times*, 28 December 2001, 1(A), 6(D).

42. Wallace, *A New Deal for New York*.

43. Frank Rich, "Ground Zero Is So Over," *New York Times*, 29 May 2005.

44. Nicolai Ouroussoff, "A Tower of Impregnability, The Sort Politicians Love," *The New York Times*, June 30, 2005.

45. Joe Mahoney and Douglas Feiden, "Nutty 9/11 Art Nixed," *The Daily News*, June 25, 2005.

46. Charles V. Bagli and Michael Cooper, "Olympic Bid Hurt as New York Fails in West Side Stadium Quest," *New York Times*, 7 June 2005.

47. Glanz and Lipton, *City in the Sky*, 205.

Bibliography

Abu-Lughod, Lila. "The Romance of Resistance: Tracing Transformations of Power Through Bedouin Women." *American Ethnologist* 17, no. 1 (1990): 41-55.

Allen, Scott. *The Cultural Economy of Cities: Essays on the Geography of Image-Producing Industries*. London: Sage, 2000.

Althusser, Louis. *Lenin and Philosophy and Other Essays*. London: New Left Review, 1971.

Anderson, Ed and Alfred Charles. "N.O., State Study Options for Dealing with Harrah's." *Times-Picayune*, 23 November 1995.

Anderson, R. *Consumer Culture and TV Programming*. Boulder, CO: Westview Press, 1995.

Andrew, Caroline, Serge Bordeleau, and Alain Guimont. *L'Urbanisation: Une Affaire*. Editions de l'Université d'Ottawa, 1981.

Anil, Samtini. "Re-Visiting the Singapore Internet Code of Practice." *Journal of Information, Law & Technology*, no. 2 (2001): 23-46.

Applebome, Peter. "As New Orleans Plans Huge Casino, Some See Promise, Others See Threat." *New York Times*, 7 July 1992.

Arevalo, Pedro. "Huaycan Self-Managing Urban Community: May Hope Be Realized." *Environment and Urbanization* 9, no. 1 (1997): 59-79.

Asia-Pacific Human Rights Network. "Singapore: Asia's Cuba." 2002. Accessed online at http://www.singapore-window.org/ sw02/020530hr.htm.

Associated Press, "Singapore Court Increases Damages for Prime Minister in Defamation Case." 17 July 1998. http://www.freedomforum.org.

Associated Press, "Washington's Efforts to Attract Sports Have Been Mixed." September 2004. http://sports.espn.go.com/espn/wire/.

Athey, Lois. *The State of Latinos in the District of Columbia: Trends, Consequences, and Recommendations*. Washington, DC: Council of Latino Agencies, 2002.

Australian Conservation Foundation. "ACF Policy Statement: Sport." October 2003. http://www.acfonline.org.au/asp/pages/document.asp?IdDoc=743.

Backerman, S. "Arts Mean Business: An Economic Survey of Vancouver's Non-Profit Cultural Industry." In *Social Planning Department*, edited by A. Niwinske. Vancouver, BC: City of Vancouver, 1983.

Bagdikian, B. *The New Media Monopoly*. Boston: Beacon Press, 2004.

Banerjee, Indrajit, and Benjamin Yeo. "Reassessing the Internet-Determinism Perspective in Democratization: A Critical Analysis of Singapore." Unpublished draft manuscript, 2002.

Bannerman, G. (2000) "Racetrack in the Park—Success or Failure: An Accident Analysis of the Realigned Public Roads in Albert Park Reserve, May 1995–December 1999." Unpublished Civil Engineering Report.

"Bank of Ireland Headquarters, Dublin: Architect's Account." *Build* (December 1972).

Barker, Chris. *Making Sense of Cultural Studies: Central Problems and Critical Debates.* Thousand Oaks, CA: Sage, 2002.

Barnekov, Timothy, and Daniel Rich. "Privativism and the Limits of Local Economic Policy." *Urban Affairs Quarterly* 25, no. 2 (December 1989): 212-38.

Barnekov, Timothy, Robin Boyle, Daniel Rich, and Robert Warren. "The New Privatism, Federalism, and the Future of Urban Governance: National Urban Policy in the 1980s." *Journal of Urban Affairs* 3, no. 4 (Fall 1981).

Barnekov, Timothy, Robin Boyle, and Daniel Rich. *Privatism and Urban Policy in Britain and the United States.* New York: Oxford University Press, 1989.

Barr, Michael. "Lee Kuan Yew and the 'Asian Values' Debate." *Asian Studies Review* 24 (2000): 309-34.

Barthes, Roland. *S/Z.* Translated by Richard Miller. New York: Hill and Wang, 1974.

Bassett, K. "Urban Cultural Strategies and Urban Regeneration: A Case Study and Critique." *Environment and Planning A* 25, no. 12 (1993): 1773-88.

Bauman, Zygmunt. *City of Fears, City of Hopes.* London: Goldsmiths College, University of London, 2003.

Bayat, Asef. "Cairo's Poor: Dilemmas of Survival and Solidarity." *Middle East Report* 202 (1997): 2-6.

———. *Street Politics: Poor People's Movements in Iran.* New York: Columbia University Press, 1997.

———. "Activism and Social Development in the Middle East." Paper prepared for World Social Summit, Geneva, August 2000.

———. "Globalizing Social Movements? Comparing Middle Eastern Islamist Movements and Latin American Liberation Theology." Unpublished paper, Cairo.

Beauregard, Robert. *Voices of Decline: The Postwar Fate of U.S. Cities.* 2nd ed. New York: Routledge, 2003.

Becker, Jörg. "Internet in Asia: Introduction." In *Internet in Asia*, edited by Sankaran Ramanathan and Jörg Becker. Singapore: Asian Media and Information Centre, 2001.

Bennett, W.L. *News: The Politics of Illusion.* 5th ed. New York: Longman, 2003.

Benson, J., and B. Alden. "The Plugola Problem." *Columbia Journalism Review* 34, no. 1 (1995): 17-18.

Bew, Paul, and Henry Patterson. *Seán Lemass and the Making of Modern Ireland: 1945-66.* Dublin: Gill and Macmillan, 1982.

Black, Daniel, Gary Gates, Seth Sanders, and Lowell Taylor. "Demographics of the Gay and Lesbian Population in the United States: Evidence From Available Systematic Data Sources." *Demography* 37, no. 2 (2000): 139-54.

Bourdieu, Pierre. *Distinction: A Social Critique of the Judgment of Taste.* Cambridge, MA: Harvard University Press, 1984.

———. *Language and Symbolic Power.* Cambridge, MA: Harvard University Press, 1991.

———. *Practical Reason.* Stanford, CA: Stanford University Press, 1998.

Boyer, M.C. "Cities for Sale: Merchandising History at South Street Seaport." In *Variations on a Theme Park*, edited by Michael Sorkin. New York: Will and Wang, 1992.

Boyer, Paul. *Urban Masses and Moral Order in America, 1820-1920.* Cambridge, MA: Harvard University Press, 1984.

Brenner, Neil, and Nik Theodore, eds. *Spaces of Neoliberalism: Urban Restructuring in North American and Western Europe.* New York: Blackwell, 2002.

Britton, S. "Tourism, Capital, and Place: Towards a Critical Geography of Tourism." *Environment and Planning D: Society and Space* 9 (1991): 451-78.

Brooks, David. *Bobos in Paradise: The New Upper Class and How They Got There.* New York: Simon and Schuster, 2000.

Brooks, Jane, and Alma Young. "Revitalizing the Central Business District in the Face of Decline: The Case of New Orleans, 1970-1990." *Town Planning Review* 64 (1993): 251-71.

Brown, Michael. "On Resisting Resistance." *American Anthropologist* 98, no. 4 (1996): 729-49.

Brown, Nathan. *Peasant Politics in Modern Egypt: The Struggles vs. the State.* New Haven, CT: Yale University Press, 1990.

Buchanan, D.R., and J. Lev. *Beer and Fast Cars: How Brewers Target Blue-collar Youth Through Motor Sport Sponsorships.* Washington, DC: AAA Foundation for Traffic Safety, 1988.

Budd, Mike, Steve Craig, and Clay Steinman, *Consuming Environments: Television and Commercial Culture.* New Brunswick, NJ: Rutgers University Press, 1999.

Bureau of Governmental Research. *BGR Outlook on Orleans: Status Report on the 1998 City Operating Budget.* New Orleans, LA: Bureau of Governmental Research, 1998.

Burns, F.P., and M. Thomas. "Governors and the Development Regime in New Orleans." *Urban Affairs Review* 39, no. 6 (July 2004): 791-812.

Burns, J.P., J. Hatch and T.J. Mules, eds. *The Adelaide Grand Prix: The Impact of a Special Event on Adelaide.* Adelaide: Centre for South Australian Economic Studies, 1986.

Burton, John. "Singapore Threatens to Sue Blogger," *Financial Times*, 9 May 2005: 6.
———. "Singapore's Arts Ambitions Caught Up in Rights Debate," *Financial Times*, 14 May 2005: 2.

Butler, Tim (with Gary Robson). *London Calling: The Middle Classes and the Re-making of Inner London.* Oxford: Berg, 2003.

Carey, James W. "Notes on the Project of (American) Cultural Studies." In *Cultural Studies in Question*, edited by M. Ferguson and P. Golding. Thousand Oaks, CA: Sage, 1998.

Carragee, Kevin. "Interpretive Media Study and Interpretive Social Science." *Critical Studies in Mass Communication* 7 (1990): 81-97.

Carroll, J. "Local TV and Newspapers Remain Most Popular News Sources." December 2004. http://www.gallup.com.

Castells, Manuel. *The City and the Grassroots.* Berkeley: University of California Press, 1983.
———. *The Rise of the Network Society*, 2nd edition. Oxford: Blackwell, 2000.

Chase, Steven. "Technically, Ottawa's Slogan Is a Disaster." *The Globe and Mail*, 3 August 2001: A1.

Chatterton, Paul, and Robert Hollands. "Theorizing Urban Playscapes: Producing, Regulating, and Consuming Youthful Nightime Spaces." *Urban Studies* 39, no. 1 (2002): 95-116.
———. *Urban Nightscapes: Youth Cultures, Pleasure Spaces, and Corporate Power.* New York: Routledge, 2003.
———. "Will the Real Creative City Please Stand Up?" *City* 4, no. 3 (2000): 390-97.

Chikritzhs, T.N., H.A. Jonas, T.R., Stockwell, P.F. Heale, and P.M. Dietze. "Mortality and Life-Years Lost Due to Alcohol: A Comparison of Acute and Chronic Causes." *The Medical Journal of Australia* 174, no. 6 (2001): 281-84.

Chee, Soon Juan. "Media in Singapore." Paper presented at the Conference on the Media and Democracy. Sydney, Australia: Sydney University, 24 February 2000.

CIA. *World Fact Book*. Washington, DC: CIA, 1992.

City of New Orleans. *Operating Budget for Calendar and Fiscal Year 2002*. New Orleans: City of New Orleans, 2002.

————. *Operating Budget for Fiscal Year 1976*. New Orleans: City of New Orleans, 1976.

Cohen, R. "Cities in Developing Societies." *Introduction to the Sociology of Developing Societies*, edited by H. Alavi and T. Shanin, 366-86. London: Macmillan, 1982.

Cohen, R.M. "The Corporate Takeover of News: Blunting the Sword." In *Conglomerates and the Media*, edited by E. Barnouw, et al., 31-59. New York: The New Press, 1997.

Cole, Mike, and Dave Hill. "Games of Despair and Rhetorics of Resistance: Postmodernism, Education, and Reaction." *Journal of Sociology of Education* 16, no. 2 (1995): 133-50.

Collins, D.J., and H.M. Lapsley. "The Social Costs of Drug Abuse in Australia in 1988 and 1992." August 1996. http://www.health.gov.au/pubhlth/publicat/document/mono30.pdf.

Crompton, J. "Sponsorship of Sport by Tobacco and Alcohol Companies: A Review of the Issues." *Journal of Sport and Social Issues* 17, (1993): 148-67.

Daly, Mary. *Dublin, The Deposed Capital: A Social and Economic History, 1860-1914*. Cork: Cork University Press, 1984.

Davis, Mike. "Planet of Slums: Urban Involution and the Informal Proletariat." *New Left Review* 26, (March-April 2004): 5-34.

————. *The Planet of Slums*. New York: Verso, 2005.

Davis, Susan. "Space Jam: Media Conglomerates Build the Entertainment City." *European Journal of Communication* 14, no. 4 (1999): 435-59.

DC Agenda. "Issue Scan—Full Report: An Annual Report Examining Changes in Neighborhood Conditions in the District of Columbia." October 2004. http://www.dcagenda.org/dc_pub.html.

Degen, Monica. "Fighting for the Global Catwalk: Formalizing Public Life in Castelfield (Manchester) and Diluting Public Life in el Raval (Barcelona)." *International Journal of Urban and Regional Research* 27, no. 4 (2003): 867-80.

Delaney, Kevin, and Rick Eckstein. *Public Dollars, Private Stadiums: The Battle Over Building Sports Stadiums*. New Brunswick, NJ: Rutgers University Press, 2004.

Donald, B., and D. Morrow. *Competing for Talent: Implications for Social and Cultural Policy in Canadian City Regions*. Hull, Quebec: Department of Canadian Heritage, 2003.

Donaldson, Loraine. *Development Planning in Ireland*. New York: Frederick A. Praeger Publishers, 1966.

Dora, C. "A Different Route to Health: Implications of Transport Policies." *British Medical Journal* 318, (1999): 1686-1689.

Draper, Hall. *Karl Marx's Theory of Revolution*. New York: Monthly Review Press, 1978.

Dublin Tourism. *Golfing Around Dublin: A Visitor's Guide to Golfing in and Around Dublin*. Dublin: Dublin Tourism, 2001.

Eagleton, Terry. *The Great Hunger*. New York: Verso, 1995.

Eggler, Bruce. "Preservationists Reject Casino Hotel." *Times-Picayune,* 8 October 2003.

Éireann, Dáil. "Parliamentary Debates." March 1970. www.oireachtas-debates.gov.ie

Eisinger, Peter. "City Politics in an Era of Federal Devolution." *Urban Affairs Review* 33, no. 3 (1998): 308-25.

———. "The Politics of Bread and Circuses: Building the City for the Visitor Class." *Urban Affairs Review* 35, no. 3 (January 2000): 316-33.

Entman, Robert and Andrew Rojecki. *The Black Image in the White Mind.* Chicago: University of Chicago Press, 1999.

Escobar, Ernesto. *Encountering Development.* Princeton, NJ: Princeton University Press, 1995.

Fannie Mae Foundation. *The Poorest become Poorer: A Report on Patterns of Concentrated Neighborhood Poverty in Washington, D.C.* Accessed online at www.fanniemaefoundation.org.

———. "Calculators: How Much House Can You Afford?" September 2004. www.fanniemae.com.

Fannon, Frantz. *The Wretched of the Earth.* Harmondsworth, UK: Penguin, 1967.

Featherstone, Mike. "Postmodern City Cultures." In *Post-Fordism: A Reader*, edited by Ash Amin. Oxford: Blackwell, 1994.

Federal Communications Commission. *The Telecommunications Act of 1996: Broadcast Ownership and Dual Network Operations.* July 2003. Accessed online at http://www.fcc.gov/telecom.html.

———. "FCC Sets Limits on Media Concentration: A Summary of the Broadcast Ownership Rules Adopted on June 2, 2003." 22 July 2003. Accessed online at http://www.fcc.gov/ownership.

Fisher, A.J. Hatch, and B. Paix. "Road Accidents and the Grand Prix." *The Adelaide Grand Prix: The Impact of a Special Event*, edited by T.J. Mules, 151-68. Adelaide: Centre for South Australian Economic Studies, 1986.

Fiske, John. "Ethnosemiotics." *Cultural Studies* 4 (1990): 85-100.

Fiske, John. *Television Culture.* London: Routledge, 1987.

Fitzgerald, Garret. *Planning in Ireland.* Dublin: Institute of Public Administration, 1968.

Florida, Richard. *The Rise of the Creative Class.* New York: Basic Books, 2002.

———. *Cities and the Creative Class.* New York: Routledge, 2005.

———. "Kotkin's Fallacies—Why Diversity Matters to Economic Growth." (July 2005) http://www.creative class.org/baffler_response.html.

"Folding to the Casino Industry: How Soft Money Buys Congress." *Public Citizen*, 2001. Accessed online at http://www.citizen.org/congress/campaign/special_interest/articles.cfm?ID=5771.

Foucault, Michael. *Knowledge/Power.* New York: Pantheon, 1972.

Frank, Thomas. *The Conquest of Cool: Business Culture, Counterculture and the Rise of Hip Consumerism.* Chicago: University of Chicago Press, 1997.

Fraser, Murray. "Public Building and Colonial Policy in Dublin, 1760-1800." *Architectural History: Journal of Architectural Historians of Great Britain* 28 (1985): 113.

Fredline, E., and B. Faulkner. "Variations in Residents Reactions to Major Motorsports Events: Why Residents Perceive the Impacts of Events Differently." *Event Management* 7 (2001): 115-25.

Frey, James, ed. "Gambling: Socioeconomic Impacts and Public Policy." Special Issue of *Annals of the Academy of Political and Social Science.* March 1998.

Friedman, John. "The Dialectic of Reason." *International Journal of Urban and Regional Research* 13, no. 2 (1989): 217-44.

———. *Empowerment: The Politics of Alternative Development.* London: Blackwell, 1992.

————. "Rethinking Poverty: Empowerment and Citizen Rights." *International Social Science Journal* 148, (1996): 161-72.

Friedman, Michael, David Andrews, and Michael Silk. "Sport and the Façade of Redevelopment in the Postindustrial City." *Sociology of Sport Journal* 21 (2004): 119-39.

Gaffikin, Frank, and Barney Warf. "Urban Policy and the Post-Keynesian State in the United Kingdom and the United States." *International Journal of Urban and Regional Research* 17, no. 1 (1993): 67-84.

Garnham, Nicolas. *Capitalism and Communication: Global Culture and the Economics of Information*. London: Sage, 1990.

————. "Political Economy and Cultural Studies: Reconciliation or Divorce?" *Critical Studies in Mass Communication* 12 (1995): 62-71.

Gastil, J., and P. Levine. *The Deliberative Democracy Handbook: Strategies for Effective Civic Engagement in the Twenty-First Century*. San Francisco: Jossey-Bass, 2005.

Gay, du Paul, and Michael Pryke, eds. *Cultural Economy: Cultural Analysis and Commercial Life*. London: Sage, 2002.

Geertz, Clifford. *Local Knowledge: Further Essays in Interpretive Anthropology*. New York: Basic Books, 1983.

George, Cherian. *Singapore: The Air-Conditioned Society*. Singapore: Landmark Books, 2000.

Ghannam, Farha. "Relocation and Use of Urban Space." *Middle East Report* 202 (1997): 17-20.

Gibbons, G. Stephen, and Gregory L. Price. "Politics and Prison Development in a Rural Area." *Prison Journal* 75, no. 3 (1995): 380-90.

Gibson, Timothy. *Securing the Spectacular City: The Politics of Revitalization and Homelessness in Downtown Seattle*. Lanham, MD: Lexington Books, 2004.

Giddens, Anthony. *Sociology*. Oxford: Polity Press, 2000.

Gitlin, Todd. *Inside Prime Time*. New York: Pantheon, 1983.

Godlee, F. "Transport: A Public Health Issue." *British Medical Journal* 304, no. 6818 (1992): 48-50.

Gomez, James. *Self-Censorship: Singapore's Shame*. Singapore: Think Centre, 2000.

————. *Internet Politics: Surveillance and Intimidation in Singapore*. Singapore: Think Centre, 2002.

Gordon, David. "The Global Economy: New Edifice or Crumbling Foundations?" *New Left Review* 1988, no. 168: 24-64.

Gotham, Kevin Fox. "Representations of Space and Urban Planning in a Post-World War II U.S. City." In *Constructions of Urban Space*, edited by Ray Hutchison. Stamford, CT: JAI Press Inc., 2000.

————. *Critical Perspectives on Urban Redevelopment, Volume Six of Research in Urban Sociology*. New York: Elsevier Press, 2001.

————. "Marketing Mardi Gras: Commodification, Spectacle, and the Political Economy of Tourism in New Orleans." *Urban Studies* 39, no. 10 (September 2002): 1735-56.

————. "Theorizing Urban Spectacles: Festivals, Tourism, and the Transformation of Urban Space." *City: Analysis of Urban Trends, Culture, Theory, Policy, Action* 9, no. 2 (July 2005).

————. "Tourism Gentrification: The Case of New Orleans's Vieux Carre." (French Quarter) *Urban Studies* 42, no. 7 (June 2005): 1099-1121.

Gottdiener, Mark, ed. *New Forms of Consumption: Consumers, Culture, and Commodification*. Lanham, MD: Rowman & Littlefield, 2000.

———. *The Theming of America: American Dreams, Media Fantasies, and Themed Environments.* 2nd ed. Boulder, CO: Westview Press, 2001 [1997].

Graeme, Evans. "Hard-Branding the Cultural City—From Prado to Prada." *International Journal of Urban and Regional Research* 27, no. 2 (2003): 417-40.

———. "Measure for Measure: Evaluating the Evidence of Culture's Contribution to Regeneration." *Urban Studies* 43, no. 5/6 (2005), 959-83.

Graham-Rowe, D. "Too Hot to Handle: It's Not Just the Speed That Makes Motor Racing Dangerous." *New Scientist* 170, no. 2293 (2001): 13.

Green Motorsport. "GreenMotorsport.com: The Home of Environmentally Friendly Motorsport." 10 December 2003. http://www.btinternet.com/~keneth.foat/greenmotorsport/.

Grossberg, Larry. "Cultural Studies vs. Political Economy: Is Anybody Else Bored with This Debate?" *Critical Studies in Mass Communication* (1995): 72-81.

Gruneau, Richard, and David Whitson. *Hockey Night in Canada.* Toronto: Garamond, 1993.

———. "Upmarket Continentalism: Major League Sport, Promotional Culture, and Corporate Integration." In *Continental Order? Integrating North America for Cyber-Capital*, edited by V. Mosco and D. Schiller. Lanham, MD: Rowman & Littlefield, 2001.

Hackworth, Jason. "Progressive Activism in a Neoliberal Context: The Case of Efforts to Retain Public Housing in the United States." *Studies in Political Economy* 75 (Spring 2005): 29-51.

Haines, Andrew, T. McMichael, R. Anderson, and J. Houghton. "Fossil Fuels, Transport and Public Health." *British Medical Journal* 321 (2002): 1168-69.

Hall, Stuart. "Encoding/Decoding." In *Culture, Media, Language*, ed. S. Hall et al. London: Hutchinson, 1980

———. "The Problem of Ideology: Marxism without Guarantees." In *Marx: 100 years On*, ed. B. Matthews. London: Lawrence and Wishart, 1983.

Hall, Stuart, Chas Critcher, Tony Jefferson, John Clarke, and B. Robert. *Policing the Crisis: Mugging, the State, and Law and Order.* New York: Holmes & Meier, 1978.

Hamilton-Hart, Natasha. "The Singapore State Revisited," *Pacific Review* 13 (2000): 195-216

Hammer, J. "A Season of Sleaze in TV News." *Newsweek* 115, no. 24 (1990): 71.

Hamnett, Chris, and Noam Shoval. "Museums as Flagships of Urban Development." In *Cities and Visitors: Regulating People, Markets and City Space*, edited by Lily M. Hoffman, Susan S. Fainstein, and Dennis R. Judd. Malden, MA: Blackwell Publishing, 2003.

Hannigan, John. *Fantasy City: Pleasure and Profit in the Postmodern Metropolis.* London: Routledge, 1998.

———. "Symposium on Branding, the Entertainment Economy, and Urban Place Building: Introduction." *International Journal of Urban and Regional Research* 27, no. 2 (June 2003): 352-60.

———. "Boom Towns and Cool Cities: The Perils and Prospects of Developing a Distinctive Urban Brand in a Global Economy." Paper presented at the Leverhulme International Symposium 2004: The Resurgent City, London School of Economics and Political Science, April 2004, 19-21.

———. "Diversity Without Tears: Marketing the Multicultural in the Gentrified City." Paper presented at the Seminar on "Takeaway Cultures." Centre de Cultura Contemporània, Barcelona, December 2004.

Harvey, David. "From Managerialism to Entrepreneurialism: The Transformation in Urban Governance in Late Capitalism," *Geografiska Annaler B* 71 (1989): 3-17.

———. *The Condition of Postmodernity: An Enquiry into the Origins of Cultural Change.* Oxford: Blackwell, 1989.

———. "Flexible Accumulation Through Urbanization: Reflections on 'Postmodernism' in the American City." In *Post-Fordism: A Reader*, edited by Ash Amin. Oxford: Blackwell, 1994.

Harvey, J. "Sports and Recreation: Entertainment or Social Right?" *Horizons* 5, no. 1 (2002): 26-28.

Havens, Timothy. "'It's Still a White World Out There': The Interplay of Culture and Economics in the International Television Trade." *Critical Studies in Media Communication* 19 (2002): 377-91.

Headrick, Daniel. *The Tools of Empire: Technology and European Imperialism in the Nineteenth Century.* New York: Oxford University Press, 1981.

Heath, Joseph, and Andrew Potter. *The Rebel Sell: Why Culture Can't Be Jammed.* Toronto: HarperCollins, 2004.

Herivel, Tara, and Paul Wright, eds. *Prison Nation: The Warehousing of America's Poor.* New York: Routledge, 2003.

Herman, Edward, and Noam Chomsky. *Manufacturing Consent: The Political Economy of the Mass Media.* New York: Pantheon Books, 1988.

Hickey, N. "Money Lust." *Columbia Journalism Review* 37, no. 2 (1998): 28-37.

Hoc, Lim. "Cultural Strategies for Revitalizing the City: A Review and Evaluation." *Regional Studies* 27, no. 6 (1993): 592.

Hoffman, Lily, Susan Fainstein, and Dennis Judd, eds. *Cities and Visitors: Regulating People, Markets, and City Space.* New York: Blackwell Publishing, 2004.

Holcomb, Briavel. "Marketing Cities for Tourism." In *The Tourist City*, edited by Dennis Judd and Susan Fainstein. New Haven, CT: Yale University Press, 1999.

Holcomb, Briavel, and Robert Beauregard, *Revitalizing Cities.* Washington, DC: Association of American Geographers, 1981.

Hollie, Shaw. "Mega-Mall for Mirabel?" *Financial Post*, 27 August 2005: FP1, 5.

Hoodfar, Homa. *From Marriage to Market.* Berkeley: University of California Press, 1997.

Hoogvelt, Ankie. *Globalization and the Postcolonial World.* Baltimore, MD: Johns Hopkins University Press, 1997.

Horswill, M. "How to Have a Car Crash." Public lecture, 27 February 2001, Department of Psychology, University of Reading.

Horswill, M.S. and M.E. Coster. "The Effect of Vehicle Characteristics on Driver's Risk-Taking Behaviour." *Ergonomics* 45, no. 2 (2002): 85-104.

Hourcade, Bernard. "Conseillisme, Class Sociale, et Space Urbain: Les Squatters Du Sud de Tehran 1978-1981." *Urban Crisis and Social Movements in the Middle East*, edited by K. Brown et al. Paris: Editions L'Harmattan, 1989.

Huntington, S. *Political Order in Changing Society.* Ithaca, NY: Yale University Press, 1968.

Huntington, S., and J. Nelson. *No Easy Choice: Political Participation in Developing Countries.* Cambridge, MA: Harvard University Press, 1976.

ICF Consulting, *Choosing a Future: A New Economic Vision for Ottawa.* Ottawa: ICF Consulting, 2000.

ILO. *World Employment Report, 1998-1999.* Geneva: ILO, 1999.

Indergaard, Michael. *Silicon Alley: The Rise and Fall of a New Media District*. New York: Routledge, 2004.

Ipsos Public Affairs. "Press Release: New Poll for "No D.C. Taxes for Baseball." Coalition Shows: D.C. Voters Oppose Public Funding, Strongly Oppose Giveaway, Reject Ballpark Tax on Business, Want D.C. Council to Make Major Modification of Contract." November 2004. http://www.nodctaxesforbaseball.org.

Jacobs, Kerrie. "Why I Don't Love Richard Florida." 22 February 2005. Accessed online at www.metropolismag.com.

Jessop, Bob. "Post-Fordism and the State." In *Post-Fordism: A Reader*, edited by Ash Amin. Oxford: Blackwell, 1994.

Jhally, Sut, and Justin Lewis. *Enlightened Racism: The Cosby Show, Audiences, and the Myth of the American Dream*. Boulder, CO: Westview Press, 1992.

Johnson, Richard. "What Is Cultural Studies, Anyway?" *Social Text* 6, no. 1 (1987): 38-80.

Johnston, I. "Educating Drivers About Speed." In *Australian College of Road Safety*, edited by Road Safety Workshop on Speed, National Museum, Canberra, 2003.

Judd, Dennis. "Constructing the Tourist Bubble." In *The Tourist City*, edited by Dennis Judd and Susan Fainstein. New Haven, CT: Yale University Press, 1999.

Judd, Dennis, and Susan Fainstein, eds. *The Tourist City*. New Haven, CT: Yale University Press, 1999.

Judd, Dennis, and Todd Swanstrom. *City Politics: Private Power and Public Policy*. New York: HarperCollins, 1994.

Kalathil, Shanthi and Taylor Boas. *Open Networks, Closed Regimes: The Impact of the Internet on Authoritarian Rule*. Washington, DC: Carnegie Endowment for International Peace, 2003.

Kearns, Kevin. *Georgian Dublin: Ireland's Imperilled Architectural Heritage*. London: David and Charles, 1983.

Kearns, G., and C. Philo, eds. *Selling Places: The City as Cultural Capital, Past and Present*. Oxford: Pergamon Press, 1993.

Kellner, Douglas. "Overcoming the Divide: Cultural Studies and Political Economy." In *Cultural Studies in Question*, edited by Marjorie Ferguson and Peter Golding. London: Sage, 1998.

Kennedy, M., and P. Leonard. "Dealing with Neighborhood Change: A Primer on Gentrification and Policy Choices: A Discussion Paper Prepared for the Brookings Institution Center of Urban and Metropolitan Policy." 14 October 2004. http://www.brookings.edu./urban.

King, Ronette, and Stewart Yerton. "But Long-Term Economic Impact Is Still a Wild Card." *Times-Picayune*, 24 October 1999.

Klein, N. *No Logo*. New York: Picador USA, 1999.

Knauss, Tim. "MDA Seeks to Marry Creativity and Renewal." *(Syracuse) Post-Standard*, 26 February, 2004.

Knott, T. "Mayor's 'City Living, DC Style' Vision Shortsighted." *Washington Times*. 6 November 2003. http://washingtontimes.com.

Kotkin, Joel. *The New Geography: How the Digital Revolution Is Reshaping the American Landscape*. New York: Random House, 2000.

Kuo, Eddie, Alfred Choi, Arun Mahizhnan, Lee Wai Peng, and Christina Soh, *Internet in Singapore: Study on Usage and Impact*. Singapore: Times Academic Press, 2002.

Kuppinger, P. "Giza Spaces." *Middle East Report* 202 (1997): 14-16.

Kurtz, H. "Local TV News: Now Part of Sales?" *Washington Post*, 3 November 2003.

Laponce, J.A. "Ottawa, Christaller, Horowitz and Parsons." In *Capital Cities/Les Capi-tales*, edited by John Taylor, Jean Lengellé, and Caroline Andrew. Ottawa: Carleton University Press, 1993.

Lash, Scott, and John Urry. *The End of Organized Capitalism*. Madison: University of Wisconsin Press, 1987.

———. *Economies of Sign and Space*. London: Sage, 1994.

Lauria, Mickey, Robert Whelan, and Alma Young. "The Revitalization of New Orleans." In *Urban Revitalization: Policies and Programs*, edited by Fritz Wagner, Timothy Joder, and Anthony Mumphrey. Thousand Oaks, CA: Sage Publications, 1995.

Lav, Iris, and Andrew Brecher. "Passing Down the Deficit: Federal Policies Contribute to the Severity of State Fiscal Crisis." *Center on Budget and Policy Priorities*, 2004. http://www.cbpp.org/5-12-04sfp.htm.

Lee, Terrance. "Emulating Singapore: Towards a Model for Internet Regulation in Asia," in *Asian Cyberactivism: Freedom of Expression and Media Censorship*, edited Steven Gan, James Gomez, and Uwe Johannen. Bangkok: Friedrich Naumann Foundation, 2004.

Lee, T. Waipeng. "Singapore." In *Internet in Asia*, edited by Sankaran Ramanathan and Jörg Becker. Singapore: Asian Media and Information Centre, 2001.

Leeds, A. "The Concept of the 'Culture of Poverty': Conceptual, Logical, and Empirical Problems with Perspectives from Brazil and Peru." In *The Culture of Poverty: A Critique*, edited by E.B. Leacock. New York: Simon and Schuster, 1971.

Leeds, A., and E. Leeds. "Accounting for Behavioral Differences: Three Political Systems and the Responses of Squatters in Brazil, Peru, and Chile." In *The City in Comparative Perspective*, edited by J. Walton and L. Magotti, 193-248. London: John Wiley, 1976.

Leeds, Jeff, and Louise Story. "Radio Payoffs Are Described as Sony Settles." *New York Times*, July 26, 2005.

Lees, Loretta. "The Ambivalence of Diversity and the Politics of Urban Renaissance: The Case of Growth in Downtown Portland, Maine." *International Journal of Urban and Regional Research* 27, no. 3: 613-34.

Lefebvre, Henri. *The Production of Space*. Cambridge, MA: Blackwell, 1991.

Lenhart, H. "The Race to the Bottom." *Oregon Business*, May 1997, 31.

Lenin, V.I. *What Is to Be Done*. Peking: Foreign Language Press, 1973.

Lenskyj, Helen. *Inside the Olympic Industry* Albany: SUNY Press, 2000.

———. "Sport and Corporate Environmentalism." *International Review for the Sociology of Sport* 33, no. 4. (1998): 341-54.

Levander, Michelle. "Singapore to Relax Censorship Laws As It Seeks to Expand Internet Access." *Wall Street Journal*, 1 September 1999.

Levine, E. "Toward a Paradigm for Media Production Research: Behind the Scenes at General Hospital." *Critical Studies in Media Communication* 18 (2001): 66-82.

Lewis, Oscar. *Five Families: Mexican Case Studies in the Culture of Poverty*. New York: Basic Books, 1959.

———. *The Children of Sanchez: Autobiography of a Mexican Family*. New York: Random House, 1961.

———. *La Vida: A Puerto Rican Family in the Culture of Poverty*. New York: Random House, 1966.

Lim, Hoc. "Cultural Strategies for Revitalizing the City: A Review and Evaluation," *Regional Studies* 27, no. 6 (1993): 589-94.

Livingstone, Sonia. "The Rise and Fall of Audience Research: An Old Story with a New Ending." *Journal of Communication* 43, no. 4 (1993): 5-12.

Lloyd, Richard. "Grit as Glamour: Neo-Bohemia and Urban Change." Unpublished manuscript, University of Chicago, 2000

———. "'Neo-Bohemia': Art and Neighborhood Redevelopment in Chicago." *Journal of Urban Affairs* 24, no. 5 (2002): 521.

Lloyd, Richard, and Terry Nichols Clark. "The City as an Entertainment Machine." In *Critical Perspectives on Urban Redevelopment*, vol. 6, *Research in Urban Sociology*, edited by Kevin Fox Gotham. New York: Elsevier Press, 2001.

Logan, John, and Harvey Molotch. *Urban Fortunes: Towards the Political Economy of Place*. Berkeley: University of California Press, 1987.

Louisiana State University Agricultural Center Research and Extension. "About Allen Parish." 1999. http://www2.lsuagcenter.com/parish/allen/About_the_Parish.htm.

Lowes, Mark. *Indy Dreams and Urban Nightmares: Speed Merchants, Spectacle, and the Struggle Over Public Space in the World-Class City*. Toronto: University of Toronto Press, 2002.

———. "Major League Sports, Civic Discourse and the 'World-Class' City." In *Civic Discourse and Cultural Politics in Canada: A Cacophony of Voices*, edited by S. Fergusson and L. Shade. Westport, CT: Ablex Publishing, 2002.

Lowry, Dennis, T. Nio, and D. Leitner. "Setting the Public Fear Agenda: A Longitudinal Analysis of Crime Reporting, Public Perceptions of Crime, and FBI Crime Statistics." *Journal of Communication* 53, no. 1 (2003): 61-73.

Macek, Steve. *Urban Nightmares: The Panic Over the Post-Industrial City in the Media and Public Discourse*. Minneapolis: University of Minnesota Press, 2006.

Mackenzie, Suzanne. "Building Women, Building Cities: Towards Gender Sensitive Theory in the Environmental Disciplines." In *Life Spaces*, edited by Caroline Andrew and Beth Moore Milroy, 13-30. Vancouver, BC: UBC Press, 1988.

Malton, James. *Malton's Dublin*. Dublin: The Dolmen Press, 1987.

Martin, H. "Payola Controversy Heats Up." *Radio Magazine Online*, 13 March 2003. http://beradio.com/ar/radio_payola_controversy_heats/.

Mason, C. "Transport and Health: En Route to a Healthier Australia?" *The Medical Journal of Australia* 172, no. 5 (2000): 230-32.

Mattick, R.P., and T. Jarvis. *An Outline for the Management of Alcohol Problems: Quality Assurance Project*. Canberra: AGPS, 1993.

McAdam, D., S. Tarrow, and C. Tilly. "Towards an Integrated Perspective on Social Movements and Revolution." In *Comparative Politics: Rationality, Culture, and Structure*, edited by M.J. Linchbach and A. Zuckerman. Cambridge: Cambridge University Press, 1997.

McAllister, M.P. "Television News Plugola and the Last Episode of Seinfeld." *Journal of Communication* 52, no. 2 (2002): 383-401.

McChesney, Robert W. *Rich Media, Poor Democracy: Communication Politics in Dubious Times*. New York: The New Press, 1999.

———. *The Problem of the Media: U.S. Communication Politics in the 21st Century*. New York: Monthly Review Press, 2004.

McDonald, Frank. *The Destruction of Dublin*. Dublin: Gill and Macmillan.

McGee, T.G. "The Persistence of Proto-Proletariat: Occupational Structures and Planning of the Future of Third World Cities." In *Comparative Politics: Rationality, Culture, Structure*, edited by M. Linchbach and A. Zuckerman. Cambridge: Cambridge University Press, 1997.

McNally, David. "Globalization on Trial: Crisis and Class Struggle in East Asia." *Monthly Review* 50, no. 4 (1998): 1-13.

Meehan, Eileen. "Leisure or Labor?: Fan Ethnography and Political Economy." In *Consuming Audiences? Production and Reception in Media Research*, edited by I. Hagen and J. Wasko. Cresskill, NJ: Hampton Press, 2000.

Meisel, John. "Capital Cities: What Is a Capital?" In *Capital Cities/Les Capitales: Perspectives Internationales/International Perspectives*, edited by J. Taylor, J.G. Lengellé, and C. Andrew. Ottawa: Carleton University Press, 1993.

Mele, C. "The Materiality of Urban Discourse: Rational Planning in the Restructuring of the Early-Twentieth Century Urban Ghetto." *Urban Affairs Review* 35, no. 5 (2000): 628-48.

Melucci, A. "A Strange Kind of Newness: What's 'New' in New Social Movements?" *New Social Movements*, edited by Enrique Larana, Hank Johnston, and Joseph R. Gusfield. Philadelphia, PA: Temple University Press, 1994.

Mommaas, Hans. "Cultural Clusters and the Post-Industrial City: Towards the Remapping of Urban Cultural Policy." *Urban Studies* 41, no. 3 (2004): 507-32.

Moores, Shaun. "Texts, Readers, and Contexts of Reading: Developments in the Study of Media Audiences." *Media, Culture, and Society* 12 (1990): 1-22.

Morley, David. "Active Audience Theory: Pendulums and Pitfalls." *Journal of Communication* 43, no. 4 (1993): 13-21.

Mosco, Vincent. *The Political Economy of Communication: Rethinking and Renewal.* Thousand Oaks, CA: Sage, 1996.

"Most of the City's Workers Fall into Service Jobs: Orleans Poverty Rate Among the Worst in the U.S." *Times-Picayune*, 20 November 2001: 1.

Mowbray, Rebecca. "Harrah's Bill Passed, But Hand Isn't Over Yet." *Times-Picayune*, 15 March 2001.

———. "The Art of the Deal." *Times-Picayune*, 18 April 2001.

———. "Harrah's In Negotiations to Buy Casino Rival Caesar's." *Times-Picayune*, 14 July 2004.

———. "Harrah's Building Nightclub." *Times-Picayune*, 8 March 2005.

———. "State Approves Harrah's, Caesar's Merger Plan." *Times-Picayune*, 16 March 2005.

———. "Revenue from Gaming Grows Slowly." *Times-Picayune*, 16 July 2003.

Murdock, Graham. "Base Notes: The Conditions of Cultural Practice." In *Cultural Studies in Question,* edited by Marjorie Ferguson and Peter Golding. London: Sage, 1998.

Nakamura, David, and Thomas Heath. "Amended Deal on Stadium Approved: Council Seals Return of Baseball to DC." *Washington Post*, 22 December 2004: A1.

Nakamura, David. "Selling a Hipper Image: Marketing Campaign Seeks to Attract Upscale Residents." *The Washington Post*, 19 June 2003: T10.

National Low Income Housing Coalition, *Out of Reach 2003: America's Housing Wage Climbs.* 24 September 2004. http://www.nlihc.org/oor2003.

Nelson, Joan. "The Urban Poor: Disruption or Political Integration in Third World Cities." *World Politics* 22: 393-414.

New Straits Times (Malaysia) "Film Festival to Showcase Human Rights Issues," 26 June 2005: 22.

Newburn, Tim. "The Commodification of Policing: Security Networks in the Late Modern City." *Urban Studies* 38, no. 5-6 (2001): 829-48.

O'Cleireacain, C, and Alice Rivlin. "Envisioning a Future Washington: A Brookings Institution Research Brief." 18 November 2004. Accessed online at http://www.brookings.edu.

Office of the Chief Financial Officer, *Tax Rates and Tax Burdens in the District of Columbia—A Nationwide Comparison*. Washington, DC: Office of the Chief Financial Officer, 2004.

Ono, K., and D. Buescher. "Deciphering Pocahontas." *Critical Studies in Media Communication* 18, no. 1 (2001): 23-41.

Ozawa, C.P., ed. *The Portland Edge: Challenges and Successes in Growing Communities*. Washington, DC: Island Press, 2004.

Pabico, Alecks. "Southeast Asian Regimes Seek to Control Internet: Results Mixed." March 1998. A special report online at: www.freedomforum.org.

Park, Robert. "Human Migration and Marginal Man." *American Journal of Sociology* 33, no. 6 (1928): 881-93.

Parker, D.J.T., Reason, A.S.R. Manstead, and S.G. Stradling. "Driving Errors, Driving Violations and Accident Involvement." *Ergonomics* 38, no. 5 (1995): 1036-48.

Parker, D., and S. Stradling. "Influencing Driver Attitudes and Behaviour: Road Safety Research Report." London: Department of the Environment, Transport and the Regions, 2001.

Pear, Robert. "Buying of News by Bush's Aides is Ruled Illegal." *New York Times*, 30 September 2005: 1.

Pearlman, J. *Myth of Marginality*. Berkeley: University of California Press, 1976.

Pelofsky, J. "FCC Vote Prelude to Appeal." *Houston Chronicle*, 31 May 2003. Retrieved 15 June 2003 from Lexis-Nexis.

Pew Research Center. "News Media's Improved Image Proves Short-Lived: The Sagging Stock Market's Big Audience." August 2002. http://people-press.org.

Phillips, Susan, ed. *How Ottawa Spends 1995-96: Mid-Life Crises*. Ottawa: Carleton University Press, 1995.

Phinney, Richard. *Links of Heaven: A Complete Guide to Golf Journeys in Ireland*. New York: Baltray Books, 1996.

Pile, Steve. "Opposition, Political Identities, and Spaces of Resistance." In *Geographies of Resistance*, edited by S. Pile and M. Keith. London: Routledge, 1997.

Piore, Michael and Charles Sabel. *The Second Industrial Divide*. New York: Basic Books, 1984.

Piven, F. and R. Cloward. *Poor People's Movements: Why They Succeed, How They Fail*. New York: Vintage, 1979.

Poe, Edgar. "Oakdale, with 30.2 Percent Jobless, Seeks Alien Detention Center." *Times-Picayune*, 14 August 1982.

———. "Boost For Allen Parish." *Times-Picayune*, 23 February 1983.

Pope, John. "As the Mill Stench Left, So did the Town's Jobs." *Times-Picayune*, 14 August 1982.

———. "Unemployment in Allen Parish Highest in LA." *Times-Picayune*, 16 May 1982.

Pound, Richard. "The IOC and the Environment." *Olympic Message* 35 (March 1993).

Press, Andrea, and Elizabeth Cole. *Speaking of Abortion: Television and Authority in the Lives of Women*. Chicago: University of Chicago Press, 1999.

Procar Australia. "Formula Green: Brock and Brabham Target Help for Environment." 10 December 2003. http://www.procar.com.au.

Project for Excellence in Journalism. "The State of the News Media, 2004." 19 July 2004. www.stateofthenewsmedia.org.

Putnam, R.D., and L.M. Feldstein. *Better Together: Restoring the American Community.* New York: Simon & Schuster, 2003.

Quinn, Michael. "1916: Progress Backwards." *Build* (January 1966).

Radway, Janice. *Reading the Romance: Women, Patriarchy, and Popular Literature.* Chapel Hill: University of North Carolina Press, 1984.

Radio and Television News Directors Association. *RTNDA Code of Ethics.* December 2002. http://www.rtnda.org/ethics/coe.shtml.

Reeves, E.B. "Power, Resistance, and the Cult of Muslim Saints in a Northern Egyptian Town." *American Ethnologist* 22, no. 2 (1995): 306-22.

Reich, Robert. *The Work of Nations.* New York: Basic Books, 1991.

———. *The Future of Success.* New York: Basic Books, 2000.

Rein, Irving, and B.R. Shields. "Communication and Sports: Language of the City." Paper presented at the Annual Meeting of the National Communication Association. Chicago, Illinois. 10 November 2004.

Ritzer, George. *Enchanting a Disenchanted World: Revolutionizing the Means of Consumption.* 2nd edition. Thousand Oaks, CA: Pine Forge Press, 2005 [1999].

Robertson, K. "Downtown Redevelopment Strategies in the United States: An End-of-the-Century Assessment." *Journal of the American Planning Association* 61, no. 4 (1995): 429-37.

Rodale Publishers. "About *Bicycling*/About *Mountain Bike.*" 13 September 2004. http://www.bicycling.com/about us/0,3291,s1,00.html.

Rodan, Garry. "The Internet and Political Control in Singapore," *Political Science Quarterly* 113 (1998): 63-89.

———. "Asian Crisis, Transparency and the International Media in Singapore," *Pacific Review* 132 (2000): 215-42

———. "Singapore: Globalisation and the Politics of Economic Restructuring," In *The Political Economy of South-East Asia: Conflicts, Crises, and Change*, 2nd Edition, ed. Gary Rodan, Kevin Hewison, and Richard Robison. Melbourne: Oxford University Press, 2001.

Romer, D., K.H. Jamieson, and S. Aday. "Television News and the Fear of Crime." *Journal of Communication* 53, no. 1 (2003): 88-104.

Rosaldo, R. *Culture and Truth.* Boston: Beacon Books, 1989.

Rosenstiel, T. C. Gottlieb, and A. Finlayson. "The Magic Formula: Five Proven Steps to Financial Success in the News." *Columbia Journalism Review* 40, no. 4 (2001): 5-7.

Rubin M.S. and C. Bragitikos. "Destination Development Arrives." *Urban Land* 60, no. 2 (2001): 40-49.

Sack, Kevin. "New Orleans Casino Is Halted in Bankruptcy Filing." *Times-Picayune*, 23 November 1995.

Santagata, W. "Cultural Districts, Property Rights and Sustainable Urban Growth." *International Journal of Urban and Regional Research* 26, no. 1 (2002):19.

Sassen, Saskia. *The Global City: New York, London, Tokyo.* Princeton, NJ: Princeton University Press, 1991.

Schedler, Andreas. "The Menu of Manipulation: Elections Without Democracy," *Journal of Democracy* 13 (2002): 36-50.

Scott, Allen. *The Cultural Economy of Cities.* London: Sage, 2000.

Scott, James. *Weapons of the Weak: Everyday Forms of Peasant Resistance.* New Haven, CT: Yale University Press, 1985.

———. "Everyday Form of Peasant Resistance." *Journal of Peasant Studies* 13, no. 2 (1986): 5-35.

Schulberg, P. "KGW's Barry Is Still an Anchor in Local Waters." *Portland* [Oregon] *Tribune*, 2 August 2005. http://www.portlandtribune.com.

Schuurman, F., and T. Van Naerssen. *Urban Social Movements in the Third World*. London: Croom Helm, 1989.

Sennett, Richard. *The Conscience of the Eye*. New York: Knopf, 1991.

——. *The Uses of Disorder: Personal Identity and City Life*. London: Faber & Faber, 1996.

Shenon, Phillip. "2-Edged Sword: Asian Regimes on the Internet," *New York Times*, 29 May 1995.

Singerman, Diane. *Avenues of Participation: Family, Politics, and Networks in Urban Quarters of Cairo*. Princeton, NJ: Princeton University Press, 1995.

Smith, Neil. *The New Urban Frontier: Gentrification and the Revanchist City*. London: Routledge, 1996.

Smith, Peter Michael, and Marlene Keller. "'Managed Growth' and the Politics of Uneven Development in New Orleans." In *Restructuring the City: The Political Economy of Urban Redevelopment*, edited by Susan Fainstein et al. New York: Longman 1986, 126-66.

Sorkin, Micahel ed., *Variations on a Theme Park: The New American City and the End of Public Space*. New York: Hill and Wang, 1992.

Stabile, Carol. "Nike, Social Responsibility, and the Hidden Abode of Production." *Critical Studies in Media Communication* 17, no. 2 (2000): 186-204.

Steeves, Leslie, and Janet Wasko. "Feminist Theory and Political Economy: Toward a Friendly Alliance." In *Sex & Money: Feminism and Political Economy in the Media*, edited by E. Meehan & E. Riordan, Minneapolis, MN: University of Minnesota Press, 2002.

Steven, Miles, and Malcolm Miles. *Consuming Cities*. Houndsmills, Basingstoke, Hampshire: Palgrave Macmillan, 2004.

Steven, Miles, and Ronan Paddison. "Introduction: The Rise and Rise of Culture-Led Urban Regeneration." *Urban Studies* 42, no. 4/5 (2005): 833.

Stonequist, Everett. "The Problem of the Marginal Man," *American Journal of Sociology* 41 (1935): 1-12.

Sussman, Gerald. "The 'Tiger' from Lion City: Singapore's Niche in the New International Division of Communication and Information." In *Transnational Communications: Wiring the Third World*, edited by Gerald Sussman and John A. Lent. Newbury Park, CA: Sage, 1991.

——. *Communication, Technology, and Politics in the Information Age*. Thousand Oaks, CA: Sage Publications, 1997.

Sweeney, K. "Spotlight On: Video News Releases. What's Next for VNRs? The War is Over, But Stations are Still Choosy About What to Air." *Public Relations Tactics*. June 2003. http://www.prsa.org.

Sydney Olympic Bid Committee. "Environmental Guidelines for the Summer Olympic Games." 12 November 2003. http://www.greenpeace.org.au/archives/olympics/reports/enviroguide.pdf.

Tai, Y.F., J.B. Saunders, and D.S. Celermajer. "Collateral Damage From Alcohol Abuse: The Enormous Cost to Australia." *The Medical Journal of Australia* 168, no. 1 (1998): 6-7.

Tan, Tarn Han. "Rules on e-Campaigning Spelt Out." *Straits Times*, 18 October 2001. http://straitstimes.asia1.com.sg.

Teesson, M.W. Hall, M. Lynskey, and L. Degemhardt. "Alcohol and Drug-Use Disorders in Australia: Implications of the National Survey of Mental Health and Wellbeing." *The Australian and New Zealand Journal of Psychiatry* 34, no. 2 (2000): 206-13.

"The Drake Works." *Eye*, 30 December 2004, 11.

"The Government's Annual Survey on Infocomm Usage in Households and by Individuals for 2004." www.ida.gov.sg.

Thomas, Graham, and Sally Wyatt. "Access Is Not the Only Problem: Using and Controlling the Internet." In *Technology and In/Equality*, edited by Sally Wyatt, Flis Henwood, Nod Miller and Peter Senker. New York: Routledge, 2000.

Thompson, J.B. *Studies in the Theory of Ideology*. Berkeley: University of California Press, 1984.

———. "Introduction" In *Language and Symbolic Power*, edited by Pierre Bourdieu. Cambridge, MA: Harvard University Press, 1991.

Thornely, David. "Ireland: The End of an Era?" *Studies* 53 (1964): 1-17.

"Toronto Race Site Is Similar to Hastings Park." *Vancouver Sun*, 17 January 1997, E1, E3.

Tranter, Paul. "Motor Racing in Australia: Health Damaging or Health Promoting?" *Australian Journal of Primary Health* 9, no. 1 (2003): 50-58.

Tranter, Paul, and T.J. Keeffe. "Zero Road Toll—A Dream or a Realistic Vision." Report prepared for the 24th Australasian Transport Research Forum, Hobart, Australia: Tasmanian Department of Infrastructure, Energy and Resources.

Troutman, Parke. "A Growth Machine's Plan B: Legitimating Development When the Value-Free Growth Ideology Is Under Fire." *Journal of Urban Affairs* 26, no. 5 (2004): 611-22.

Tsaprailis, Ellen. "Luring the Endangered Tourist." *Ottawa*, June/July (2005): 44.

Tuchman, Gaye. *Making the News: A Study in the Construction of Reality*. New York: Free Press, 1978.

Turner, M.A., G.T. Kingsley, K. Pettit, and N. Sawyer. *Housing in the Nation's Capital*, 2004. Washington, DC: Fannie Mae Foundation and the Urban Institute, 2004.

Turow, Joseph. "Hidden Conflict and Journalistic Norms: The Case of Self-Coverage." *Journal of Communication* 44, no. 2 (1994): 29-46.

Urie, C. "Doctors Working Group Report on the Health Impact of the Albert Park Grand Prix." 2004. http://www.save-albert-park.org.au.

Urry, John. *The Tourist Gaze*. 2nd edition. London: Sage Publications, 2003.

U.S. Census Bureau, *Census of Population and Housing, 1980 and 1990*. http:// www.census.gov.

———. "Census of Population and Housing: New Orleans." Data supplied by the State of the Cities Data System, http://socds.huduser.org.

———. "State and County Quick Facts: District of Columbia." 14 September 2004. http://quickfacts.census.gov/qfd/states.

U.S. General Accounting Office. *Report to Congressional Requesters: District of Columbia Structural Imbalance and Management Issues*. Washington, DC: U.S. General Accounting Office, 2004.

Valentine, C. *Culture and Poverty: Critique and Counter Proposals*. Chicago: University of Chicago Press, 1968.

Vandemoortele, J. "The African Employment Crisis of the 1990s," in *The Employment Crisis in Africa*, edited by C. Grey-Johnson. Harare: African Association for Public Administration and Management, 1990.

Wasko, Janet. *Understanding Disney*. Cambridge, MA: Polity Press, 2000.

Water, John. *An Intelligent Person's Guide to Modern Ireland.* London: Duckworth, 1998.

Watson, G.L., and J.P. Kopachevsky. "Interpretations of Tourism as Commodity." *Annals of Tourism Research* 21, no. 3 (1994): 643-60.

Webster, Neil. "The Role of NGDOs in Indian Development: Some Lessons from West Bengal and Karnataka," *The European Journal of Development Research* 7 (1995): 407-33.

Weissman, Stephen, Jamie Willmuth, and Frank Clement. "Betting on Trent Lott: The Casino Gambling Industry's Campaign Contributions Pay Off in Congress." *Public Citizen*, June 1999. http://www.citizen.org/congress/campaign/special_interest/ articles.cfm?ID=6544.

Whelan, Robert. "New Orleans: Mayoral Politics and Economic-Development Policies in the Postwar Years, 1945-1986." In *The Politics of Urban Development*, edited by C.N. Stone and H.T. Sanders. Lawrence: University Press of Kansas, 1987.

————. "New Orleans: Public-Private Partnerships and Uneven Development." In *Unequal Partnerships*, edited by Gregory D. Squires, 222-29. New Brunswick, NJ: Rutgers University Press, 1989.

Whelan, Robert, and Alma Young. "New Orleans: The Ambivalent City." In *Big City Politics in Transition*, edited by H.V. Savitch and John Clayton Thomas. Newbury Park, CA: Sage Publications, 1991.

Whelan, Robert, Alma Young, and Mickey Lauria. "Urban Regimes and Racial Politics in New Orleans." *Journal of Urban Affairs* 16, no. 1 (1994): 1-21.

Whitt, J. "Mozart in the Metropolis: The Arts Coalition and the Urban Growth Machine." *Urban Affairs Quarterly* 23, no. 1 (1987): 15-36.

Wide Streets Commission, *City of Dublin: Wide and Convenient Ways, Streets and Passages* (Dublin: Wide Streets Commission, 1802).

Wilbon, Michael "D.C. Baseball in Foul Territory." *Washington Post*, 6 November 2004.

Wilks-Heeg, S., and P. North. "Cultural Policy and Urban Regeneration: A Special Edition of Local Economy." *Local Economy* 19, no. 3 (2004): 305-11.

Williams, Anthony. "Mayor Williams" Second Inaugural Address: One City, One Future." 29 September 2004. http://www.dc.gov/ mayor/speeches/ speech.asp?cp=1&id=76.

Williams, A.F. and B. O'Neill. "On-the-Road Driving Records of Licensed Race Drivers." *Accident Analysis and Prevention* 6 (1974): 263-70.

Williams, D. "Synergy Bias: Conglomerates and Promotion in the News." *Journal of Broadcasting & Electronic Media* 46, no. 3 (2002): 453-72.

Williams, Raymond. *Marxism and Literature.* Oxford: Oxford University Press, 1977.

Wilson, J.Q. and George Kelling. "Broken Windows." *The Atlantic Monthly* (March 1982): 29-38.

Wilson, Mark. "Information Networks: The Global Offshore Labor Force." In *Global Productions: Labor in the Making of the Information Society*, edited by G. Sussan and J. Lent. Creskill, NJ: Hampton Press, 1998.

Wilson, David. "Metaphors, Growth Coalition Discourses and Black Poverty Neighborhoods in a US City." *Antipode* 28 (1996): 72-96.

Wilson, David, and Jared Wouters. "Spatiality and Growth Discourse: The Restructuring of America's Rust Belt Cities." *Journal of Urban Affairs* 25, no. 2 (2003), 128.

Winston, Brian. *Misunderstanding Media.* Cambridge, MA: Harvard University Press, 1986.

Worsley, Peter. *The Three Worlds.* London: Weidenfeld and Nicolson, 1984.

Wright, J. *Fixin to Git*. London: Duke University Press, 2002.

Zeitlin, Arnold. "Singapore's New Restrictions on International Broadcasters Assailed at Conference." 23 May 2001. http://www.freedomforum.org.

Zukin, Sharon. *The Cultures of Cities*. Cambridge, MA: Blackwell, 1995.

———. *Landscapes of Power: From Detroit to Disneyland*. Berkeley: University of California Press, 1991.

Index

About the Contributors

Caroline Andrew is the director of the Centre on Governance and a professor in the School of Political Studies at the University of Ottawa. Her research areas are municipal government, urban development, and women in local politics. She is currently involved in an action research project between the city of Ottawa and community-based women's groups, City for All Women Initiative, as well as research projects looking at the management of diversity in Montreal and in Ottawa, the idea of "best practices" in the management of diversity in Ottawa, and the evaluation of "Québec en forme." Professor Andrew sits on the boards of the Lower Town Community Resource Centre, Inter Pares, the Ottawa Crime Prevention Council, and the City of Ottawa advisory committee on French-language services.

Asef Bayat is the academic director of the International Institute for the Study of Islam in the Modern World (ISIM) and ISIM Professor at Leiden University in the Netherlands. Before joining Leiden, Asef Bayat taught sociology and Middle East studies at American University in Cairo, Egypt. His areas of interest include political sociology, social movements, urban societies in transition, international development, comparative Islamist movements, and Muslim Middle East. He is the author of *Workers and Revolution in Iran* (London, 1987), *Work, Politics and Power* (London and New York, 1991), *Street Politics* (New York, 1998), and *Making Islam Democratic: Social Movements and Post-Islamist Turn* (forthcoming).

Timothy A. Gibson is an assistant professor of communication at George Mason University in Fairfax, Virginia. Professor Gibson has authored a number of publications on the media and politics of urban development, including *Securing the Spectacular City*, a book about the political struggles waged over revitalization, civic space, and homelessness in downtown Seattle during the 1990s. His most recent research explores the relationship between local development debates, local media coverage, and the imperatives of global urban promotion.

Kevin Fox Gotham is an associate professor in the department of sociology at Tulane University in New Orleans. He is currently serving as a program director for the Social and Political Sciences Cluster of the National Science Foundation (NSF). He is the author of *Race, Real Estate, and Uneven Development: The Kansas City Experience, 1900-2000* and the editor of *Critical Perspectives on Urban Redevelopment*. His current research interests are in the areas of political economy, real estate, housing, and urban tourism.

John Hannigan is professor of sociology at the University of Toronto. He is widely published on issues of the environment and urbanism. His book, *Fantasy City: Pleasure and Profit in the Postmodern Metropolis* deals with the consequences of building entertainment mega-projects in urban areas. More recently, he organized, edited, and wrote the introduction to a special symposium on "Branding and the Global Entertainment Economy" published in the *International Journal of Urban and Regional Research*. The second, revised edition of his popular text, *Environmental Sociology*, is due to come out in April, 2006.

Jeannie Haubert is a Ph.D. candidate at Tulane University in New Orleans. She is a North Carolina native who completed her undergraduate studies at Furman University in Greenville, South Carolina. Ms. Haubert specializes in immigration, racial and ethnic relations, and social stratification and has a particular interest in Latinos in the United States. She is currently working on a dissertation entitled "Discrimination in the rental market: A focus on Latinos" and anticipates completing the Ph.D. in December 2006.

Carey L. Higgins is a television newscast director currently at KGW-TV and previously at KPTV/KPDX Fox affiliates in Portland, Oregon. She has nine years of television newsroom experience in the United States. Ms. Higgins holds an M.S. in communication studies from Portland State University and a B.A. in journalism/telecommunication arts from the University of Georgia.

Andrew Kincaid is an assistant professor of English at the University of Wisconsin-Milwaukee. He earned his Ph.D. in 2001 from the department of cultural studies and comparative literature at the University of Minnesota. He has published articles in *The Journal of Commonwealth and Postcolonial Studies, College Literature*, and *REA: A Journalof Religion, Education & the Arts*. His book, *Postcolonial Dublin: Imperial Legacies and the Built Environment*, will appear in May 2006.

Mark Lowes is an associate professor of communication at the University of Ottawa. He is the author of *Inside the Sports Pages*, an ethnographic study of the work routines and professional ideologies of sports journalists and their editors. His most recent book, *Indy Dreams and Urban Nightmares: Speed Merchants, Spectacle, and the Struggle Over Public Space in the World-Class City*, examines the role megasport events play in the economic and cultural growth strategies of emerging "world-class" cities. His current research explores the viability of sports tourism as a vehicle for fostering social cohesion in Canada's rural communities.

Vincent Mosco is Canada Research Chair in communication and society at Queen's University. Professor Mosco graduated from Georgetown University (Summa Cum Laude, Phi Beta Kappa) in 1970 and received his Ph.D. in sociology from Harvard University in 1975. Professor Mosco is the author of numerous books, articles, and policy reports on the media, telecommunications, computers, and information technology. His most recent book, *The Digital Sublime: Myth, Power, and Cyberspace*, won the 2005 Olson Award for outstanding book in the field of rhetoric and cultural studies. He is also the coeditor (with Dan Schiller) of *Continental Order? Integrating North America for Cybercapitalism*, and the author of *The Political Economy of Communication: Rethinking and Renewal*. In 2004, Professor Mosco received the Dallas W. Smythe Award for outstanding achievement in communication research.

Gerald Sussman holds a Ph.D. in political science and is professor of urban studies and communications at Portland State University. He has been an active scholar on the political economy of communications and media. He has produced four books and three monographs, in addition to many journal articles dealing with the international and political aspects of information systems. His latest book, *Global Electioneering: Campaign Consulting, Communications, and Corporate Financing*, looks at the industrialization, commodification, and transnationalization of the American electoral system and the particular influence of corporate power and the hegemonic state in the national and global political process. Professor Sussman's next book project will deal with U.S. democracy assistance programs in Europe and the Third World.

Paul Tranter is a senior lecturer in geography at UNSW@ADFA—the University of New South Wales at the Australian Defense Force Academy—in Canberra, Australia. There he lectures in social geography and transport geography. His research interests include the themes of child-friendly environments and sustainable cities, the public health impacts of motorsport, and the promotion of active transport through the concept of 'effective speed.' He has recently investigated links between illegal street racing and experience with motorsport in Christchurch, New Zealand. As well as a research and teaching interest in active transport and sustainable cities, Paul enjoys cycling, commuting by public transport, and walking around his neighborhood, and appreciates the links between active transport, social contact, and healthy communities.